B
AST   Thomas, Bob, 1922—

Astaire, the man,
the dancer

DATE

ASTAIRE

Also by Bob Thomas
NONFICTION

If I Knew Then (with Debbie Reynolds)
The Art of Animation
The Massie Case (with Peter Packer)
King Cohn
Thalberg
Selznick
The Secret Boss of California (with Arthur H. Samish)
The Heart of Hollywood
Winchell
Howard: The Amazing Mr. Hughes (with Noah Dietrich)
Marlon: Portrait of the Rebel as an Artist
Walt Disney: An American Original
The Road to Hollywood (with Bob Hope)
Bud & Lou: The Abbott and Costello Story
The One and Only Bing
Joan Crawford
Reflections: A Life in Two Worlds (with Ricardo Montalban)
Golden Boy: The Untold Story of William Holden

FICTION

The Flesh Merchants
Weekend 33

FOR CHILDREN

Walt Disney: Magician of the Movies
Donna DeVarona, Gold Medal Winner

ANTHOLOGY

Directors in Action

ASTAIRE

THE MAN,
THE DANCER

By Bob Thomas

St. Martin's Press
New York

Special thanks to the following for the use of photographs: ABC Television, The Academy of Motion Picture Arts and Sciences, American Film Institute, Columbia Pictures, Golden Films, MGM-UA, NBC Television, Paramount Pictures, RKO, 20th Century-Fox, Universal Pictures, and Warner Brothers.

Grateful acknowledgment is made for permission to reprint from the following.

"Excerpt from lyrics of "Let's Face the Music and Dance" by Irving Berlin. © Copyright 1935, 1936 Irving Berlin. © Copyright renewed 1962, 1963 Irving Berlin. Reprinted by special permission of Irving Berlin Music Corporation.

"Top Hat, White Tie and Tails" by Irving Berlin. © Copyright 1935 Irving Berlin. © Copyright renewed 1962 Irving Berlin. Reprinted by special permission of Irving Berlin Music Corporation.

"Isn't This a Lovely Day" by Irving Berlin. © Copyright 1935 Irving Berlin. © Copyright renewed 1962 Irving Berlin. Reprinted by special permission of Irving Berlin Music Corporation.

Credits continued on page 331.

Editor: Toni Lopopolo
Assistant Editor: Andrew Charron
Managing Editor: Carol E.W. Edwards
Copy Editor: Erika Schmid
Designer: Manuela Paul

Library of Congress Cataloging in Publication Data

Thomas, Bob, 1922-
    Astaire the man, the dancer.

    I. Astaire, Fred.   2. Dancers—United States—Biography.   I. Title.
GV1785.A83T46   1984   793.3′2′0924 [B]   84-11735
ISBN 0-312-05783-0

First Edition

10 9 8 7 6 5 4 3 2 1

To Sam Weisbord

Contents

Acknowledgments

The kindness of Fred Astaire made this biography possible. I am grateful to others who have shared their memories and observations. Among them: Robyn Smith Astaire, Pandro Berman, Michael Black, Hal Borne, John Bubbles, George Burns, Joan Caulfield, Saul Chaplin, Cyd Charisse, Barrie Chase, Jack Cummings, Stanley Donen, Irene Dunne, John Green, John Houseman, Ross Hunter, Alf Kjellin, Joan Leslie, Perry Lieber, Joseph McBride, Hermes Pan, Gregory Peck, Eric Rhodes, Mark Sandrich, Jr., William Self, Sidney Sheldon, Red Skelton, Emily Torchia, Craig Wasson, Robert Wise, Bud Yorkin.

Joe McBride was especially helpful. He was researcher and co-writer of the script for the American Film Institute tribute to Astaire. He provided access to the Joseph McBride Collection at the State Historical Society of Wisconsin. John Hall of the RKO Archives and Audrey Malkin of the UCLA Theatre Arts Library also contributed assistance. Other valuable sources: the Academy of Motion Picture Arts and Sciences Library, Beverly Hills; the Library of the Performing Arts at Lincoln Center, New York; the Central Library, Los Angeles. Lee Margulies provided some much-needed research.

The Astaire autobiography, *Steps in Time,* is an invaluable guide to his life and career. Another helpful book is Hugh Fordin's *The World of Entertainment,* a fact-filled account of the Arthur Freed unit at MGM. Benny Green's *Fred Astaire* provides the best account of the stage and screen credits.

Introduction

June 14, 1945. MGM studio, Culver City.

A young reporter was escorted onto the set of *Yolanda and the Thief,* where a production number was undergoing a dress rehearsal. All of the dancers were attired in brightly colored tropical costumes except for Fred Astaire, who wore a pink shirt with a towel tied around the neck, gray flannel slacks with a colorful scarf as a belt. During a break in the rehearsal, Astaire talked mostly about racehorses and a new song he had written, "Oh, My Aching Back," the title based on the popular phrase of American soldiers in the European theater of war.

The production number was "Coffee Time," and Astaire remarked that it was a difficult dance to perform. "You see, the music is four-four rhythm, but the dancing is five-four, with a lot of handclaps thrown in."

In the years since that first meeting, I have seen Fred during many phases of his life and career, in periods of elation as well as times of deep sorrow. Four decades after our first encounter, Fred, with his customary kindness, granted me a series of conversations for this biography. The indented comments within the text are the result of our conversations.

1
Fred
Now

*Our only god was Fred Astaire. He was
everything we wanted to be: smooth, suave, debonair,
dapper, intelligent, adult, witty, and wise. We saw his
pictures over and over, played his records until they
were gray and blurred, dressed as much like him as we
dared. When any crises came into our young lives, we
asked ourselves what Fred Astaire would do and we
did likewise. We thought we were hot stuff but we were
very young in those days.*

—*Patrick Dennis,* Auntie Mame

"Did you see the tennis yesterday?"

Fred Astaire was talking about a championship match in which two dynamic athletes had contended evenly until one began to pull ahead. His opponent seemed to lose his spirit, and then the title.

"I've never seen anything like the way that fellow quit," said Astaire, with a look of astonishment on his face. "Brilliant player. But he can't take it when he flops. He hurt himself when he was winning. He was about to step in and take over. Then he did double faults! He's a nervous kind of a guy, and he's young. Very high-strung. He did practically the same kind of thing last year. If his service starts to go, he gives up. There was a time when I thought he could fight back, but he let balls go by, didn't even make an effort to reach out.

"I've never seen anyone behave the way he did yesterday. Six-love! Now his serve alone is going to get him a couple of games in a set. He got to the point where he didn't care. And he was probably so hot that he said, 'To hell with it! If I can be that bad, I'm not good enough to be champion.' That's the way his mind works."

The matter of self-defeat had come to Astaire's mind as he discussed some of the stunts that he had worked hard to achieve in dance numbers for films. He recalled a routine in which he had to roll up an umbrella, fasten it, then toss it across the room into an umbrella stand, hitting it on the musical beat.

"I did it forty-five times, and it always hit the edge," he said. "So I said, 'That's it! Tomorrow morning, first thing, I'm coming back, and I'm going to get that son of a bitch.' And I did! I came back the next morning fresh as a daisy, and that umbrella went into the stand on the first take."

Astaire added, "I somehow or other applied [the tennis star's experience] to myself. You get to the point where you say, 'What the hell's the use of wasting any more time?' Only this guy was wasting the championship; he might have been champion if he had stuck one more time. When he had the other fellow 5-4, all he had to do was get to 6-4. . . . And he double-faulted! He quit. He said, 'My God, if it doesn't come naturally to me at this point, I must be bad.' I felt sorry for him, I really did."

The Astaire work ethic does not countenance defeat. During nearly eighty years in every major entertainment medium, he has persevered, and excelled. He never quit, never passed up an opportunity to push himself and the dance to new levels of achievement. He has been accorded every honor a performer can receive, every tribute, including George Balanchine's: "Fred is the greatest dancer who ever lived." The name itself has become a superlative: Astaire.

He lives in Beverly Hills, on a hillside cluttered with luxury houses of varied architectural styles. The Astaire house stands on the high side of a road, affording a view over the Beverly Hills Hotel to the vast sprawl of the Los Angeles plain.

One sweltering August afternoon, Fred Astaire stood at the front door of the broad, low, gleamingly white house as I arrived for an interview. Three others were with him: his wife Robyn, her Spanish teacher and the teacher's father, an Argentine who could speak no English. "Don't worry." Fred smiled assuringly, indicating that the visitors were leaving. Robyn, slender as a boy but with feminine beauty, carried three golf clubs and was going off to hit some balls at the Bel Air Country Club. Fred gave her an affectionate kiss and turned to lead me into the house.

The interior is what you would expect in the house of Fred Astaire. Burnished leather and shining chrome. Brightly colored paintings of racecourse scenes. Terrazzo floors and deep rugs. The den, where Fred sat at a suede-covered game table, provided some evidence of his career: the Oscar and the Emmys, videotapes of his film musicals, bound volumes of photographs from the movies. There were no photographs of Fred performing. An oil portrait of Triplicate, his most successful racehorse, hung over the mantel. Near the bar area were paintings by Irving Berlin, curious clownlike figures in top hat and bow tie (an allusion to the famed Berlin-Astaire collaboration) and unearthly birds. Fred explained: "Irving told me the birds just came to him and he had to paint them. I guess that's what it's like to be a genius." In the center of the room stood a tournament-size billiard table.

He was eighty-four in the summer of 1983, and on those rare days when the desert air of Los Angeles turned humid, he could feel the abuse that his bones had taken through his lifetime. "When I built this house, I didn't think I needed air-conditioning because the wind always blew on this hill," he said. "This is the first year I felt I needed it."

He walked deliberately, with a certain stiffness in the upper body, as though he were carrying a filled drinking glass on his head. But from the waist down, he moved with a feline grace, the Astaire walk. The vision was completed by the classic attire: pink shirt with paisley scarf at the neck; full-waisted gray flannel slacks, belted with a matching paisley scarf; black suede loafers with silver buckles. The style is distinctly his, unique and unmatched; he has followed his own fashion for fifty years, yet his clothes always seem totally contemporary. His face was pink, the complexion clear. The eyes were alert but aqueous, another symptom from the weather, as was the husky voice. A sudden impression: The ears, though flat to the head, seem oversized. How could an actor with such ears have become a movie star?

Fred had tried to discourage me from undertaking a biography. "Who'd want to read a book about such a dull, ole character like me?" he asked. I refused to accept his assessment, and in the end he agreed to be interviewed. Never an easy interview, he proved remarkably candid, and rarely did his memory falter. Once he rebelled.

"The one thing I hate is talking about myself," he complained. "I just don't take myself that seriously. The only things I take seriously are my work and my family, and that end of it. As far as reading my notices, I don't enjoy them. Because most of the time you look for something that you think is going to be all right, you get a [bad] review. That happens to everyone in the business, and it's always hard to take. Everyone likes to have good notices. You spend a lot of time writing something, and you want your reviews to be good, don't you?

"I've had my share of good ones, and sometimes they've been controversial. You have to forget them, get 'em out of your mind. I have no complaints. The only thing about it is that it's difficult for me to talk about myself, because I just simply don't *like* to. I never have liked to. . . .

"I've [talked about myself] so many times that I can't even remember myself what I did. I don't know. I've never been too impressed. I would have liked it to have been a lot better. And I don't know what that means. I don't think you ever sit back and say, 'Well, I knocked that off, that's it!' Once in a while an item in a picture looks good, and I didn't think that number would be as good as that. But surprisingly, it's good. You don't sit back and say, 'That's okay.' It's *supposed* to be okay. That's what you're supposed to deliver. I was never glamour-struck by the whole thing."

Indeed, Fred Astaire, among the most glamorous figures in the history of American entertainment, seems to have striven throughout his career to avoid any semblance of glamour. His personal life has been as private as he could make it. After going into films, he never returned to performing in public, never felt the need for the applause of an audience. Throughout most of his career, he never hired a publicist. A shy, diffident man, he sufferingly endured the personal appearances and probing interviews requisite of stardom. (He is so self-protective that he long ago inserted a provision in his will prohibiting his heirs from authorizing a film based on his life.)

He was feverishly competitive, but always against himself. He detested the thought of repeating a dance he had already created, always believed he could discover some new achievement. And did.

Gazing backward on a long career, Astaire commented:

"I have never had anything that I can remember in the business—and that includes all the movies and the stage shows and everything—that I didn't enjoy. I didn't like some of the small-time vaudeville, because we weren't going on and getting better. Aside from that, I didn't dislike anything.

"You do a movie and a lot of good things happen. Some turn out better than others; you put a big effort into some that don't get the result you think they should, everybody has that. I never remember anything except that I was always anxious to get there and get at it and *do* it.

"There was nothing heroic about it. The reason I decided to do a show was that I thought it would be the best thing that I'd done so far. You find out in the middle of it that it's rocky going and you wonder if it's going to work out. Well, you can't start pouting about it. You gotta still like it as much as when you started.

"I've always thought, what a lucky life it is to be in and work at! And be paid so well. Yes, and to entertain people. But I must say that although I always tried to please an audience, I was trying my hardest to please myself. Because I felt that if I could do that, then I automatically was pleasing others. You're not doing it just for them, you're doing it for *yourself.* That's a part of the game."

He doesn't dance anymore. An inner-ear problem has made his balance uncertain, and he is afraid of falling. He fell one day on a Beverly Hills street and didn't realize he was hurt until he reached his office and a secretary said he was bleeding. He won't dance, even for Robyn, who is belatedly enthralled with the Astaire musicals. "I love to watch Fred's dances in the old movies," his wife says. "I plead with him, 'Tap for me.' But he just does a few steps and walks away. Fred has never liked to be known as just a tap dancer."

The Astaires spend much of their time at home. They occasionally dine out with friends—Fred has never liked to entertain at his own house. Both Fred and Robyn detest parties, and they attend only special occasions, such as George Burns' anniversary celebration and the dinner for Queen Elizabeth. Astaire can never appear in public without a stream of admirers wanting to pay homage, and for an extremely shy man, that becomes an ordeal.

"As far back as I can remember, it has always been the same, anywhere I go, any country where I go," he said. "Sometimes you have to be confined to your quarters or your hotel, just because you can't go outside your room. I took a trip to Japan with Ava, and we couldn't go anywhere." Robyn points out that Fred's fans, unlike the followers of rock stars, are not limited by age. They range from teenagers, who have seen his movies on television, to those who saw the films the first time around. To all of them, of course, Fred is unfailingly polite.

During his later years, Astaire had avoided seeing his film musicals, largely because he feared he would find things he wished he had done better. But because of Robyn's interest in his dancing, he has looked at some of the old movies. Surprisingly, he has not been displeased.

"He's beginning to appreciate his work for the first time," Robyn observes. "He's starting to take pride in what he's done."

Fred cited a television interview with pop singer Lionel Richie, who remarked, "I've just begun to realize that I look in the mirror now and I like that person."

Fred added: "That's how I feel when I see some of my films."

2

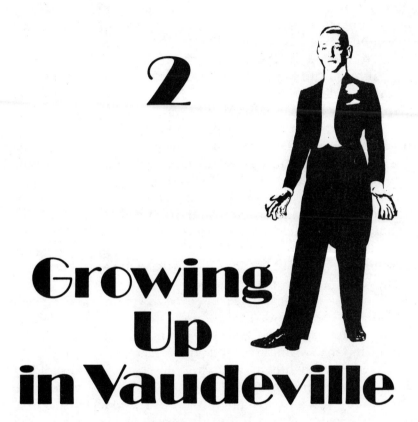

Growing Up in Vaudeville

You're the nimble tread
Of the feet of Fred Astaire. . . .

—*Cole Porter, "You're the Top"*

November 28, 1917. The premiere of *Over the Top* at the Forty-fourth Street Roof promised more than the usual excitement of a New York theater opening. The theater was new; the Shuberts had converted a rooftop dance palace, once Castles in the Air, home of Vernon and Irene Castle, into a playhouse. The Shuberts were also trying an innovation: a nine-o'clock curtain time in an attempt to draw the late-dining society crowd. Just the thing for a New York exhilarated by the war to end all wars.

The revue had originally been called *Oh, Justine* to capitalize on the fame of its gorgeous star, Justine Johnson. Then it became *The Nine O'Clock Revue,* and finally *Over the Top,* a jaunty reference to the new war.

The title changes were indicative of the makeshift nature of the revue. It contained a featherweight plot concerning the star's imaginary visit to her lover, played by Colin Campbell. The comedian T. Roy Barnes appeared intermittently to explain and resolve the plot. Sigmund Romberg provided most of the songs, and the production numbers imitated the Ziegfeld Follies and the Winter Garden revues. "The Land of Frocks and Frills" featured showgirls in elegant costumes. A hastily added spectacle depicted American planes attacking German trenches.

The cast was largely recruited from vaudeville. The acts included the song-and-dance team of Joe Laurie and Aileen Bronson, mind readers Harry and Emma Shamrock, and a youthful dance team, Fred and Adele Astaire.

Fred was eighteen, his sister eighteen months older. They had recently been succeeding in big-time vaudeville after many years of struggle. *Over the Top* marked the first time they had performed outside of vaudeville houses, and they danced three numbers as well as appearing in sketches.

Newspaper critics found *Over the Top* labored and artificial, but a few bestowed praise on the Astaires. Lewis Sherwin wrote in the *Globe:* "One of the prettiest features of the show is the dancing of the two Astaires. The girl, a light, sprite-like little creature, has really an exquisite floating style in her caperings, while the young man combines eccentric ability with humor."

T. Roy Barnes decided that his role was not in keeping with his status as a comedy star, and he withdrew from *Over the Top.* He was replaced by Ed Wynn, who contributed his zany humor and helped extend the run to seventy-eight performances. The show toured and enjoyed enthusiastic audiences, especially in Washington, D.C., which was bustling with wartime activity.

"Charles Dillingham's out front!"

Everyone backstage at the Garrick Theater shared the excitement of the news. All knew who Dillingham was: the Episcopal minister's son who had drifted into the theater from drama criticism became Daniel Frohman's press agent and assistant before producing his first musical, *The Office Boy,* in 1903. Dillingham's well-produced shows made him a rival of the Shuberts and Florenz Ziegfeld. The cast of *Over the Top* realized that Dillingham's approval could mean prosperity for their careers, and they performed that night with repeated glances to the upper left box where Dillingham gazed down at the stage.

The youngest members of the company were the ones who caught the showman's eye. Dillingham was entranced by the airy grace and antic humor of Fred and Adele Astaire.

"I want you to do a show for me," Dillingham told the Astaires.

"But we've agreed to do another revue for the Shuberts," Fred replied.

"That's all right; I'll wait," the producer said with a paternal smile.

It was thrilling, Fred believed, for a big-shot Broadway producer to volunteer to sponsor their careers. Adele agreed that it was nice; as always, she failed to share her brother's concern for their future. But Fred was convinced that Dillingham's sponsorship would mean a giant step toward the success they had been seeking ever since they departed from Omaha.

According to family legend, Frederick Austerlitz left Austria as a result of a dispute with his older brother Ernest. Both were officers in the Emperor's army, but Ernest held a higher rank, and when Frederick didn't salute him, the younger brother was arrested. Enraged by the indignity, Frederick decided to emigrate to the land of freedom. He arrived in New York in 1895, remaining only briefly after his release from Ellis Island. Friends in Vienna had arranged a job for him in the leather trade in Omaha, Nebraska.

Like many Europeans, Frederick Austerlitz traveled west with apprehension. But he encountered no marauding Indians, not even cowboys. By 1895 Omaha was a booming railroad center of a hundred thousand, its mills, stockyards and factories prospering. Austerlitz soon discovered he disliked dealing in leather, and he found work as a salesman for the Storz Brewing Company. It was ideal work for the hearty, gregarious Viennese, whose family had been brewers. Austerlitz became a favorite with his customers, who enjoyed his thickly accented humor.

"There are only two kinds of Austrians: rascals and musicians," he often said. "And I play the piano."

Austerlitz became a popular figure at parties among Omaha's young people. One night he met a pretty girl of Alsatian parentage named Ann Gelius, only recently graduated from a Catholic high school. Although there was ten years' difference in their ages, they fell in love and married within a few months. They moved into a wood frame house on North Nineteenth Street, a short distance from downtown Omaha. Their daughter Adele was born September 10, 1897. On May 10, 1899, Ann Austerlitz gave birth to a son, named after his father.

> FRED: I remember very little about Omaha. I can recall how my father used to take me for rides in the buggy, and we'd go downtown and visit the stores. There was a cigar store called Sachs, where he would chat with friends.
>
> The old days were all very . . . pleasant. Fortunately, I have no recollection of anything terrible.
>
> I don't remember seeing any stage shows in Omaha. I have vague recollections of going down to the school where my sister was taking dancing lessons. It was not a professional school, just a place where little girls took dancing lessons. I didn't know what I was looking at, and I didn't give a damn. I was very young, perhaps three. I didn't know what the hell was going on.

Adele studied dancing at the Chambers Dancing Academy, and Fred went along because his mother had no one to leave him with. She liked to tell the story of how Freddie found a pair of ballet slippers in a corner of the dance studio, put them on and imitated his sister in a toe dance. If it happened, he doesn't remember it.

At first Adele's dancing lesson seemed nothing more than a little girl's diversion, but her teachers and her mother soon recognized that Adele was gifted. Even at six she displayed a natural grace and an infectious gaiety that set her apart from all the other girls in the Chambers Dancing Academy.

Frederick Austerlitz delighted in his daughter's talent. He had grown up with the operettas and concerts of Vienna, and he was entranced by the vigor of American entertainment. Ann Austerlitz recognized the potential of Adele's dancing skill. Though she had been reared in a family that considered entertainers a sinful breed, Mrs. Austerlitz realized that a dancing career could provide release from the provincial life in Omaha, Nebraska. Her ambitions were aided, unexpectedly, by the forces of prohibition.

In 1904, the God-fearing citizens of Nebraska were convinced by their pastors and temperance zealots to ban alcoholic beverages from the state. That put the Storz brewery out of business and Frederick Austerlitz out of work. He and his wife had long, late-night discussions about their future. They finally decided that Adele's talent deserved better training than she could get in Omaha. Ann would take the two children to New York City; Frederick would stay in Omaha to earn money to support them.

> FRED: It was basically my father's idea that we should go to New York. He thought it would be good because my sister had talent. I was too young to know anything. When I went east, I just came along for the ride. That's what I thought I was doing.
>
> I didn't know I was going there for a purpose. You don't know all the things that are going on at that age. There was no way I could have thought, "Oh, we're going on the stage!" I didn't know what a stage was, I guess. I was four and a half at the time.

The railroad journey to New York took two and a half days, with a change of trains in Chicago. Mrs. Austerlitz and the two children took a hansom cab from Pennsylvania Station to the Herald Square Hotel. For a few days they visited the sights of the huge, bewildering city, then Mrs. Austerlitz decided they must attend to the reason they had come to New York: for Adele to train as a dancer. Also Fred. Since he had displayed some cleverness in imitating his sister's steps and because it was easier than hiring a baby-sitter, Fred would take lessons, too.

Adele and Fred were enrolled in Claude Alvienne's dancing school in the Grand Opera House building at Eighth Avenue and Twenty-third Street. Their father had picked the place from an ad in a theatrical paper to which he subscribed. Between lessons, Adele and Fred studied grammar, arithmetic and other subjects with their mother. She had been trained to be a school teacher, and she decided that the children should not be distracted from their dancing by the necessities of public school.

Fred proved to be a willing student. After he had become a movie star, Ann Austerlitz told an interviewer a story about her son at the age of five: "Adele, who was a year and a half older than Freddie, was studying her lessons regularly. Freddie wanted to learn, too, but he was so young that I'm afraid I didn't give him the attention I should have. I felt there was plenty of time. He would sit close by while Adele recited her lessons, never saying anything, just listening. Then one morning something happened that seemed to be the keynote to Freddie's character through all the years that have followed.

"It was very early. I heard some sound in the living room, and I found Freddie in his pajamas, lying on his stomach in front of the fireplace with the *Sunbonnet Primer* in front of him. When I came in, he was whispering to himself. 'Pretending to read,' I thought. But when he saw me, I learned differently. He could really read.

"'Mom, ' he said, 'hear me read!' And read he did. He rattled the sentences off for a page or two. My surprise—it wasn't feigned—delighted him.

"'How did you learn, Freddie?' I asked him. 'I "tudied,"' he told me. 'I asked Delly some of the words, but mostly I "tudied."'"

Fred at five in a dance school recital

The most pleasurable part of the education of Adele and Fred Austerlitz was seeing the New York shows. Their mother reasoned that if they were to become stars, they needed examples to aspire to. She took them regularly to Broadway theaters, where the musical comedy was bursting into full flower during the first decade of the century. The prolific George M. Cohan was bringing new vitality to the theater, and Florenz Ziegfeld introduced his garish revues. Among the attractions: Victor Herbert's *Babes in Toyland,* Cohan in *Little Johnny Jones,* Fritzi Scheff as *Mlle. Modiste,* Nat M. Willis in *The Duke of Duluth,* Victor Moore in Cohan's *45 Minutes from Broadway,* David Montgomery and Fred Stone in *The Red Mill.*

The show that most influenced Fred was *The Soul Kiss,* starring Adeline Genée. The producer, Flo Ziegfeld, billed her as "the world's greatest dancer," and although she was past her prime, she dazzled audiences at the New York Theater with her ballet artistry. She could even dance beautifully in hunting boots during a hunt ballet. Fred recalls that his mother took him and Adele to *The Soul Kiss* again and again, "hoping it would rub off on us."

The education of Fred and Adele Austerlitz also included the drama, and their mother took them to see the stars of the Broadway theater: John Drew, Ethel Barrymore, Maude Adams, William Gillette, Maxine Elliott, E. H. Sothern. Students of the Alvienne school were expected to perform in plays, and Fred and Adele were cast in a scene from *Cyrano de Bergerac*. Fred, to his never-ending ignominy, was forced to perform as Roxanne to the Cyrano of his sister, who was three inches taller. Fortunately, their *Cyrano de Bergerac* lasted only one performance.

If there had been any doubt about the role of brother and sister, it was soon resolved. Adele was unswervingly feminine, and Fred, perhaps in compensation for the pursuit of dancing that some of his playmates considered sissy, was totally male.

Through their career together, Fred and Adele seemed content in their relationship, avoiding the competitiveness that has afflicted and often destroyed show-business teams. At the height of their Broadway fame, they gave a light-hearted interview backstage before a performance of *The Band Wagon.*

"It's funny," Fred said, "but there was a time—I was six and Adele was seven—when I used to think of her with contempt. She couldn't play ball, or chin herself, or whistle through her teeth. She couldn't even spit! I used to pray at night for God to turn her into a brother. Why, one day she even tied a pink ribbon in my hair."

"I remember that," said Adele, "and I remember the sock in the eye you gave me."

"Then," Fred continued, "when we had the first contest at dancing school, Adele, I remember, put in some crazy little jiggers that we hadn't prepared at all. I was all primed for murder—until the judges gave us the first prize, with special mention for Adele. Then it began to dawn on me that she had her way of getting results and I had mine. Gradually that idea sank in, until I understood that we got along together best if we admitted that we were two separate people."

"From that first sock in the eye," said Adele, "I realized you could never be a sister to me. I decided to just accept you as a brother and let it go at that. Maybe, if you *had* been a sister, we'd have turned out to be a couple of boop-oop-a-doop girls. And if I'd been a brother, we'd be a pair of novelty acrobats."

Ann Gelius Austerlitz did not fit the traditional pattern of stage mother: the demonic woman, frustrated in her own ambitions to be a performer, willing to sacrifice anything and anybody to further her children's careers.

> FRED: She was not that kind of person at all. She didn't do any pushing; she just maintained the career as it was being formed. She brought us east, and she was always an influence of importance to us. She was not at all a pro. She was one of the most lovely persons you could ever imagine. She was very gentle, and very amusing. Her sense of humor was always there.
>
> She was always a little surprised when there might be something shocking. "Why do they have to do that?" she would ask. [In later years] I used to take her to shows in New York. Once in a while we would see one that was not like a present-day shocker but used words that to my mind were a bit rough. She would tolerate it, but asked, "Why do they do it?" I'd tell her, "Well, writers and the press think they have to do this and that. . . ." She'd laugh at it sometimes. But sometimes she just said, "I think it's dreadful!"

Fred recalls that it was his father who suggested a name change for his talented children, having conceded that Austerlitz would lack appeal on theater marquees. Fred believes that the name came from an Alsace-Lorraine uncle named L'Astaire. Although Adele was older and taller, she would take second billing to Fred; tradition dictated that the male member of a dance team was listed first. So the billing would read: Fred and Adele Astaire.

The two prodigies from Nebraska became the stars of the Alvienne dance academy. Both of them, but especially

Fred's first top hat, in the bride and groom vaudeville act, 1906

Adele, seemed so naturally gifted that Alvienne believed they could go immediately into show business. Mrs. Austerlitz drew from her savings to buy props and costumes for the act that Alvienne had devised. Adele and Fred would play a miniature bridal couple, she in satin wedding gown, he in evening dress, including—fatefully—top hat, white tie and tails.

The props were two wedding cakes, equipped with bells and electric lights. Fred and Adele danced up and down the cakes, playing "Dreamland Waltz" on the bells with their hands and feet. The cakes lighted up at the end of the dance. Adele performed a solo while Fred changed into his lobster costume for his own solo. Adele returned as a champagne glass, and they performed an eccentric duet, concluding with tunes played on the wedding-cake bells.

Their act was a sensation at the dance academy recital. Ann Austerlitz was radiant with pride. Only a year before, against all the warnings of her friends and relatives in Omaha, she had brought her two children to New York with the blind hope that they could find careers as dancers. Now the dream seemed possible.

"Mrs. Austerlitz," Claude Alvienne announced, "I believe Fred and Adele are ready to face real audiences."

In 1905, that meant vaudeville.

By the first decade of the new century, vaudeville had become the people's entertainment. Every American city had at least two vaudeville theaters, every town had one. The cities offered the prestigious two-a-day, with eight high-class acts accompanied by full orchestra. Smaller cities featured five acts of lesser quality, appearing three or four times a day with a five-piece accompaniment. In the small towns, a couple of acts ground out five or six shows daily, to the music of a pianist and a trap drummer.

Vaudeville was as stratified as English society. There was big-time vaudeville, and there was small-time, and the gulf between them was enormous. Even within the two-a-day cast, lines of demarcation existed. The aristocracy was the next-to-closing act: famed comedians, singing stars, Broadway actors in sketches, such as Ethel Barrymore in *The Twelve-Pound Look*. At the lower end of the ladder were the opening and closing acts—jugglers, acrobats, animals, new performers who lacked the audience's full attention as it entered and departed.

Keyport, New Jersey, was far from the big time. The vaudeville theater was on a pier at the summer resort, and it offered four acts and a four-piece orchestra. The management was willing to give new acts a tryout, and Mr. Alvienne managed to book Fred and Adele for a half-week engagement at $50. Alvienne crated the wedding cakes and Mrs. Austerlitz carefully packed the costumes, and they departed with the two children on the train trip to Keyport.

While the other acts waited for their own rehearsal time, Ann Austerlitz directed the assembling of the wedding cakes and cued the electrician for the split-second timing of the lights. The matinee performance went smoothly, neither Astaire betraying a moment of nervousness. The evening show brought strong applause, and the local reviewer proclaimed, somewhat grandly: "The Astaires are the greatest child act in vaudeville."

On the strength of the Keyport opening, Alvienne found bookings for the Astaires in small towns in New Jersey, Pennsylvania and New York, and he continued perfecting the act. Frederick Austerlitz, who had misgivings about the adventure during the year of separation from his wife and children, was thrilled by the success of Adele and Fred. He came to New York to share the excitement and plan for their future. An expansive, outgoing man, Austerlitz made connections with important theatrical figures. He convinced the booker for the Orpheum circuit to view the Astaire act in Paterson, New Jersey. The result: a twenty-week contract at $150 a week, plus train fares for the Astaires and their mother.

The Orpheum circuit was big-time. Fred and Adele found themselves on bills with Elsie Janis, Joe Cook, Mr. and Mrs. Carter DeHaven, Pat Rooney and other headliners. The Astaires were only an opening act, but they were treated with courtesy and affection by the other performers. Adele spent most of her spare theater time in the dressing room, but Fred was intensely curious about the other acts, particularly the acrobats, jugglers and tap dancers. He made friends with some of the juvenile performers, but his mother was vigilant in protecting him from any bad influence. As soon as their show was over, Mrs. Austerlitz hurried Adele and Fred back to their quarters, usually a third-rate hotel or theatrical boardinghouse.

> FRED: Big-time vaudeville was a pretty damn fine institution. We got into it very soon, when we were pretty young kids. We never played the small-time circuits, like the Loew's or the Pantages. They were three-a-day and sometimes more.
>
> We played the Orpheum circuit, starting in Chicago, then working our way through the Middle West and up into Canada—Edmonton and Calgary were a split week. Then Seattle, Portland and San Francisco. Except that we couldn't play San Francisco because of the labor law. So the rest of the company would play San Francisco, and we'd play Oakland; for some reason the law didn't apply there. Then we came down to Los Angeles and played the old Orpheum Theater. Hollywood was just a bud then, nothing there but lemon groves. Somebody asked if I wanted to go out to see it, and I wasn't interested.
>
> It was a high-class form of entertainment, vaudeville was. The big time was kind of glamorous . . . I don't remember ever suffering about anything

Adele, eleven, and Fred, ten, show their early style in clothes

at all. Maybe we didn't get as many bookings as we wanted to. That used to worry me a little, because we needed the money at that point. When we outgrew that and had a position and were in demand, it was a different story.

The problem in San Francisco was repeated in other cities, especially New York. The cause was Elbridge T. Gerry, whose name became an epithet to child performers and their parents. He was a New York lawyer and self-appointed guardian of public morals whose Gerry Society crusaded against cruelty to children. Gerry considered the theater too sinful and exploitive of children, and he persuaded lawmakers in New York and elsewhere to forbid use of children on the stage until they were sixteen—eighteen in some cities.

Fred tried to fool the Gerry Society by wearing long pants and trying to look older, but his efforts usually failed.

In some cities, like Los Angeles, Mrs. Austerlitz was able to obtain a waiver from the Gerry Society by proving that Fred and Adele were well supervised and receiving a good education. Her efforts were unavailing in New York City, where the act needed to be seen in order to impress bookers and producers.

The act had another problem. Adele was approaching her teens and growing fast. Fred was three inches shorter, and the difference bordered on the ludicrous when they danced together. Frederick Austerlitz made another of his journeys to New York, and he and his wife agreed that their children should temporarily retire from performing.

They found a house in Highwood Park, a suburb of Weehawken, across the Hudson River from Manhattan. For the first time in their lives, Adele and Fred were enrolled in public school. Fred entered the fourth grade at Hamilton Grammar School, but his mother's lessons in trains and hotel rooms had been so good that he was quickly promoted to the fifth grade.

The towers of Manhattan could be seen from Highwood Park, but for two years Fred Astaire enjoyed a boyhood far removed from big cities and vaudeville houses. His mother made him continue dance practice and learn French as well, but otherwise he could live and play like any of the other boys of the Hamilton school. Fred adored his new life. His one great embarrassment came when schoolmates, aware of his theatrical experience, urged him to sing or dance for a school entertainment. His face turned red; he sank his hands in his pockets and stammered his reluctance. If no escape was possible, he obliged with a pseudo-bass rendition of "Asleep in the Deep."

"Never once did he discuss his dancing with us boys," recalled a former playmate after Fred had become a movie star. "That was a thing apart, and he wanted us to forget all about it when we played.

"He was one of the best-natured boys on the block. I remember when we both were about eleven, his dad sent him a lovely bag of marbles from out west. They were real agates and made swell shooters. When I admired them and asked him to let me shoot with them, he gave me a half dozen, including the best shooter in the lot, a pure blood-red one."

*Vaudeville
veterans, 1912*

The suburban idyll ended. Fred had grown to Adele's
height, and their mother decided it was time to start pursuing their careers again. The family moved to a West Fifty-
fifth Street boardinghouse, and Fred and Adele were enrolled at Ned Wayburn's dancing school three blocks away.
Wayburn had been a Broadway stage manager as well as
dancer, and his school was considered one of the best in New
York. Fred returned to the familiar routine of daily lessons,
with his mother tutoring him. At least he wasn't traveling all
the time, and he could play baseball in the street with neighborhood friends.

Mrs. Austerlitz paid the show-wise Wayburn a thousand
dollars to create a new act that would be less juvenile than
what Fred and Adele had performed on the Orpheum circuit. After months of delay, he produced "A Rainy Saturday."
The tiny plot introduced Fred as a baseball player thwarted
from a neighborhood game because of rain. His kid sister
convinces him to play house, and they take the roles and
costumes of adults in the courting and marriage stages.

Fred and Adele rehearsed "A Rainy Saturday" week after week until it was ready for an audience. But Ann Austerlitz could not find an agent who would even review a performance. "Not interested in kid acts," she was told. Finally Wayburn booked the Astaires on a benefit program he was staging at the Broadway Theater. The reviews were favorable, and "A Rainy Saturday" was given a one-week engagement at Proctor's Fifth Avenue, a vaudeville theater at Broadway and Twenty-eighth Street.

Fred was elated. It was their first booking in an important New York theater. And they would be sharing the bill with Douglas Fairbanks, who was appearing in a sketch, "A Regular Business Man." Fairbanks was an idol for Fred, who had seen his portrayals of energetic, go-getter Americans in Broadway plays.

The Astaires rehearsed with the orchestra for "A Rainy Saturday," and prepared for the first matinee with growing excitement. Then the crushing news: They had been assigned to open the show.

"How can they do this to us!" Fred groaned. "People will be walking in, and they'll miss all our dialogue."

"Oh, come on, Freddie," his sister said. "We'll just have to be so terrific that the manager will have to give us a better spot for the evening show."

They agreed to give their best effort, but they faced an impossible situation. When they danced onto the stage, their hearts fell at the sight of rows of empty seats. The balcony was more populated but inattentive. Neither the jokes nor the singing and dancing drew response from the audience. The concluding applause was not enough for Fred and Adele to make it into the wings.

> FRED: We were on that show for only one performance. After the matinee we were canceled. I remember coming back to the theater and looking at the bill. "We were there before and now we're not—why?" I said to the manager. "Because you're off the bill," he said.
>
> I remember after the matinee, I watched Doug Fairbanks from the side. That was the last chance I had to look at anything. We had to leave the theater.

Years later I got to be friends with Doug. He didn't remember that years before we had been on a bill together. He said, "Oh, I was so preoccupied in those days, I didn't look at anything but myself and my career."

Back to the road. But this time it wasn't a deluxe tour of the Orpheum circuit. Nothing travels as fast in show business as news of failure, and word spread among bookers and agents that those Astaire kids who were so cute a few years ago had flopped at Proctor's Fifth Avenue.

Fred and Adele played a few split-week dates on the outskirts of New York. During one unforgettable New Jersey engagement, rowdies in the balcony threw coins at them. Finally an agent named Lew Golder managed to book them on the small-time United Booking Office circuit. When bookings were lean, the Astaires even played the infamous Gus Sun circuit, smallest of the small-time. With their father's work faring poorly in Omaha, they had to accept whatever work they could find. Rarely did they earn more than $150 a week, and out of it came room, board and train fare for Fred, Adele and their mother. They continued to improve the act, eliminating dialogue for a smoother song-and-dance flow.

Years afterward, Fred and Adele could laugh about their travails while touring with "A Rainy Saturday." During an interview, Adele remarked that they weren't always the opening act. There was that time in a tiny hamlet in Pennsylvania.

"We didn't open, Delly dear, because there were only two acts on the bill," Fred reminded her. "The other one was a dog act. And we had to climb a ladder to our dressing room. There was only one dressing room on stage level, and the dogs got that because they couldn't climb the ladder."

For Adele, traveling was a lark; she found enjoyment no matter where they played. Fred was constantly concerned that their career was becalmed. There were times he felt they were progressing, then they would be slapped down again. The specter of the Proctor's failure haunted him.

"We were playing small-time houses on the Keith circuit, and they always put us in the opening position," Fred recalled in 1928. "We opened more shows for Keith than any other act. Finally we hit the palace in Chicago and we went over big. After the Monday matinee they moved us up to a better spot. We had arrived. We felt great.

"The next week we played St. Louis. 'Ha!' we said, 'they'll have heard about Chicago: Wait and see, we'll have a soft spot on this bill.' We opened the show again. It was heartbreaking. Especially when we went back to Chicago later and played the Majestic theater. We were in the opening spot!"

Fred blamed himself. He felt that he was the weak half of the brother-sister team, and the reviews reflected that. Time after time critics rhapsodized over Adele's gamine charm, her youthful verve, her joyful, spontaneous spirit, dismissing her brother as an adequate partner.

The Detroit *Free Press:* "For sheer personality and charm, Adele Astaire outshines anyone who has appeared here in months."

The Philadelphia *North American:* "The bill began with a pair of excellent dancers, the girl, who was also the possessor of remarkably good looks, being especially graceful of movement."

The Boston *Record:* "Fred and Adele Astaire gave a fine exhibition of whirlwind dancing, although it would be wished that the young man give up some of the blasé air which he carries constantly with him. He is too young for it and deceives none."

Fred Astaire in his midteens was a dancer in search of a style. One thing he knew: He didn't want to dance ballet. Though he had been inspired by Adelaide Genée and had undergone a few weeks of ballet training, he disliked the formality of ballet, the constriction of performing a movement in the same classic way. For a boy whose favorite pastimes were playing baseball and shooting pool, the effeminacy of ballet was intolerable. Ballet in the early decades of the century focused on the ballerina; only Nijinsky brought male vitality to the medium, and Fred never saw him dance.

Vernon and Irene Castle, who were revolutionizing American social dancing in the pre-war years, were an important influence on the young Fred Astaire.

> FRED: They were ballroom dancers, and I did a picture about them later on. They danced in nightclubs,

but we were too young to go to nightclubs. They also appeared in Broadway shows, and that's where we saw them. Vernon Castle was an eccentric dancer, but they made a classy pair. They were very stylish, and they established a lot of dances that society took up. They were a terrific craze.

Although Fred admired the Castles (he helped Irene create dances after Vernon's death as a flier in World War I), he didn't want to be a ballroom dancer. Something else was stirring in him, something that he traced back to Claude Alvienne's dance studio during the earliest days in New York. During the lessons, Professor Alvienne beat rhythm to the pianist's music, pounding a wooden stick against the back of a chair. The pounding beat made a lasting impression on the five-year-old Fred.

Growing up in vaudeville, Fred sometimes played on bills with jazz bands. He stood in the wings listening to their thumping rhythms, his feet tapping irresistibly. He also studied the black tap dancers, whose response to the ragtime and jazz music seemed effortless and natural. He made friends with some of them, including the sublime Bill Robinson.

> FRED: Bill Robinson was a buck dancer [somewhat akin to clog]. I admired him, but I didn't do what he did—the wooden-shoe up and down the stairs. John Bubbles was different. I don't know whether he used tap shoes or not, but he was stylish. I used to meet him occasionally and we'd try steps together, but at that point in my career I wasn't doing much tap dancing.

As he hunted for his own style, Fred was also seeking a new direction for the Astaires' vaudeville act. After two years with "A Rainy Saturday," Fred was fifteen and Adele was sixteen and a half. Both looked older than their years, Fred with his slicked-back hair and assured manner, Adele with her beauty in full bloom. They could no longer play kids, and as brother and sister, romantic duets became perilous, even when they were play-acting as adults.

Fred and Adele finally outgrew A Rainy Saturday

From the start of their vaudeville act, the major feature had been the Astaires' toe dancing. Finally, at the age of sixteen, during an engagement at Feltmann's restaurant in Coney Island, Fred rebelled."I'm not going to dance on my toes anymore," he announced. "It's too sissy."

Despite an occasional triumph, such as the Chicago Palace, they were far from headliners. Their salary remained stuck at $150 a week.

Even though they were financially hard-pressed, Ann Austerlitz insisted that Fred and Adele take the summer off. They spent some time at the Delaware Water Gap in Pennsylvania, and Frederick Austerlitz joined them for a family vacation such as they hadn't known before. Fred began his lifelong love affair with golf, and he and Adele swam and rode horses and became acquainted with the society swells who frequented the resort. It was their first close-up view of how the rich lived and played, and both Fred and Adele were fascinated.

In the summer of 1914, as the family were gathered at the Delaware Water Gap, their nighttime discussions centered on the future of the act. Adele was little concerned; she was usually boating or dancing with one of the rich young socialites. Fred argued that something drastic had to be done if he and Adele were ever to escape from the small-time. His mother agreed, and his father suggested that they needed expert advice in rebuilding the act.

Frederick Austerlitz found the right person: Aurelia Coccia who with his wife had starred in a highly successful "flash act" (vaudeville term for an act with special scenery, dancers and singers). Coccia understood what dazzled audiences, and he convinced the Astaires to junk the baseball act and start anew. He added the latest dances and new songs, with Fred playing the piano. After six months of polishing the dances and songs, Coccia announced that Fred and Adele were ready for a tryout.

Fred himself helped pick out the songs. He had developed a remarkable feel for music and liked to practice the latest hits from Tin Pan Alley on the piano. Whenever he was in New York, he made a tour of the music publishers. A favorite stop was Waterson, Berlin and Snyder, because it published songs of the prolific and immensely popular Ir-

Fred in a Buster Brown pose

ving Berlin. Fred had bought two Berlin songs, "I Love to
Quarrel with You" and "I've Got a Sweet Tooth," and once he
met Berlin in the publishing offices.

Remick's was another publisher on Fred's rounds. One day he struck up a conversation with a young man who was demonstrating songs at a piano. He introduced himself as George Gershwin and said, "I write songs, too; I'll play one for you." The vaudevillian and the songwriter formed an immediate rapport, and before Fred left the office, Gershwin mused, "Wouldn't it be great if some day I would write a musical and you'd be in it?"

The teenage Fred evidences the Astaire style and chin.

Fred gave the new act the grand title, "Fred and Adele Astaire in New Songs and Smart Dances," and they tried it out in summer resorts. Audience response was good, and the Astaires launched a tour of New England. Again the act proved a crowd pleaser, especially in New Haven, where Yale students were entranced by Adele.

The Astaires traveled across America with their new songs and smart dances, and the reaction ranged from good to show-stopping. Fred was elated but not complacent. He continued polishing the dances, forcing Adele to rehearse between performances. They were good enough to play the Palace, Fred believed. Indeed there was interest from the management of the Palace, the ultimate goal of all vaudevillians from its opening in 1913. But Fred let it be known that he and Adele would not accept the opening spot, and the Palace made no offer.

The Astaires' tour of 1915–1916 was triumphal. They were earning $350 a week and playing the top vaudeville houses of the country. Fred bought a back-page ad in *Variety* so the show world could read the critics' encomiums.

The tour proved that Fred and Adele Astaire had an unlimited future in vaudeville. The wedding-cake act and the Rainy Day act had exhibited their precocity: cute kids doing grown-up things. But the sophistication of their dancing could not be fully appreciated until they had become young adults.

Their style was something new. It wasn't ballroom dancing, like the Castles'. It wasn't adagio or tap or ballet. The Astaires had their own special grace, a lighthearted flow of movement that seemed to spring spontaneously from the gay spirits of the dancers.

A week after the Astaire ad appeared in *Variety,* an agent called with the offer of a contract with the Shuberts. Adele was twenty and Fred was eighteen when they opened in *Over the Top* at the Forty-fourth Street Roof. Their vaudeville days were over.

3

Broadway and London

He is the most interesting, the most inventive, the most elegant dancer of our times. . . . You see a little bit of Astaire in everybody's dancing—a pause here, a move there. It was all Astaire's originally.

—George Balanchine

THE PASSING SHOW OF 1918
It is a whale—without Jonah
A HUGE WHIZZING
ENTERTAINMENT!
A brilliant Array of Talent with
The Winter Garden's famous
WIGGLING WAVE OF WINSOME WENCHES!!!
130 PEOPLE 2 ACTS 25 SCENES

The press agent's hyperbole heralded the second Broadway show of Fred and Adele Astaire. It was a standard Shubert revue, remembered principally for introducing the wartime song hit "Smiles," by J. Will Callahan and Lee S. Roberts. The rest of the score was by Sigmund Romberg, Jean Schwartz and Harold Atteridge, and reflected the current music: "The Galli-Curci Rag," "Trombone Jazz," et cetera. Frank Fay, Willie and Eugene Howard and Charles Ruggles supplied the comedy.

Before starting their contract with Charles Dillingham, Fred and Adele had to fulfill their commitment for one more show for the Shuberts. After their success in *Over the Top,* they were disappointed with *The Passing Show of 1918.* They had only two numbers, including one in which they flitted around the stage in bird costumes, singing, "Twit, twit, twit, you'd better do your little bit, bit, bit. . . ." Fred detested the costume and the number, and so did Adele.

They also performed a tango from their vaudeville act, and it helped them attract good notices. Heywood Broun commented that the Astaires "made the show pause early in the evening with a beautiful loose-limbed dance. It almost seemed as if the two young persons had been poured into the dance."

The Passing Show was overshadowed by *The Ziegfeld Follies of 1918,* starring Will Rogers, Eddie Cantor, W. C. Fields and Ann Pennington, but the Shubert revue lasted 124 performances before going on the road. Frank Fay dropped out of the tour, and Fred assumed his role.

The tour ended on a triumphal note: a return to the Palace Theatre in Chicago, scene of their first big hit in vaudeville and now a legitimate house. Fred celebrated by buying a used Mercer sports car, which he drove until *The Passing Show* folded in June 1919.

Fred could afford such a luxury. The Astaires' salary had risen from $250 a week in *Over the Top* to $350 in *The Passing Show,* and Charles Dillingham had promised a leap to $550. No more the $15 suits that he had bought in the vaudeville small-time. Now he could afford the well-tailored Brooks Brothers suits, the kind worn by the sons of the rich at Ivy League colleges.

In 1919 Fred was twenty—he had been too young to be drafted in the war—and his personal style had developed. Like many other performers of the period, he was influenced by the distinctive, enormously successful George M. Cohan. Fred adopted the dancer's saunter, the smart clothes, the brisk, wise-cracking manner. In the theatre, as at school in Highwood Park, he was "one of the boys." He shot craps with his fellow performers, took part in the horseplay and practical jokes. He became an expert pool player, and during the run of *The Passing Show* was introduced to the excitement of the race track.

> FRED: The first horse race I ever went to was at Belmont Park in New York. Gordon Dooley, who was one of the famous Dooley family, and Charlie Foy, one of the Seven Little Foys, and I went out to Belmont one day. That was before I went to London. I got involved over there with some racing people, a couple of jocks I got to know, and I started racing a couple of animals there. I began with moderate type of material. I wasn't expecting to win any derby; I didn't know enough about it.

Fred was comfortable amid the raucous male camaraderie of dressing rooms. Elsewhere he was intensely, almost painfully, shy. His entire life had been concentrated on performing for the stage, and that he could do, confident in his talent. But in social situations he found himself stammering, as if aware that he lacked the polish and education of those he admired.

Broadway success brought with it the glare of publicity, and press agents came to realize the discomfort with which

Fred endured interviews. Fortunately, Adele more than made up for him with her unfailing vivacity. She adored talking to interviewers and often spouted outrageous remarks.

Adele delighted in the prominence that the Broadway theater was bringing to her. Most of her life had been spent in traveling from one city to the next. At last she could remain in New York and enjoy the beaux who showered her with gifts and took her to the finest restaurants. For Fred, his shyness precluded romance. He mooned over certain chorus beauties but doubted his chances of winning out over their wealthy suitors. With his long chin, narrow face, large ears, already receding hairline and skinny frame, he never considered himself handsome.

Ann Austerlitz had long before relinquished the role of stage mother, and Fred now handled most of the business affairs. But she remained close to Adele and Fred, and with the new prosperity from the theater, all three moved into the Hotel Majestic on Seventy-second Street, occupying a suite overlooking Central Park West. They pleaded with Frederick Austerlitz to join them. But his Austrian pride would not allow him to live off the earnings of his children. He remained in Omaha.

Apple Blossoms was the Astaires' first show for Charles Dillingham. It was pure operetta, and the producer was taking a chance. The Austro-German operetta, for twenty years a Broadway staple, had been banished because of wartime animosities. With his showman's instinct, Dillingham figured the operetta was due for a comeback in late 1919, and he proved himself right.

John Charles Thomas and Wilda Bennett starred in a remarkably literate script by William LeBaron, who also wrote the lyrics. Half of the music was composed by Fritz Kreisler, half by Victor Jacobi. The Astaires did not take part in the story. They contributed two importance dance numbers, one to a Jacobi song, the other to be written by Kreisler.

He was the leading violin virtuoso of the day, an Austrian whose love of the theatre compelled him to write songs for operettas. He invited Fred and Adele to his studio and asked, "What sort of music do you want for your dance?" Fred hummed a few bars of the tango they had used in their act. "I don't get it; can you play it for me?" the composer asked.

Fred sat down at the piano and played the tango. Kreisler listened thoughtfully, then said, "Would this fit your dance?" He played his noted composition "Tambourin Chinois," and Fred and Adele agreed it would be perfect. A few days later, Kreisler appeared at rehearsal with a new arrangement, which he played as the Astaires plotted the dance with the choreographer, Edward Royce.

Another rehearsal pianist appeared at the Globe Theater: George Gershwin.

Although his first musical, *La La Lucille*, had been produced in May of 1919, Gershwin delighted in playing rehearsal piano because of his friendship with Fritz Kreisler. George and Fred renewed an acquaintance that had begun in the Remick publishing office, and George repeated his desire to compose a show for the Astaires.

Apple Blossoms enjoyed a good tryout in Baltimore and opened in New York on October 7 to critical and audience acclaim. The operetta had been redeemed.

For the first time, reviewers made mention of Fred's contribution to the dancing team. Alexander Woollcott of *The New York Times* commented: "There should be a half a dozen special words for the vastly entertaining dances of the Adaires [sic], in particular for those of the incredibly nimble and lack-a-daisical Adaire named Fred. He is one of those extraordinary persons whose sense of rhythm and humor have been all mixed up, whose very muscles, of which he seems to have an extra supply, are downright facetious."

Apple Blossoms continued drawing crowds into May of 1920. In September, a full season's tour began, with the Astaires receiving $750 a week.

FRED: I found [a long run] a tedious thing. I didn't like it. If you had a long run, you started thinking, 'What are we gonna do next? What's it gonna be?' But then you hadn't really started to plan. It wasn't like a movie: When you get halfway through, you can start planning for the next one. You can't do that on the stage. We played in New York for a year and a half; in London, two years. Then you had to go elsewhere, tour with it. You began to say, "Gee whiz, we're using up a lot of years here. . . ."

[About staying fresh in a long run] There was a different thing every night. You'd get some nights with a very dull audience. They wouldn't be too enthusiastic, without knowing it. You can't get them all.

Another time you get an audience where they can't get enough of you, and they laugh twice as loud. There were always things happening in live shows. In a musical, you didn't have time to get down about it. I just worried about the work. I'd say, "I didn't do this or that so well tonight; I'd better come in tomorrow and rehearse it."

After you've been doing something for a year, you don't *want* to come in and rehearse it. . . . As I remember, you would always have room for improvement in a show. You mustn't let it get too ad-libby or too [mechanical]. We were very conscientious about giving a good performance, both Delly and I were. I was, more than Delly. She'd say, "Aw, to hell with it, I don't feel like it tonight." But she would do it, always well, because she was a real pro, a wonderful performer.

Charles Dillingham tried to repeat the hit of *Apple Blossoms* with a 1921 operetta, *The Love Letter.* Again Victor Jacobi contributed songs, William LeBaron wrote the book and lyrics, John Charles Thomas starred, and the Astaires danced. The story was derived from a Ferenc Molnár play, *The Phantom Rival.*

Sensing that the production wasn't going well, Dillingham poured money into lavish costumes and elaborate sets. But the expense couldn't cure the anemic script. Reviews were halfhearted, and the public was apathetic. Dillingham closed *The Love Letter* after thirty-one performances.

Yet the show marked a significant advance for Fred and Adele Astaire. Reviewers again praised their dances. The *Herald:* "Next to the star, the Astaires once more dancing about him like fireflies made the high score of the evening, getting four encores for their entertaining singing and nutty dancing to 'Upside Down' and revealing in this and other whirlwind numbers they have developed a penetrating comedy touch with their lips as well as with their always ambitious feet."

The Love Letter also proved an important show for the Astaires because it provided their signature number: the Runaround.

It was the inspiration of Edward Royce, who directed the dances for *The Love Letter*. During rehearsal, Royce asked Adele to run in large circles with her hands up as if bicycling. While the pianist played a series of *oompahs*, Fred joined Adele in the running. Royce was delighted with the result, and devised a silly dance that culminated in the runarounds and a dash offstage. Overnight Jacobi and LeBaron wrote a song, "Upside Down," to fit the dance.

FRED: It became a trademark for us, and whenever we went into it the audience would applaud. We would get numerous encores from it. There was a little tag at the end and they'd want more: "Come out and do it again!"

It had to be planted a certain way. First we did the song, a nutty number. Then we'd start by walking. [He demonstrated with the first two fingers of his hands on a tabletop.] The music would go Oompah! Oompah! Then we'd break into a sort of trot. Oompah! Oompah! Oompah! Then we'd keep going around and around and around, and the people would laugh and applaud and all that sort of thing. Then we'd go off. They'd want an encore, so we'd come back and find a way of getting into the run again.

It was simple as hell. It was a "dumb" number—oompah, oompah, oompah—first we'd walk, then the orchestra would go faster and we'd run. My sister is the one who was really the reason for it being so good. She was very funny the way she did it, and I would go along beside her. She was a good comedienne.

I did a little bit of the runaround with Gracie Allen in *Damsel in Distress*. It wasn't the same thing; it couldn't be the same in a movie because you can't stop and do encores and ad-lib.

With Fred and Adele prospering on Broadway, Frederick Austerlitz could no longer resist joining them to share their fame. After fifteen years, the family was reunited. In the next few years Austerlitz engaged in a number of business enterprises, none successful. His natural cheerfulness began to fade, and he underwent periods of depression. The cause of his decline, Fred believed, was his failure to fulfill the Old World percept that a man should support his family.

Fred Astaire has always been a shopper. Not necessarily a buyer. A shopper. Throughout his lifetime he has enjoyed looking in shop windows, browsing through jewelry stores, inspecting all the merchandise in haberdasheries. It became a form of relaxation for him, an escape from the pressures of the show world.

One day as *The Love Letter* was limping to a close, Fred decided to escape the misery of being in a flop. He dropped into Finchley's men's furnishing shop to buy a tie. The young salesman recognized him and began making suggestions about the Astaires' career.

"I think you ought to get out of those revues and operettas and do a real musical comedy like *Oh Boy*," said the salesman, referring to the Jerome Kern hit.

Fred agreed with the reasoning but thought the tie salesman presumptuous to be handing out career advice. Then the young man identified himself as Alex A. Aarons, part owner of the store, son of a noted theater executive. Young Aarons had produced George Gershwin's first show, *La La Lucille*, and wanted to do another with the brilliant composer—and the Astaires.

Fred thought nothing more of the encounter until he and Adele were coming to the end of a tour with *The Love Letter*. Aarons said he was preparing a show and wanted the

The Astaires had their first speaking roles in For Goodness Sake, *1922.*

Astaires in it. Since Charles Dillingham had nothing ready
for them, he agreed to release Fred and Adele to Aarons.

For Goodness Sake, which opened February 20, 1922, at
the Lyric Theater, was another advance for the Astaires. It
marked the first time they had speaking roles, as the second-

ary romantic couple. Another first: Fred took part in the devising of their dances. He decided to repeat the run-around routine, this time to the song "The Whichness of the Whatness and the Whereness of the Who." Fred was disappointed that George Gershwin was occupied with another show and contributed only two songs. But the score by William Daly, Paul Lannin and Arthur Jackson provided serviceable numbers for Fred and Adele.

Though not the stars of *For Goodness Sake,* the Astaires drew the biggest praise from the critics. Their dances drew "storm after storm of applause," reported the *Evening Telegram.* The *Morning American* reported that the Astaires "can speak a little, act a little and dance a quart. They are as nice a twain as one would want to see." Wrote Robert Benchley in *Life* magazine: "When they dance, everything seems brighter, and their comedy alone would be enough to carry them through even if they were to stop dancing (which God forbid!)."

For Goodness Sake lasted fifteen weeks and would have gone longer except for the heat wave that closed most of the uncooled Broadway theaters in the summer of 1922. After playing the show in Chicago for a few weeks, Fred and Adele prepared to return to their mentor, Charles Dillingham.

The Bunch and Judy was a disappointment for Fred and Adele. It was to be their first starring vehicle, and Dillingham assembled the elements with his customary taste. Jerome Kern was engaged to write the songs. The plot, an eerie foreshadowing of future events, concerned an American dancing star who abandons her career for a British nobleman. During rehearsals, the show's shortcomings began to manifest themselves. The script creaked, the songs failed to elevate, the Astaires kept falling off a banquet table on which they were to dance.

The Philadelphia tryout justified everyone's apprehensions. The critics complained about the plot, found the Kern songs undistinguished. The *Inquirer* mispelled the Astaires' name, and the *Bulletin* grumbled that they danced too much.

Dillingham tried to bolster the show by injecting specialty acts, including six brothers who played saxophones, but the additions merely exposed the flimsiness of the plot. During the final week in Philadelphia, the comedian Joseph

Cawthorne rushed out of his dressing room to get to the stage and fell down the stairs. He suffered a broken kneecap and was replaced by Johnny Dooley, brother of Fred's racetrack buddy, Gordon Dooley. A sister, Ray Dooley, was already in the *Bunch and Judy* cast, and Fred thought two brother-sister teams might be lucky.

The opening at the Globe in New York was postponed one night until November 28, 1922, Dillingham hoping that an additional performance would help get the show in shape. It didn't. Although the reviews were kind, the public detected the mishmash nature of *The Bunch and Judy*, and ticket sales were slow.

Dillingham tried to keep the show going. He staged an elaborate party for Adele's "twenty-first" birthday (in fine theatrical tradition, she had already taken three years off her age). The seventy members of the *Bunch and Judy* cast gathered on the last-act cabaret set after a Tuesday night performance for a lavish supper to which the press was invited. Adele counted up eighty-one birthday gifts, including one that attracted press notice: a ton of coal "from a young Pittsburgh admirer." According to newspaper reports, Adele donated the coal to Mr. Dillingham to help heat the Globe Theater and received a bouquet of orchids in return.

The show's press agent issued publicity about Adele that was just as fanciful as her alleged age. This was duly printed, and among the misinformation:

Real name: Adele Astaire.
Born: Omaha, Nebraska, December 5, 1901.
Educated: Omaha and Boston public schools.
Occupation before going on stage: music student.
Stage debut: amateur night, Columbia Theater, Boston.
First actual engagement: dancing in vaudeville with brother Fred, Orpheum Theater, Omaha, October 11, 1916.
First New York engagement: vaudeville, Palace Theater, 1917.
Salary: $1750, divided with brother Fred.
Favorite author: Stephen Leacock.
Favorite newspaper: the ones that print pictures of Adele Astaire.

Publicity could not save *The Bunch and Judy*, and it lasted only sixty-three performances. Dillingham tried to save some of his investment by touring the show, but audiences on the road were equally apathetic. The closing notice was posted.

Fred gained a minor satisfaction on closing night. Throughout the run of *The Bunch and Judy,* he had been required to perform the "Pale Venetian Moon" number in a white satin knickerbocker costume with white periwig. He detested the costume, especially the wig. When the curtain went down on his final performance of "Pale Venetian Moon," he pulled off the wig and hurled it the length of the stage.

The Astaires returned to New York in defeat, and Fred agonized over their future. He worried whether Charles Dillingham would exercise the next contract option, raising their weekly salary from $1,000 to $1,250. The producer decided not to.

Again Alex Aarons came to the rescue after an Astaire flop.

The enterprising young producer had the notion that *For Goodness Sake* might succeed in London. He made the suggestion to Fred during the waning days of *The Bunch and Judy,* then sailed to London to see if he could arrange a production.

Fred was distraught over his and Adele's failure in their first starring show. He declined a lucrative offer for the Astaires to dance in a Manhattan supper club. He also turned down a chance for them to appear at the Palace, once their greatest ambition. Fred and Adele decided to indulge themselves in their first real vacation—not counting their summer layoffs at eastern resorts. Then Aarons cabled that he had succeeded in promoting a London production of *For Goodness Sake.* For Fred and Adele, whose only trips outside the United States had been for vaudeville dates in Canada, the chance was irresistible.

Ann Austerlitz was concerned about her husband's health, which had been declining, and she felt she should remain in New York with him. But he argued that she had worked hard for Adele and Fred and deserved to see them triumph in England. He promised he would join them as soon as he felt better. But, in truth, he was suffering the first stages of cancer. The voyage on the *Aquitania* was joyful though beset with rough seas. Both Fred and Adele became enamored with England immediately. He could spend hours browsing through the shops, especially the clothing stores on Savile Row. She indulged herself by buying new frocks to wear at the tea dances in the Savoy Hotel, where they stayed. Alex Aarons and his English partner, Sir Alfred Butt, entertained them in great style. They attended their first London show, *Battling Butler,* starring Jack Buchanan, who impressed Fred with his airy elegance and comedic style. Fred was also impressed by the audience.

> FRED: We hit London when it was more glamorous than it is today. I was always aware, and it amused me, that they would dress up so much to go out. I've mentioned this a lot of times, and it isn't that I was awe-struck, because I don't think anybody in our business gets awe-struck that people would dress up. I was amazed to see an audience where the men were all in white ties! This would not only be on opening night. A successful show would have all of the front rows—the stalls, they call them—in evening dress. White tie, not a dinner jacket, but white tie, full dress. The ladies in their jewels and gowns. It was quite exciting.
>
> I've been back to London since then, not on the stage or anything. But I've been to a couple of shows, and it's nothing like that now. [The English] are nonchalant about it. They don't think about dressing at night—unless they're going to some private party maybe.

Fred once remarked that he had a sure gauge for when a London show was starting to decline: black ties began replacing white ties in the stalls.

During their early period in London, the Astaires had an alarming experience at the Empire Theatre. They attended the opening night of a revue that failed to find favor with the audience. Patrons in the gallery talked back to the actors, boos and whistles punctuated the performance. The curtain brought a chorus of disdain. Fred and Adele stared at each other with trepidation, but Aarons assured them that no such disturbance would greet *For Goodness Sake.*

Work began on the show, which acquired a new title, *Stop Flirting*. The script was Anglicized, an English cast was recruited, and the score was bolstered with a Gershwin song, "I'll Build a Stairway to Paradise," which had been written for *George White's Scandals of 1922*. Rehearsals progressed smoothly, and the tryout tour began in Liverpool. The response was enormous, especially to the runaround by Fred and Adele. Audiences demanded encore after encore.

The secret was in how Fred and Adele flew offstage at the end of the runaround. Fred's years in vaudeville had taught him the wisdom he imparted to his English understudy: "Always think of the exit. The exit's the thing that kills 'em. You can make your whole show by your exit."

Stop Flirting moved to Glasgow and Edinburgh, where the Scots were charmed by the American accents of the Astaires. An exuberant interviewer wrote: "When I danced around to the stage door of the King's last night—what's that? Danced? Yes, danced; I couldn't walk after watching the Astaires all evening—I found them coming off the stage, where they had just been having their photograph taken. The photographer must have had his quickest lens working, for if ever feet twinkled, the Astaires have 'em." Adele introduced the reporter to her mother, about whom he wrote: "It was difficult to believe the tall, beautiful young woman who greeted me was the mother of these two."

Critics were equally struck by the Astaires. One commented that the two young Americans introduced a new art: "Grotesque and eccentric dancing is familiar, but humor combined with vivacity and art and nimble daintiness is a novelty which was last night rewarded by enthusiastic recalls."

Stop Flirting opened on May 30, 1923, at the Shaftesbury Theater in London. During the first act, Fred feared that the premiere audience was cool. The gallery wasn't responding with any enthusiasm. But at least, he consoled himself, there were no catcalls.

Everything changed in the second act, when Fred and Adele had their best numbers. For the duet of "Oh Gee, Oh Gosh, Oh Golly, I Love You" the reaction was enthusiastic. Then came "The Whichness of the Whatness." The runaround captivated the Londoners, stalls and gallery, and they began chanting "Oompah! Oompah! Oompah!" as the Astaires circled crazily around the stage.

"Columbus may have danced with joy at discovering America," wrote the London *Times*, "but how he would have cavorted had he also discovered Fred and Adele Astaire!"

The *Times* continued, with total lack of British reserve, that the Astaires "typify the primal spirit of animal delight that could not restrain itself, the vitality that burst its bounds in the Garden of Eden. They are as lithe as blades of grass, as light as gossamer, as odd as golliwogs."

Other reviews were equally hyperbolic. The *Star* remarked that Adele "could dance the depression out of an undertaker." St. John Ervine declared, "I could have willingly watched Miss Astaire dance for the whole evening and so, judging from the applause, could the rest of the audience." The *Pall Mall Gazette* critic observed that the Astaires "neither look nor behave like regular dancers," and added, "Their final shoulder-to-shoulder gallop not only brings down the house but is one of the funniest things of its kind I can remember."

London had embraced Fred and Adele in a way that New York never had. No wonder they were crazy about everything English.

The Prince of Wales came to *Stop Flirting* ten times and invited the Astaires to join him for supper. The Duke and Duchess of York, Prince George and other members of royalty attended the show and became acquainted with Fred and Adele. The American visitors were adopted by stars of the London stage and invited to night-club parties and weekends in the country. When America's royalty, Douglas Fairbanks and Mary Pickford, visited London with clamorous acclaim, they were taken to *Stop Flirting* by Lord and Lady Mountbatten. Fred and Adele were invited to their box between acts.

While Adele led an active social life with dashing young noblemen, Fred was busy with his own new friends, who ranged from bookmakers and jockeys to Prince George and Noel Coward.

Two years before, Coward had come backstage after a performance of *The Love Letter* in New York and had urged Fred to appear in London. Coward was delighted by the Astaires' London success. While he never lacked confidence in his own talents, he admitted, "Freddie, when I see you dance it makes me cry."

Fred confessed his own desire to be a songwriter. "Then you must have some music lessons, Freddie," Coward announced. "And so must I."

Coward was a self-taught pianist who had written a few songs and was preparing more for a revue, *London Calling!* Years later, Coward recalled:

"I have only had two music lessons in my life. These were the first steps of what was to be a full course which Fred Astaire and I enrolled for at the Guildhall School of Music, and they faltered and stopped when I was told by my instructor that I could not use consecutive fifths. He went on to explain that a gentleman named Ebenezer Prout had announced many years ago that consecutive fifths were wrong and must in no circumstances be employed. At that time Ebenezer Prout was merely a name to me (as a matter of fact he still is, and a very funny one at that), and I was unimpressed by his Victorian dicta.

"I argued back that Debussy and Ravel used consecutive fifths like mad. My instructor waved aside this triviality with a pudgy hand, and I left his presence forever with the parting shot that what was good enough for Debussy and Ravel was good enough for me."

The music lessons ended, but Fred gave Coward expert instruction in the dance. Coward was having trouble with two dances he and Gertrude Lawrence were rehearsing for *London Calling!* Fred gladly supervised the choreography and also staged Coward's solo number, "Sentiment." It drew a comment from the *Sunday Express:* "Mr. Coward cannot compose and should sing only for his friends' amazement."

The Astaires' London success was shadowed by one thing: reports of their father's worsening illness in America. Ann Austerlitz became so concerned that she left England to rejoin her husband.

One evening before a performance, Sir Alfred Butt came to Fred's dressing room without his customary cheerfulness. "You know that your father has been sick, Fred," the producer said. "Would you be surprised to learn that he was very sick?"

"No," Fred replied with mounting apprehension. "I

would not be surprised. He has been ill for some time. But what are you trying to tell me?"

"Fred, your father has died."

As Fred struggled to comprehend the news, he heard Sir Alfred saying he would be willing to close down the show for a period.

"No," Fred replied. "We'll just keep right on going."

He and Adele managed to get through the performance, and they continued the run without interruption. It was the first real tragedy that had befallen the Astaires, and for weeks they numbly tried to deal with it. For Fred, particularly, it was a brutal, bewildering event. He had never really known his father. The memories of Omaha were dim, almost too distant to recapture. In his growing-up years, Fred knew him as an occasional presence, a hearty man who was proud of his son's and daughter's accomplishments. During the brief time he lived with his family, Frederick Austerlitz seemed defeated by life. His children had grown up. Too late to be a father.

For a year and a half, London continued its love affair with Fred and Adele, and *Stop Flirting* might have surpassed *Chu Chin Chow,* the long-run record holder. Adele, a confirmed anglophile, would not have minded. Fred was equally fond of the English and had even acquired a modest accent to accompany his Savile Row wardrobe. But he worried about their lengthy absence from the Broadway theater. He realized that their last three New York shows had been flops. It was time to go home and prove themselves.

Reporters were on hand when the S. S. *Homeric* arrived in New York, and they questioned the Astaires about their London triumph. Adele sidestepped inquiries about her dancing with the Prince of Wales, snapping that he and the royal family "were very kind to my brother and me and I'm not going to talk about it for publicity purposes."

Alex Aarons wanted to put the Astaires to work. Now he was the partner of Vinton Freedley, who had played the juvenile in *For Goodness Sake* as well as investing in it. Their new show bore the tentative title of *Black-Eyed Susan,* and

George Gershwin and his brother Ira were writing the songs, their first collaboration. Fred hated the title but was delighted that George's prediction, expressed years before when he played the piano at Remick's, would finally come true.

The title became *Lady, Be Good!* and the show proved a milestone for the Astaires, the Gershwins and the American musical.

For Fred and Adele it was their first chance to be unquestioned stars. Theirs were the two leading roles, and happily, they were cast as brother and sister. In their midtwenties, with their relationship known to all theatergoers, they could no longer act as sweethearts.

The book by Guy Bolton and Fred Thompson was lamely plotted, but it gave Adele the chance to display her rare talent as a comedienne, especially in concert with Walter Catlett. *Lady, Be Good!* provided Fred with his first opportunity to shine as a solo performer in a Broadway show. His number "The Half of It, Dearie, Blues" proved to be a highlight.

The Gershwin songs were new and fresh and vital, perfectly attuned to 1924 America. Ragtime and jazz had been introduced to Broadway before, but the *Lady, Be Good!* songs transcended the popular music of honky-tonks and cabarets. George had combined Negro music with his own syncopation. And Ira's lyrics, perfectly cadenced to the complicated music and brilliantly rhymed, gave it a finish of worldly sophistication.

Lady, Be Good! seemed blessed from the start. Philadelphians cheered the tryout premiere, and little repair work seemed necessary. One of Adele's songs was eliminated. When she and Fred were tossed onto the street for nonpayment of rent, Adele sang about an imaginary lover she hoped would come into her life. Some believed the song slowed down the show; Adele thought she was considered too young-looking to sing it. George Gershwin theorized: "It lacks a soothing, seducing rhythm; instead, it has a certain slow lilt that subtly disturbs the audience instead of lulling it into acceptance." A few years later the song redeemed itself: "The Man I Love."

The *Lady, Be Good!* score still contained, as *The New York*

Times remarked, "a number of tunes the unmusical will find hard to get rid of." They included "Lady, Be Good!," "Fascinating Rhythm," "So Am I" and "Oh, What a Lovely Party." The songs were enhanced immeasurably by an innovation in the orchestra pit: twin pianos played by Phil Ohman and Vic Arden. They provided a new and exciting sound that perfectly suited the Gershwin melodies.

The New York Times noted the change in Adele since her London triumph: "When she left she was a graceful dancer—and she has returned not only with all her glorious grace but as a first-rate comedienne in her own right. Miss Astaire in the new piece is as charming and entertaining a musical comedy actress as the town has seen on display in many a moon. Fred Astaire too makes a good account of himself."

The *Herald-Tribune* reported that when the Astaires "sang and danced 'Fascinating Rhythm' the callous Broadwayites cheered them as if their favorite halfback had planted the ball between the goalpost after an 80-yard run. Seldom has it been our pleasure to witness so heartfelt, spontaneous and so deserved a tribute."

"Fascinating Rhythm" was introduced early in the second act, when Cliff Edwards strolled into an argument between Fred and Adele and started singing the song to the accompaniment of his famed ukulele. The Astaires dropped their quarrel and danced to the intricate melody. It was a perfect union of words, music and movement.

> Fascinating rhythm,
> You've got me on the go!
> Fascinating rhythm,
> I'm all a-quiver.
>
> What a mess you're making!
> The neighbors want to know
> Why I'm always shaking
> Just like a flivver. . . .

After almost twenty years as performers, Fred and Adele Astaire had achieved the unquestioned status of stars.

Lady, Be Good! proved the most original musical in a season that included *The Student Prince, Rose Marie, Big Boy,* with Al Jolson, as well as such revues as *Ziegfeld Follies, George White's Scandals, Earl Carroll's Vanities, The Passing Show, Music Box Revue* and *Garrick Gaeities,* which introduced the team of Lorenz Hart and Richard Rodgers to Broadway.

Lady, Be Good! seemed certain for a long run, and Fred was relieved that their eighteen-month absence in England had not harmed the Astaires' reputation. Although their dances drew immense applause at every performance, Fred resisted complacency.

Adele once said: "Opening night I'd do it the way Fred wanted, and then after the show had been running awhile, I'd start missing. Maybe I'd miss a step, so in getting to the wings, I'd stroll off frightfully blithe, acting very cute (I thought) outfoxing him, telling myself, 'Now, never mind. He won't notice that—it was such a little thing.'

"But he'd be waiting for me. 'Babe, you missed a step tonight,' he'd say, very patiently. 'Don't you think we'd better stay after the show and rehearse?'

"And somehow, no matter what I wanted to do instead, no matter where I thought I had to go, there he'd have me rehearsing for hours, teaching me the routine all over again."

On rare occasions Adele rebelled, particularly when an intriguing man was waiting for her at the stage door. Fred worried about some of her suitors, fearful that they might take advantage of his sister. She shrugged off his concerns, arguing that he always found something to worry about: their performances, future contracts, her beaus. "Moaning Minnie," she called him.

Fred found his own diversions. He dated actresses and showgirls, though he was serious about none of them. He visited the night spots with his old friend from summer vacations, Philadelphia socialite James Artemus. They were joined by Artemus' friend from Yale, Jock Whitney. Fred and Whitney formed what was to be a lifelong friendship, and Fred met Mrs. Payne Whitney, Jock's mother and owner of a prestigious racing stable. When Fred couldn't get to the racetrack, he placed bets through bookmakers and even cabled London to wager on English races.

Fred and Adele sail for London and Lady, Be Good! *(Wide World Photos)*

During the run of *Lady, Be Good!* the Astaires were visited by a young Nebraskan named Leland Hayward. He had dabbled in writing publicity and scripts for the movies, but in 1925 was broke and jobless. Making the rounds of Manhattan night clubs, Hayward had encountered a friend, Mal Hayward (no relation), who complained that business at his Trocadero was rotten. Leland Hayward's suggestion: Why not hire Broadway's hottest act, Fred and Adele Astaire?

The Astaires were intrigued by the proposal, and Fred insisted on a $5,000 weekly salary so they could make enough to buy a new Rolls-Royce. Hayward clinched the deal.

The engagement was a success, putting the Trocadero back in business. The Astaires bought the Rolls on their next trip to England, but they decided night clubs were not for them. They never played another one.

As for Leland Hayward, he set up a talent agency, with the Astaires as his first clients. He built one of the biggest agencies before selling out to MCA and becoming a top stage and film producer.

April 14, 1926. The Empire Theater on Leicester Square, London. English first-nighters could not remember a premiere as tumultuous as *Lady, Be Good!*, starring Fred and Adele Astaire. They were cheered when they first appeared onstage. When they danced a witty Charleston, the audience squealed delightedly. Fred's solo, "The Half of It, Dearie, Blues," caused joyful shouts. The runaround brought the show to a delirious halt.

The *Evening Standard* rhapsodized: "Miss Adele Astaire is, I think, the most attractive thing on any stage. . . . She dances with an intelligence, with a gaiety, with a grace and delight . . . she is a comedienne in her toes and in her fingertips and in every line of a vivid and lovely little body." The *Daily Sketch* predicted a year's run despite the show's weak book, adding, "Fred and Adele Astaire have only to appear and everybody is blissfully happy. . . . Their dancing was uproarious. Fred's solo dance was one of the biggest things of the night."

Producers Aarons and Freedley had carefully tailored *Lady, Be Good!* to the English audience. The Gershwins had written "I'd Rather Charleston" to exploit the dance sensation that had swept England. The pace of the show was slowed to fit English taste. "Londoners want their measure of novelty, but they will not tolerate anything revolutionary in the theater," said Aarons. The script had to be reworked to eliminate words that were harmless in America but obscene in England.

Aarons added: "We put a new prologue in *Lady, Be Good!* at the Empire, in order to get Fred and Adele on the stage later than they appeared in New York. Like George Gershwin, the Astaires have a large London society following, and as these people came to the theater even later than they do in New York, we felt it would be better to hold off the entrance of the stars until the house was in."

Society and royalty embraced the Astaires once more. Even George V and Queen Mary attended *Lady, Be Good!*, a rare occurrence. The Prince of Wales was a frequent visitor, in the royal box and backstage, as were Prince George and the Duke and Duchess of York.

Adele received a hand-written letter from the Duchess: "I have just got back today from the country, and I wondered whether you would like to come in and see the baby sometime tomorrow—Tuesday. Would you and your brother like to have luncheon about 1:30?—or about 6 P.M.? It would be so nice to see you both. . . . Elizabeth." The Astaires paid the visit and saw the baby, who would be the future queen.

The London newspapers adopted Adele as the ideal American flapper, and she obliged them with sprightly, sometimes outrageous comments, which were duly reported in the American press.

Like many visiting celebrities, Adele was received by George Bernard Shaw. Trying to make conversation with the legendary playwright, she inquired, "What do you think of actors?"

"Nothing!" Shaw replied with a waggle of his beard. "If it wasn't for us authors, there wouldn't be any."

After their meeting, Adele told reporters, "I feel that my stay in England is complete. If it didn't make any difference to Mr. Shaw, I'd like to follow him around all day."

Adele had tea with Sir James Barrie, who announced afterward that she was his choice to play Peter Pan in the next Christmas production of the Barrie play. The novelist Hugh Walpole also was overwhelmed by Adele's ingenuous charm. Both John Galsworthy and his wife kissed Adele when she left after a visit with them.

Fred's pursuits were less literary. He became a good friend of a noted jockey Jack Leach, who introduced him to the major jockeys and trainers in England. On most non-matinee days, Fred motored to the racetrack in his new Rolls-Royce and spent the afternoon analyzing bet prospects with the experts. He even bought half-interests in two horses, Dolomite and Social Evening. Fred was undaunted that neither showed particular promise. He was enraptured by the entire racing scene.

Lady, Be Good! continued to be the most popular show in London. After more than two years in the same production—by far their longest run—Fred and Adele were weary of it. They were not displeased when the closing was announced, because the venerable Empire Theater was to be demolished and supplanted with a movie palace.

The final performance was set for January 22, 1927, and tickets were scarce, so much so that the Prince of Wales had to appeal to Fred for help in acquiring a box. All royal efforts had failed. Sir Alfred Butt managed to displace another party, and the Prince was reported to have danced to his favorite tunes in the rear of the box.

The rest of the audience was equally entranced. Affectionate shouts punctuated the performance, and the ovations were more overwhelming than Fred and Adele had ever known. The Empire was filled with notables, including Adeline Genée, who had been one of the theater's stars. In his curtain speech, Fred acknowledged her as the early inspiration in the careers of Fred and Adele Astaire.

The Prince of Wales invited Fred, Adele and their friends to a party at St. James' Palace after the show. The party continued until early morning and included a vigorous demonstration of the new Black Bottom dance by Jock Whitney, who had left his Oxford studies for the celebration.

After a tour of *Lady, Be Good!* in England, Wales and Scotland, Fred and Adele returned to the United States in June to prepare for another show.

Alex Aarons and Vinton Freedley had used their profits from *Lady, Be Good!* and two other Gershwin shows, *Tip Toes* and *Oh, Kay!*, to build a new theater on West Fifty-second Street. They combined their first names and called it the Alvin. The producers wanted another Gershwin-Astaire show for the premiere, and they commissioned Robert Benchley and Fred Thompson to compose a script. The title: *Smarty.*

Everything went wrong in Philadelphia. The dialogue fell flat, and the scenery threatened to as well. Cues were missed, tempos went awry, costumes tore. The public responded by staying away.

Washington was worse. Robert Benchley resigned when a reviewer observed that Benchley helped create the kind of turkey he had assailed for years as a drama critic. Paul Gerard Smith was summoned to help with the rewrite.

"Gee, it was terrible," Fred remarked in a 1928 *Collier's* article. "In Washington, we were playing one version and rehearsing another. Every performance was different from the one before it.

"There were times when I used to carry my lines typed on cards. I'd have to look down into my hand before I dared open my mouth. you know—look at the card—'and so-and-so and so-and-so, Herbert'; then another look at the card, then 'so-and-so and so-and-so, Herbert'; then another look at the card, then 'so-and-so and so-and-so.' Honest, I never thought we'd make it to New York. We even asked them to chuck the whole thing.

"But that's where Alex Aarons and Vin Freedley were keen managers. They knew, even when we didn't, that we had something, and instead of junking it, they kept working over it and working it until—well, you saw how it was received. My sister and I were never so discouraged in our lives—except once."

The other big discouragement came when he and Adele finally escaped being an opening vaudeville act when they scored a hit at the Chicago Palace, then returned there later—as an opening act.

The final stop of *Smarty* before Broadway was Wilmington, Delaware. The title was changed to *Funny Face,* which coincidentally was Fred's nickname for Adele. The new title seemed to signal a change in the show's fortunes. Victor Moore had been added to the cast, and his presence boosted the comedy. The Gershwins added new songs, including a comedy number for Fred and Adele, "The Babbitt and the Bromide."

The song concerned two old acquaintances who meet by accident and exchange a string of clichés. They meet ten years later, then twenty years afterward in heaven, always spouting the same tired phrases:

> Hello!
> How are you?
> Howza folks?
> What's new?
> I'm great!
> That's good!
> Ha! Ha!
> Knock wood.
> Well! Well!
> What say?
> Howya been?
> Nice day!
> How's tricks?
> What's new?
> That's fine!
> How are you?

Originally the Astaires sang Ira's lyrics in unison, deadpan, as if neither was listening to the other. The song worked better when they alternated the lines. The number was surefire, climaxed by the Astaire runaround.

> FRED: *Funny Face* was one of those shows that came
> to life when it got to New York. We had trouble with
> it on the road. It had to be remade, and one day
> we'd be doing one version, the next day at the
> matinee we'd be doing another version of the first
> act or whatever it was. Finally we went into Wilming-
> ton, Delaware, for a three-night stand. We were
> changing it and changing it, and we really didn't
> know what we had. But we were due in at the Alvin
> Theater, and we had a smash hit. We had the show
> right [in Wilmington] but we didn't know what we
> had.

The critics were rapturous, though some deplored the creaky, jewel-robbery plot. Fred played the guardian of Adele, whose jewels were stolen. Victor Moore was capital as the bumbling thief, and the Gershwins had never before written such a tuneful score. The hit was "'S Wonderful," sung by Adele and her romantic interest, Allen Kearns. They also sang "He Loves and She Loves." Besides "The Babbitt and the Bromide," the Astaires did "Funny Face," and Fred performed "My One and Only" with Gertrude McDonald and Betty Compton.

Funny Face proved a significant advance in the career of Fred Astaire. He established himself as a solo performer with a wider range than merely dancing duets with his sister. The "High Hat" number presaged the movie Fred Astaire. Resplendent in tuxedo, hands planted in his pockets, Fred performed a rousing tap number with a black-tie chorus of two dozen male dancers repeating his steps. Besides being a show-stopper, the number underscored his versatility and displayed a virility he had rarely had a chance to show before.

> FRED: At that point, I wasn't doing much tap danc-
> ing. Finally I started at the end of the run of *Lady, Be*

Good! We played it about a year, and in the last week
I decided to try something different. I had a solo
number with the ingenue girl, not Delly. Suddenly,
after fiddling around with tap, I made up my own
way of doing it.

I remember the first night I tried it out. It
stopped the show! So it stayed in. We went to London with the show, and I did it over there. Then I
did more and more of it. I didn't do so much with
my sister, because she wasn't a tap dancer. I did
solos. It was kind of my own way of handling that
form. It came in handy in all of the shows I did after
that.

It was strictly a sideline; I did so many other
kinds of dances. When I'm called "a tap dancer," it
makes me laugh. Because I *am* in a way, but that is
one of the kinds of dancing I do. I happened to have
some outstanding, successful numbers in the tap, so
people remember. . . . I had a little different treatment of how to *apply* it. I didn't just set out and hop
into the "buck." I'd move around and do things.

Funny Face opened on November 22, 1927, six weeks
after the premiere of the movie *The Jazz Singer.* When the
audience heard Al Jolson say, "Come on, Ma! Listen to this,"
the talkie revolution was on. Many persons, including Fred
Astaire, were convinced that sound motion pictures would be
a passing novelty. But the sensation created by *The Jazz Singer*
prompted the Hollywood studios to begin converting to
sound. Their major planning concerned musicals, the only
form of entertainment that had been impossible in silent
films.

The studios hunted through the Broadway theater for
singers, dancers, directors, choreographers and songwriters
to create the coming wave of film musicals. Walter Wanger,
head of the New York office of Paramount Pictures, asked
the Astaires to make a screen test. They reluctantly agreed,
and agonized when they saw themselves on the screen. Both
were relieved when Paramount made no offer for a contract.

Funny Face further established the Astaires as stars of the Broadway musical, and producers began coveting their services. Florenz Ziegfeld sought them for a show he was planning for the 1928–1929 season. Fred was flattered to learn that Broadway's most famous producer wanted to star him and Adele. But *Funny Face* was certain to run through the season, and Alex Aarons had already scheduled a London run afterward.

"Adele and I would love to do a Ziegfeld show," Fred told Ziegfeld. "Maybe after we get back from London."

Adele had turned thirty during the tryout of *Funny Face*. She had been dancing nearly all her life, and she was beginning to tire. Fred found it harder and harder to induce his sister to stay after the performance to rehearse a dance that had lost its focus. She much preferred to go out nightclubbing with a handsome young man.

Society columnists always reported the latest romance of Adele Astaire, usually with an American millionaire. She was rumored engaged to William Gaunt, Jr., but he was said to have lost his fortune "because he paid more attention to Adele than his financial affairs." A marriage was predicted for Adele and Jock Whitney, Fred's great chum, but she was a bridesmaid at his wedding. Next came Billy Leeds.

He was a millionaire yachtsman who had once been married to a Greek princess. After *Funny Face* had closed because of the summer heat, Adele and Billy were inseparable. During a July weekend at his country place on Long Island, he invited Adele for a cruise on his new motorboat. As the motor was warming up at the dock, it suddenly exploded, smoke and burning oil shooting into the air.

Billy placed Adele on the dock, untied the rope and shoved the boat into the channel. The fuel tank exploded shortly afterward, destroying the boat.

Adele suffered burns on the face, neck and shoulders. The London opening of *Funny Face* was canceled, and it was rumored along Broadway that she would never perform again. Weeks in the hospital brought a complete recovery, her beauty undamaged. The Astaires opened in *Funny Face* at the Prince's Theatre on November 8, 1928, and they had their third straight London hit.

Funny Face lasted longer in London than on Broadway: 263 versus 250 performances. As the show finally wound down, Fred was exhilarated by the prospect of working for the great Ziegfeld. The producer had cabled the Astaires about a show that would team them with his favorite star, Marilyn Miller. She was a radiant personality and an exquisite dancer, and Fred was intrigued by the challenge of dancing for the first time with a star who wasn't his sister.

Closing night of *Funny Face* at the Prince's Theatre provided another love feast for the Astaires and the London audience. The same regulars in the gallery, cheering on their Freddie and Delly. The same sea of white ties and jewels in the stalls. Afterward the rich and the royal crowded into the Astaires' dressing rooms. Among the visitors to Adele was Prince Aly Khan, who brought along a friend, Charlie Cavendish. He was Lord Cavendish, member of an ancient noble family.

When Adele went to Paris for a fling before returning to New York with Fred, Cavendish was there. She was intrigued by him, and he was overwhelmed by her. He assured her they would be seeing more of each other, since he was planning to spend the winter in training at a Wall Street bank.

Fred was certain that *Smiles* would be another hit for him and Adele.

Ziegfeld had produced four great shows in a row—*Show Boat, The Three Musketeers, Rosalie* and *Whoopee*—and he was giving *Smiles* the same lavish treatment. The accomplished William Anthony McGuire was writing a script based on a story by Noel Coward. The songs were by Vincent Youmans, of *No, No, Nanette* fame. Marilyn Miller and the Astaires were the darlings of Broadway, and the supporting cast was first-rate.

So why did *Smiles* flop?

The tryout in Boston brought a portent of disaster. The fragile plot—about a French waif adopted by American soldiers who meet her later as a grown beauty—was smothered by the Ziegfeld-style production. Except for "Time on My

Hands," the Youmans songs were uncharacteristically flat. The show was overlong and uninspired.

Flo Ziegfeld tried major surgery. With McGuire too drunk to rework the script, Ziegfeld brought in Louis Bromfield and other writers. Ring Lardner contributed new lyrics. Walter Donaldson provided a song, "You're Driving Me Crazy," for Adele and Eddie Foy, Jr. Nothing helped.

Smiles opened November 18, 1930, and Ziegfeld staged his customary glittering premiere. Critics and audience alike recognized the emptiness on the Ziegfeld Theater stage. Though the show was panned, some reviewers praised the Astaires. Brooks Atkinson in *The New York Times:*

"Strictly speaking, the Astaires are dancers. But they have more than one string to their fiddle. With them, comedy is a comedy of manners, very much in the current mode. Free of show-stop trickery, they plunge with spirit into the midst of the frolic . . . they give dancing all the mocking grace of improvisation with droll dance inflections and with comic changes of pace. Adele Astaire is also an impish comedian; she can give sad lines a gleam of infectious good-nature. Slender, agile and quick-witted, the Astaires are ideal for the American song-and-dance stage."

Smiles contained two redeeming features: the Youmans tune, "Time on My Hands," which did not become popular until much later; and Fred's dance number "Say, Young Man of Manhattan."

The idea for the dance came to him during one of his many sleepless nights. He envisioned himself before a line of male tap dancers, with whom he performs a fast tap routine. Then he aims his cane and, with a sharp tap of his feet, guns down a member of the chorus line. Then another. And another. Finally, with his feet beating a rat-a-tat, he machine-guns the survivors. The attire of Fred and the chorus: top hat, white tie and tails.

> FRED: I do not like wearing tails. Never have. I
> worked in them a lot, and they were difficult to wear.
>   You see, when you're in tails, the collar melts. If
> you're working in a picture under all those hot
> lights, you simply wilt in a heavy, stiff shirt. It shows
> up badly, and you have to stop, dry off, change,

come back and get all sweated again. Do that four or times during the day, and you just say, "Oh, come on!"

I haven't worn tails in a long time, so I haven't been stuck with that. It gets to be dated, anyway. For two ballroom dancers to come out and do a waltz in tails and all that—time goes on, and they just don't do that anymore.

After *Smiles* had opened, Fred received a telephone call from Alex Aarons, who was producing a new Gershwin show, *Girl Crazy.* Everything seemed in shape but the "Embraceable You" number performed by Allen Kearns and a newcomer, Ginger Rogers. Would Fred drop in at the Alvin Theater and help stage it?

Fred obliged, and he restaged the number in the theater lobby. He was impressed by the vivacious redhead from Independence, Missouri, and he invited her out for dancing at the Casino in Central Park. Fred also dated Marilyn Miller, but neither she nor Ginger became a romance.

Smiles collapsed after 63 performances. Fred was devastated. He had no capacity for failure, and he blamed himself for not contributing enough to make the show succeed. Adele was less concerned. She was in love.

Lord Charles Arthur Cavendish, second son of the ninth Duke of Devonshire, was learning the stock business at J. P. Morgan Company. His family had been close to English sovereigns for centuries, and as a toddler Charlie had carried the Queen's crown at the coronation of George V in 1910. The family owned a town house in Carlton Gardens overlooking the Mall and spent their summers in County Waterford, Ireland, at the 200-room Lismore Castle, which dated back to William the Conqueror. At one time Sir Walter Raleigh lived there.

No Cavendish had married outside nobility, but Charlie was determined to make Adele his bride. She adored him and was intrigued by the prospect of being an English Lady, complete with Irish castle. At thirty-three, she realized it was time to quit the brother-sister act. Yet she resisted Charlie's entreaties to marry immediately.

"Not now," she told him. "I don't want to end my career on a flop. I want to go out with a hit."

Unable to shake his depression over the *Smiles* flop, Fred suggested to Adele that they take a trip to Europe, their first without having to work when they got there. Adele agreed, and they booked passage on the *Bremen*. Before they sailed, Max Gordon called Fred about a new revue he was producing. It was called *The Band Wagon*. Howard Dietz and Arthur Schwartz were writing the songs, and George S. Kaufman was working on the sketches with Dietz. Frank Morgan and Helen Broderick had already been cast, as well as the Viennese ballerina Tilly Losch.

"We'll sign," Fred said eagerly.

After a pleasurable trip to London and Paris, the Astaires returned to prepare for *The Band Wagon*. Max Gordon was planning an elaborate production that would employ turntables to revolve the scenery. He planned to spend $160,000, a heavy sum for a musical in the Depression days.

Dietz called on Fred at the Astaires' apartment, 875 Park Avenue, to discuss songs and sketches. Dietz noticed an accordion sitting in the corner of the room.

"Can you play that?" Dietz asked.

"Sure," Fred replied. "Used to play it in vaudeville."

"Good. Arthur and I are going to write you a song for it."

The pair produced "Sweet Music to Worry the Wolf Away," and Dietz instructed Fred to play it on the accordion every day: "You're going to know this one so well that when you dance and accompany yourself in the opening number, you'll be dazzling."

Dietz took Astaire to a Harlem night club, Step-In, to see a dancer with a complex and original tap step. When Fred duplicated the step, the dancer said to Dietz: "He can dance! Does he want a job in the club?"

When Adele made it known that she intended to retire and marry if *The Band Wagon* was a hit, the show's creators considered the possibility of her premature departure. It was decided to give Fred the heavier burden so her leaving would be less damaging to the show. Dietz discussed the matter with Ann Astaire (she had now taken her children's name), who was still advising on career matters. Mrs. Astaire agreed.

Thus Fred was given his best opportunity to display his versatility. Besides playing the accordion and dancing with Adele in "Sweet Music," he appeared as a French brat in "Hoops," performed "New Sun in the Sky" in debonair style and showed skill as a comedian in the sketches.

"The Beggar's Waltz" was his most ambitious number, portending the future Astaire. The dance opened with him as a beggar on the steps of the Vienna opera house. As the ballerina, Tilly Losch, passed into the theater, she dropped him a few coins. He fell asleep, and the set revolved to reveal a stage setting in which he danced a ballet with the woman of his dream. When the dance ended, he was again a beggar on the steps and she handed him a small purse as she walked past.

Albertina Rasch choreographed *The Band Wagon,* but as always, Fred was the major architect of the Astaire dances. He explained the creative process to an interviewer:

"Sometimes the songwriters give us a number and we work from that. The words may suggest the routine, or the music may give us the inspiration. Incidentally, it has always been impossible for us to work up anything with a poor piano player. We have to catch something from the music, and unless the pianist puts it there, we are lost.

"We listen to the song as it is played over and over again. Our feet move. We must find new steps or combinations. Against the wall must be a big, full-length mirror. We watch our feet do this or that, and we say it's good or bad. Over and over drums the music.

"Gradually we do the same steps as the same bar repeats itself. After hours, we may have half a dance. We can't get the rest. Our brains go rum-tum-tum with the music even when the piano stops. Our feet keep moving, hunting for the right thing, but the mirror tells us we are wrong. It is an impasse.

"A terrible feeling of desperation attacks us. We know there must be steps to fill into the holes, but nothing we do looks right. Our tempers fray. Our dispositions sour.

"Then it is time to go to bed. The music keeps pounding through our heads and our feet twitch under the sheets.

The *"Hoops"* number, The Bandwagon

These are the hours when most of the difficult spots are licked, for it is during the night that the inspiration we need comes to us. Early in the morning one of us may jump out of bed and find what has eluded us. The new day begins on a happy note if the mirror shows us we have what we want.

"But that is not the end.

"There are other dances, too. Day after day for as long as two months, we hammer our way through the problems. It can never be called fun. It is work of the hardest kind, requiring all day with never a thought of anything else. The grind is awful."

No wonder Adele wanted to quit.

"I want my days to be my own," she told the same interviewer. "I'm tired of having to go to parties. Just think of being able to go to Europe when I want to, instead of traveling only to fulfill a contract.

"The program is too rigid for me. I'm not one of those incurable enthusiasts who are born to the stage and never want to leave it. I was born in Omaha of parents who knew nothing about the theater, and it never really got into my blood.

"I may be a lazy sort of person and that's why I want to give it up. Getting ready for a show is a terrible job, hours and hours of trying to perfect something that doesn't go right. It takes something out of me, and I think I've done it long enough. Now I want to play, and I'm going to when this show is over."

The opening of *The Band Wagon* on June 3, 1931, erased any doubt that Adele would go out on a hit. The show drew critical praise for its brilliant score, especially "I Love Louisa," the first-act closer with the entire cast on a Bavarian carousel, and "Dancing in the Dark," sung by John Barker as Tilly Losch danced on mirrored prisms. Reviewers found the dances and sketches inspired and expressed surprise and delight at the emergence of Fred Astaire as actor and comedian. The show was so good that he and Adele didn't have to resort to their runaround.

Adele later related how she and Charlie Cavendish decided to marry: "I think I proposed to him. It was at Twenty-One, which in those days was a speakeasy. I'd had one drink, because I don't drink very much, and I said, 'Do you know, we get along so well, I think we ought to get married.' 'Right-ho,' he says and I thought no more about it. Next morning he wakes me up and he says, 'You proposed to me last night and I accepted. If you don't go through with it, I'll sue you for breach of promise.'"

Adele announced she would retire from the theater and marry Lord Charles Cavendish after *The Band Wagon* completed its Chicago run in the summer of 1932.

Now past thirty, Fred Astaire was the ideal figure of the man-about-Manhattan. He lived in a Park Avenue penthouse and drove a $22,000 Rolls-Royce (yet he took a taxi to and from the theater, always with the same driver). He hobnobbed with the ultra-rich at their Long Island estates and clubs. He was immaculately tailored, yet with a style all his own.

He attended the opening of *Flying Colors,* a revue starring his friend Clifton Webb. The first-nighters arrived in the customary full dress, except for Fred Astaire. He appeared in a gray business suit and seemed more in fashion than any man there.

Fred and Adele still lived with their mother, and she relieved them of the burdens of everyday life. Mrs. Astaire supervised the apartment staff and attended to many of the business matters. Though Fred and Adele were earning $4,000 a week, her mother allowed Adele only $100 spending money.

At the theater Fred enjoyed the services of the ever-faithful Walter—no one knew his last name. Walter traveled wherever Fred performed, though more than once he had to be sent home from London because of homesickness. "The world to Walter is Harlem surrounded by a lot of unimportant territory," Fred cracked.

Walter helped Fred make his fast changes—though for *The Band Wagon* a second dresser had to be added. Walter knew and understood all of Fred's idiosyncrasies: his abhorrence of gushy fans, his passion for horses and noodle soup—not round noodles, flat ones. Walter also fetched Fred's favorite dish after a matinee, ice cream. He screened guests, and if he knew and liked them, he would join in the dressing-room badinage.

Walter was the keeper of the Bridgeport robe. Every opening night (and later, on opening day of every movie) Walter produced the red-and-green plaid dressing gown that Fred had bought in 1922 while playing in Bridgeport, Connecticut. The Astaires had stopped the show in Bridgeport, so Fred considered the robe lucky. Without a word, Fred put it on and wore it while preparing for the first performance. Then Walter packed it away until the next opening.

The Astaire dressing room was neat and well ordered. Pasted on the mirror was a sign: "No singing or dancing around this dressing room." Also on the mirror were a few press clippings about Fred and the show. This was surprising, because he seemed to dislike publicity.

He viewed interviews as a necessary but unpleasant aspect of his career. He could be articulate when talking about his work and the show, but when asked personal questions he stammered and became embarrassed. He suffered when he saw any hint of criticism in print, especially when it was directed at Adele.

After Adele sang on Rudy Vallee's radio hour a columnist wrote an uncomplimentary review. When the columnist paid a backstage call at *The Band Wagon*, Fred pleaded: "Please, if you ever take a rap at us, direct it at me, not Adele."

Most actors made a show of their charity appearances. Not Fred. Once he attended a meeting at which he volunteered to perform with Adele for a worthy cause. He was asked to meet with reporters and photographers to announce the event. Fred declined: "We're not giving our services to get our names in the papers. We're doing it to help."

When Jock Whitney presented him with a pair of new-style, big-wheel roller skates, Fred was eager to try them out. He realized the press might discover him rolling along the Manhattan streets in daylight. So every night after a performance, much against his mother's wishes, he skated happily up and down Park Avenue. "Now, Freddie, think what will happen if you break an ankle!" Mrs. Astaire cautioned. "Oh, Mom, I'll be all right," he replied.

For relaxation, Fred often dropped into the Lambs Club,

Young Man of Manhattan

Adele Astaire (Culver)

which he had joined early in his Broadway career. He enjoyed shooting pool, a skill he had learned during his vaudeville travels, and playing bridge and rummy with veteran performers such as Charles Winninger, Hal Skelly, William Gaxton, Frank McIntyre and Thomas Meighan.

Horse racing remained his abiding passion. He kept in touch by cable with the horses he raced under his buff-and-blue colors in England. One of them, a colt named Nick the Greek, showed rare promise. During the racing season, Fred haunted the tracks near New York, and he was never more at ease than when he was talking with track people about the prospects of this horse or that.

During his youth in New York, Fred had become acquainted with Rev. Randolph Ray, who introduced him to the Episcopal faith. Fred was confirmed at the Church of the Transfiguration, known to show people as "The Little Church Around the Corner," and he has remained an Episcopalian ever since.

He met her at a party at the Long Island estate of Mrs. Graham Fair Vanderbilt. It was a luncheon to be followed by golf on Mrs. Vanderbilt's private golf course.

Fred found himself at a table with an attractive young woman he didn't know. He was intrigued by the fact that she didn't seem to know him, either. She had never seen him on the stage.

Her name was Phyllis Potter. He was attracted to her casual manner, her exquisite face, her willowy figure, the engaging way she pronounced r, so that his name came out "Fwed." She mentioned that her uncle was Henry W. Bull, and Fred made the immediate connection. He was Harry Bull, a leading figure of New York society and member of many clubs, including the Turf and Field Club, through which Fred knew him. At the end of the luncheon, Fred asked if he could call her. She agreed.

Twenty-three years before, she had been born Phyllis Livingston Baker, daughter of a prominent Boston doctor, Harold W. Baker. Her mother died and her father remarried, and from the age of ten Phyllis lived with her Uncle

Adele: "They're milder, Fred." Fred: "Taste better, too." The pose for a Chesterfield cigarette ad, 1931

Harry and Aunt Maud. They had homes in Manhattan, in Islip on Long Island and in Aiken, South Carolina, where Bull bred horses. He was a senior partner in Harriman and Company.

In 1927, Phyllis Baker was married to the prominent socialite Eliphalet Nott Potter III, and they had a son who was named Eliphalet Nott Potter IV. It was an unhappy marriage, and Mrs. Potter was separated from her husband when she met Fred at Mrs. Vanderbilt's lunch-and-golf party.

Fred and Phyllis began seeing each other, and he induced her to attend a performance of *The Band Wagon*. She approved of this show and his performance. Fred had known many infatuations, but now for the first time he was wildly, irretrievably in love. He telephoned Phyllis daily. He suffered whenever she went out with other men. Phyllis was definitely attracted to the attentive Fred Astaire. But she had been hurt by the bitter marriage to Potter, and she wasn't ready to become serious about any man.

The Band Wagon ran through the summer at the newly air-conditioned New Amsterdam Theater and into 1932. The road tour began, and Adele played her last performance at the Illinois Theatre in Chicago on March 5, 1932. Vera Marsh assumed her role. Fred was under contract to remain with *The Band Wagon* until the tour ended, so he was not able to attend Adele's wedding. Adele and Charlie were married in May in a formal ceremony attended by the upper strata of English society.

When *The Band Wagon* closed, Fred faced a double challenge: building a career as a single, and convincing Phyllis Potter to marry him.

He considered a few offers and concluded that *Gay Divorce* held the most promise. Dwight Wiman and Tom Weatherly were producing, and Fred felt the Dwight Taylor script had possibilities. He told the producers he might be interested; then he decided to go to England. Phyllis was there.

Fred visited the newly wed Cavendishes at Lismore Castle, then left for London to meet Phyllis. After a few days he received a cable asking him to return to New York for discussions about *Gay Divorce*. Fred hesitated to leave Phyllis. He was also apprehensive about facing the Broadway audience without Adele.

Phyllis advised him to return and added the first note of hope he had heard from her: "If we are going to be married, you'll have to work, won't you?"

With soaring heart Fred sailed back to New York and conversations about *Gay Divorce*. The script was unimpressive: a lame farce about a woman who hires a gigolo so she can get a divorce and a man who poses as the gigolo because he loves her. The clincher was Fred's meeting with Cole Porter. They had known each other slightly, and Linda Porter, his wife, was a distant cousin of Phyllis. When Fred heard Porter play the first song, "After You, Who?" he said, "I'll do the show."

Fred returned to Europe to spend a few weeks with Phyllis at Tourquet on the French Riviera, where she was vacationing with her family. She quieted his fears about the challenge of going it alone. When he pressed her for a marriage date, she put him off, reasoning that he had enough to worry about with the new show.

Rehearsals for *Gay Divorce* began immediately upon Fred's return to New York. He heard the completed Cole Porter score and was pleased except for one song, "Night and Day."

"I don't think I can sing it," he said.

"Sure you can," Porter answered. "I wrote it especially for your voice."

It was the first time Porter had fashioned a song for the qualities of a singer's voice. Knowing Astaire's range, he had written the melody first, the reverse of his usual procedure of starting with the lyrics. Monty Woolley arrived at Porter's apartment as he was composing and announced, "I don't know what you are writing but it is terrible and you should give it up."

Porter spent the weekend at the estate of the Vincent Astors in Newport. He told later of having lunch during a rainstorm and hearing Mrs. Astor complain about a broken eave spout: "That drip, drip, drip is driving me crazy." *Voila!* Porter sat down to the piano and completed the lyrics of "Night and Day."

"My voice will crack if I sing it," Astaire argued at rehearsals.

Tom Weatherly, the co-producer, agreed with Fred: "I think we ought to take out the song."

Porter remained firm. He was convinced that Fred could handle "Night and Day" and that it would make a worthy contribution to the show.

The new Astaire partner was Claire Luce, a blond actress and dancer who had appeared in Ziegfeld's *American Revue* in 1926. Fred wanted his dances to be entirely different from those he had performed with Adele, and he arrived at something new—and daring—for the "Night and Day" number. He and Miss Luce waltzed swiftly around a hotel suite, flying over chairs and tables. The dance resulted in many falls during rehearsals and sometimes in a performance, but it proved to be a remarkably effective number.

The cast included Erik Rhodes, Eric Blore and Luella Gear. Howard Lindsay directed the show, and Jo Mielziner created elegant hotel sets that gleamed of chrome and glass. But all of the professionalism and gloss couldn't disguise the rickety plot. And, as Fred had feared, critics lamented the loss of Adele.

In Boston, the *Transcript* commented: "An Astaire must dance and still does very well—but not for the general good is he now sisterless."

Phyllis had returned from Europe and had volunteered to join Fred in Boston. He advised against it, realizing he would be occupied with the *Gay Divorce* overhaul. All of the ministrations didn't help, and Fred approached the New York opening with more than his usual worry. He was heartened by a cable from Adele and Charlie: NOW MINNIE DON'T FORGET TO MOAN.

Minnie had much to moan about. The highly social audience was late, noisy and unresponsive. There was merely polite reaction when Fred sang the show's major song.

> Night and day,
> You are the one.
> Only you beneath the moon
> And under the sun.
> Whether near to me or far,

It's no matter, darling,
Where you are.
I think of you
Night and day.

Reviewers found *Gay Divorce* flat and cheerless, and none celebrated Fred Astaire's debut as a single. One claimed that Fred stared into the wings "as if he were hoping his titled sister, Adele, would come out and rescue him." Another concluded that "two Astaires are better than one." When he wasn't dancing, wrote another, Astaire "gives a curious impression of unemployment." Another dismissed the notion of Fred Astaire as a romantic hero—"he hasn't the hair, for one thing."

Nor did the critics predict a future for "Night and Day." The song went unnoticed, and orchestra leaders declined to play it. The forty-eight bars instead of the usual thirty-two made it too long. Singers found it difficult because of the four notes above the octave. The persistence of song pluggers finally got "Night and Day" played on the radio, beginning its career as Cole Porter's most successful song.

The popularity of "Night and Day" helped sustain *Gay Divorce,* and rewriting and restaging provided an audience-pleasing show. Fred settled in for a full season's run.

Memo from David O. Selznick, executive vice president in charge of production, RKO studio:

"Please arrange for the executives to see the test of Fred Astaire. I am a little uncertain about the man, but I feel, in spite of his enormous ears and bad chin line, that his charm is so tremendous that it comes through even in this wretched test. . . ."

Selznick had ordered a test in January 1933 after learning from Astaire's agent, Leland Hayward, that his client might be interested in leaving the theater and entering films. Selznick responded enthusiastically, declaring that "Astaire is one of the great artists of the day; a magnificent performer, a man conceded to be perhaps, next to Leslie Howard, the most charming in the American theater, and unquestionably

the outstanding young leader of American musical comedy."
One studio official responded to the test with a now classic
line.

> FRED: It has been repeated many times, usually in-
> correctly. What the man said was: "Can't act. Slightly
> bald. Also dances."

Selznick was eager to sign Astaire to a contract before his
availability was widely known. All studios were planning musicals, which had been overdone in the early talkie period
and now enjoyed renewed popularity after the hit of *42nd
Street*. Selznick predicted "a wild scramble on the part of all
studios to test Astaire."

Astaire signed a contract, dated May 27, 1933, to make
an RKO film called *Flying Down to Rio* at a salary of $1,500 a
week. If the studio exercised its option for his services, the
next two films would be made at $1,750 per week; his salary
would then rise by stages to $3,000 for the sixth film.

Flying Down to Rio would be made in the summer, at the
close of the New York run of *Gay Divorce*. Fred was committed to do the show in London. Then, if RKO exercised
the option, he would return to Hollywood.

Fred was embarking on a new, uncharted adventure,
and he didn't want to face it alone. He wanted Phyllis to be
with him always, and she agreed. But she had to do something first.

In 1932, Phyllis had gone quietly to Reno and remained
the necessary six weeks to get a divorce from Eliphalet Potter
III. The settlement granted the father three months' annual
custody of their son, who was called Peter. Phyllis realized
that when she married Fred, they would be spending ex-
tended periods in Hollywood, London or elsewhere. She
didn't want to be removed from Peter, who would remain in
New York with his father for a quarter of the year.

Phyllis filed suit in New York for greater custody of her
son. Potter, who had remarried, contested the suit, and the
case drew wide publicity. Finally an agreement was reached:
Peter would stay with his father one month each year.

On July 12, 1933, the day after the settlement was
reached, Fred and Phyllis went to the Brooklyn chambers of

Supreme Court Justice Selah B. Strong, The bride, twenty-five, wore a blue-and-white print silk frock with white crepe turban, the bridegroom, thirty-three, wore a dark blue business suit. They were married shortly after six o'clock in the evening, with her uncle, Henry Worthington Bull, giving Phyllis away.

> FRED: I never had any idea of getting married—until I met Phyllis. We married when I was making the change from stage life to the movies, so she was caught in the middle of all that.

The couple had a one-day honeymoon cruising the Hudson on the yacht of Mrs. Payne Whitney. Then they flew to California to begin their marriage and Fred's new career.

4

RKO and Ginger

*Mr. Astaire is the nearest approach we are
ever likely to have to a human Mickey
Mouse; he might have been drawn by Mr. Walt
Disney, with his quick physical wit, his
incredible agility. He belongs to a fantasy
world almost as free as Mickey's from the
law of gravity.*

—*Graham Greene,* The Spectator

With his bride clutching his arm, Fred Astaire emerged from the Ford tri-motor plane and stepped slowly down the stairs and onto the hot pavement at Burbank airport. After a twenty-six-hour Transcontinental Western Air flight, he had arrived back in California for the first time since he and Adele played the Orpheum circuit as teenagers.

"Mr. Astaire, I'm Andy Hervey of the RKO publicity department," said a short, smiling man who offered his hand. "We'd like to take some pictures of you and Mrs. Astaire for the L.A. papers."

The Astaires posed for photographs beside the airplane, then entered a limousine that took them to the Beverly Wilshire Hotel on Wilshire Boulevard in Beverly Hills. On the following day, the Los Angeles *Times* carried the news: AS-TAIRE AND BRIDE HERE FROM EAST. The story began, "Combining business with honeymoon, Fred Astaire, musical-comedy star and dancer, arrived yesterday from New York with his society divorcée bride, the former Phyllis Livingston Potter, to join Hollywood's motion-picture colony."

Fred doubted that he could become a permanent member of that colony. But at least he would have two chances. Since *Flying Down to Rio* was not ready to start, RKO allowed Fred to make an appearance in *Dancing Lady* at MGM. The producer was David O. Selznick, who had left RKO to work for his father-in-law, Louis B. Mayer. Selznick had been reluctant to do so, but Mayer had promised him independence, as well as access to MGM's huge list of stars. For his first film, *Dancing Lady,* Selznick got MGM's biggest star combination, Clark Gable and Joan Crawford.

In *Dancing Lady,* Astaire played himself and danced two duets with Joan Crawford, "Heigh-Ho, The Gang's All Here" and "Let's Go Bavarian," choreographed by Sammy Lee. Miss Crawford was thrilled to be dancing with Fred, whom she had seen onstage in New York when she was a Shubert chorus girl. She invited the Astaires to her home and filled their Beverly Wilshire suite with flowers.

> FRED: *Dancing Lady* came in handy before I did the RKO picture. Metro asked my agent, Leland Hayward, if I wanted to do that thing with Joan Crawford, and it seemed like a good idea.
>
> I was "Fred Astaire, a dancer from New York,"

"Let's Go Bavarian" with Joan Crawford in Dancing Lady *(MGM)*

and Gable introduced me. As I've said many times in the past, I always thought I had one of the best introductions to the movies anyone could have at that particular time—to have Gable introduce me.

Fred enjoyed his brief work at MGM. He had worried about performing without an audience for the first time in his career, but he found he didn't need the immediate re-

sponse. And being able to repeat a dance until he perfected it—that was an unexpected joy. His spirits were dampened when he saw himself on the screen. He wrote a note to himself: "Ponderous dancing, grotesque face."

Next he reported to RKO to begin his movie career in earnest.

Throughout its history, RKO had been the Sick Man of Hollywood, and in 1933 its health remained precarious.

The studio dated back to 1921, when two independent producers brought thirteen acres from the Hollywood Cemetery and founded Robertson-Cole Productions at the corner of Gower Street and Melrose Avenue. The company became known as FBO (Film Booking Offices) and underwent a series of convulsions until Joseph P. Kennedy bought it in 1926.

Kennedy seemed more interested in promoting Gloria Swanson's career than in building a studio, and RKO limped along until 1928. David Sarnoff of the Radio Corporation of America bought into FBO to help promote RCA's Photophone system for talkies. Unable to compete with the major theater-owning companies, Kennedy and Sarnoff gained control of the 700-theater Keith-Albee-Orpheum chain. The result of the merger was called Radio-Keith-Orpheum— RKO.

Absentee ownership helped create an unsettled atmosphere at RKO. Within four years, William LeBaron was replaced as production chief by David Selznick, who was succeeded by Merian C. Cooper. A few notable films were produced: *What Price Hollywood, Rio Rita, Cimarron, Bird of Paradise, King Kong, A Bill of Divorcement, Morning Glory.* But the lack of continuity, limited financing and paucity of new and exciting stars—except for a Selznick discovery, Katharine Hepburn—prevented RKO from competing effectively with the major studios. Poor theater business helped push RKO into equity receivership in January 1933.

Fred Astaire found RKO much different from what he had seen at MGM. For one thing, it was smaller, You could

White tie and tails followed Astaire in his first film, Dancing Lady, *with Joan Crawford (MGM).*

walk from one end of the RKO lot to the other in two or
three minutes. RKO people did not have that sense of self-
confidence and superiority that could be felt at MGM. The
atmosphere at Melrose and Gower was pervaded by hope
and aspiration, along with a feeling of resignation, like a
baseball club that had been too long in the cellar.

Flying Down to Rio was getting close to production. The
producer was a graduate of two-reel comedies, Lou Brock.
The director was a former D. W. Griffith assistant, Thornton
Freeland, who had made two other musicals, *Whoopee!* with
Eddie Cantor, and *Be Yourself,* with Fanny Brice.

The romantic stars had been announced: Dolores Del
Rio, Gene Raymond and the Brazilian singer Raul Roulien.
Astaire would get fifth billing, after a female dancer, not yet
cast.

Moaning Minnie found new worries. The script was a
romantic triangle that seemed as witless as *Smiles.* He was cast
in a lesser role as accordion player in Gene Raymond's band.
Above all, he didn't believe movies were the proper medium
for dancing. He suggested to producer Brock that there
should be a single Astaire number "because people won't
stand for more than that."

His other concern was his face, which one Broadway
critic had described as "the shape of an upside-down Bartlett
pear."

"My face didn't matter on the stage," he reasoned,
"where they don't have closeups. But if you blow it up forty
feet high on a movie screen—oh, no!" The RKO makeup
department worked on the face, but nothing could be done
to change its contours. The vanished hairline was replaced
by a subtle, flat toupee.

Fred was confident about one element of *Flying Down to
Rio:* the music. Before leaving New York, he had gone to the
apartment of Vincent Youmans, who had written the score
for *Smiles.* Youmans played the songs he had composed for
Rio: "Orchids in the Moonlight," "The Carioca," "Flying
Down to Rio," "Music Makes Me." At least, Fred consoled
himself, there would be good music to dance to.

During an early conference, Lou Brock said casually,
"We decided on the girl you're going to dance with. She's
under contract to RKO. Ginger Rogers."

"The Carioca" set the standard for Astaire-Rogers finales, Flying Down to Rio *(RKO).*

Fred was pleased. He had pleasant memories of their dates in New York, and he knew she was a facile dancer who responded to direction and learned quickly. But he suspected that she didn't want to be stuck in a musical.

Ginger didn't. Her career as a film actress, which had started when she was still playing in *Girl Crazy,* was progressing nicely. Since arriving in Hollywood in 1931, she had appeared in thirteen films. Some had been musicals, like *42nd Street* and *Sitting Pretty,* but most had afforded straight acting,

which was her abiding interest. She wanted to shed her reputation as a Charleston dancer and chorus girl. Ginger's ambition was fired by a mother who was everything that Ann
Astaire was not. With the protectiveness of a she-wolf, Lela
Rogers had guided her daughter's career since its beginnings
in Fort Worth.

Dave Gould, the dance director of *Flying Down to Rio,*
was busy preparing the spectacular finale in which beauties
would seem to fly on wingtops as biplanes soared over Rio De
Janeiro. So the job of rehearsing with Fred Astaire fell to
Gould's assistant, Hermes Pan.

He was born Hermes Panagiotopulos, son of an American
mother and the Greek consul in the South. Growing up in
Memphis and Nashville, the boy developed a fondness for
the natural, loose-limbed dancing of the blacks and a talent
for copying their movements. His father died when Hermes
was twelve, and the impoverished family moved to New York
City. Hermes went right to work, delivering packages and
dancing for tips in speakeasies.

Pan started as a singer in Broadway shows, then danced,
always asking fellow members of the chorus to teach him new
steps. "How do you do a time step?" he asked. "How do you
pirouette?" His repertoire grew.

While working in *Top Speed,* Pan became acquainted with
the ingenue Ginger Rogers. Her mother invited some of the
chorus people to a spaghetti dinner during the Philadelphia
tryout, and Pan asked Ginger her ambition in show business."I want to be a movie star," she replied. Pan recalls
thinking that she didn't seem the type.

Pan never saw Fred Astaire on the stage, but he was
repeatedly reminded of him by people who remarked, "You
look like Fred Astaire." Indeed, the resemblance was un-
canny: the same slender frame, wide forehead and narrow
chin, the same lilting movement when they walked.

When Hollywood turned to musicals, Pan, his sister and
mother drove west in an ancient Chevrolet. But dance directors had their favorites, and Pan was unable to find studio
work. He was hired to sing, dance and move scenery in a

theatrical company that lurched through the West on a rickety bus, always one city ahead of the producer's creditors. They caught up with him at Merced, California, and the hotel owner would not let the company leave until the bill was paid. Pan's mother was left behind for security while the troupe went on to Antioch to earn money to redeem her.

Back in Hollywood, Pan staged dances for a revue, then hired on at RKO as Dave Gould's assistant. On his first day at work, Pan was told by Gould: "Fred Astaire is working on Stage 8. Why don't you go up there and see if you can help him?"

With grave apprehension, Pan entered the darkened stage and found Fred Astaire in rehearsal clothes, working with a pianist.

"My name is Pan," said the newcomer. "Dave Gould said I might be able to help you."

"Hi ya, Pan," replied Fred, who ever afterward would call him Pan, seldom Hermes. "As a matter of fact, I'm working on a routine. Would you like to see it?"

"Sure."

Astaire performed some intricate steps that astounded Pan and made him wonder what he could possibly contribute.

"I'm stuck for something in the middle," Fred remarked. "I got a hole right there. Got any ideas?"

Pan reached back into his memory of dances he had learned from fellow chorus members in New York. "How about this break?"

Fred stared at Pan's feet as he tapped out the break. "Do it again," Astaire said.

"Gee, that's good," Fred commented. "I'll use that."

From then on, Fred relied heavily on Hermes Pan to help solve problems, to contribute ideas, to act as a first audience and collaborator on the dances that Fred concocted. As their partnership progressed, it became difficult to know who contributed what. They became almost mirror images, and they could communicate wordlessly, expressing themselves with movement.

Pan became Ginger Rogers' alter ego as well. Because she was occupied with other films—she made eight movies in 1933—she could not attend rehearsals with Astaire and Pan.

Her role was danced by Pan, who then taught it to Ginger when she became available.

Fred discovered he had not one dance for *Flying Down to Rio,* as he had hoped, but three: a brief tango with Dolores Del Rio to "Orchids in the Moonlight"; a fast tap solo to "Music Makes Me"; a duet with Ginger for the big production finale, "The Carioca."

The principal gimmick for "The Carioca" occurred to Hermes Pan when he heard the Edward Eliscu-Gus Kahn lyrics.

Pan devised the idea of having Fred and Ginger perform "The Carioca" with foreheads touching, performing turns without losing contact with their heads. Fred liked it, and so did Dave Gould, who was staging the spectacular dance.

When Fred saw the "Carioca" duet cut together, he was distressed. "It's awful," he complained. "Can't we do it over?" He was assured that RKO, then flirting with bankruptcy, could allow no such extravagance.

Fred was appalled at how he looked on the screen. He had been told by Marie Dressler that she felt dreadful for days after seeing herself on the screen, and Maurice Chevalier had warned him of the shock. But Fred was still unprepared for what he saw. "I have a face like a knife," he groaned, wishing he could burn all his scenes in *Flying Down to Rio.*

Filming concluded, and Fred and Phyllis prepared to leave their rented Beverly Hills house to move to London, where he was scheduled to open in *Gay Divorce* in November. Fred made the rounds of the RKO departments, and his good-byes had a note of finality.

"I don't think I'll be coming back," he said.

Londoners received *Gay Divorce* with the enthusiasm that Fred had hoped for but did not get in New York. The old-fashioned plot didn't faze the critics, nor did the absence of Adele. The show was ensured of at least a six-month run, and Fred and Phyllis leased a Mayfair house. With them was Peter, who was slowly being won over by his new stepfather.

The "Orchids in the Moonlight" tango with Dolores Del Rio (RKO)

Fred's return to England was tinged with sorrow. Adele had given premature birth to a baby girl, who died the same day. Adele remained confined to Lismore Castle for several weeks. Then she and Charlie came to London, and for the first time, Adele watched from the audience as Fred performed. She cried.

Later she wrote for a London daily: "It knocks me cold how he's developed. No, it isn't that he developed. He's always had what he's got now, but it never had a chance to show until I left. He was always staying in the background himself, always pushing me forward. He'd stand back while I got the laugh. Always playing straight for me.

"So when I finished, things came out he didn't know he could do himself. All the numbers we used to do, they were all Fred's ideas. And one day Fred is going to knock them cold with his acting. I know. I knew it first when he did the ballet with Tilly Losch in *Band Wagon*."

She added another revelation upon seeing Fred from out front for the first time: "It was also the first time I realized Fred had sex appeal. Fred! Where did he get it? He's so unconceited looking."

While triumphing nightly at the Palace Theatre, Fred found something to worry about: his movie debut. He had no concern about *Dancing Lady,* except that critics might question the brevity of his appearance. He didn't want them to surmise that he was another Broadway star who had been given short shrift by the studios.

Flying Down to Rio caused him hours of anxiety. He was still convinced he had failed in it. He felt his fears were confirmed by the fact that he had received no messages from RKO about the response at previews.

A few days after *Gay Divorce* opened in London, Fred wrote his agent asking for news of *Flying Down to Rio.* No one in England had heard about it though they knew about *Dancing Lady,* which "doesn't mean a damn to me." What about another picture? Fred hoped it would not be *Gay Divorce,* which had to be held up by "hoofing." And too much dancing was not suitable for movies.

Still there was no news from Hollywood. Fred cabled Leland Hayward to inquire about another movie in 1934; if none appeared, Fred would have to seek a New York show for the fall.

"You are a cinch, baby, for all the pictures you want," Hayward responded, advising him to make no plans to return to the stage.

Finally Fred received a cable from Hollywood telling him of a fine preview response for *Flying Down to Rio* and Fred Astaire. The message came from Pandro Berman, another figure who would play a vital role in Fred's movie career.

To Fred's distress, Rio *made the Astaire-Rogers teaming inescapable (RKO).*

Pan Berman was a boss's son who made good. When Pandro graduated from DeWitt Clinton High School in New York in 1923, he said he didn't want to go to college. He wanted to take his education at the new FBO studio in Hollywood. His father, who was general manager of FBO, consented.

The young man learned the movie business on the sets and in the cutting rooms. During the RKO period he became assistant to the studio heads, first William LeBaron, then David Selznick, then Merian Cooper. He also produced films, the first being the estimable *Symphony of Six Million*. While *Flying Down to Rio* was being made, Berman became acquainted with Fred Astaire. Alone among RKO executives, Berman saw great promise in films for the Broadway dancer.

The brilliant, erratic Merian Cooper suffered a slight heart attack and said to Berman, "I'm going on a vacation. I'll be on a mountaintop in Hawaii, but I won't tell you where, so don't try to reach me. You're in charge of the studio."

Pandro Berman took charge. Encouraged by the huge response at previews of *Flying Down to Rio,* he foresaw a series of films co-starring Fred Astaire and Ginger Rogers. Berman knew of Fred's success with *Gay Divorce* in London. He sent for a script.

Berman considered *Gay Divorce* adaptable to the screen, and he suggested it to Lou Brock, who had produced *Rio.* Brock returned to Berman's office, tossed the copy of *Gay Divorce* on the desk and said, "I can blow better scripts out of my nose."

Undeterred, Berman contemplated producing *Gay Divorce* himself. He decided to confer with Fred in London. Stopping in New York, he attended a performance of the new Jerome Kern musical *Roberta,* which he believed might be another vehicle for Fred Astaire and Ginger Rogers.

Fred was happy to hear from Pan Berman the promising news about *Flying Down to Rio.* Fred also agreed with the suggestion of filming *Gay Divorce.* But he exploded at Berman's proposal of teaming with Ginger.

"I am fond of Ginger, but I absolutely do not want to be teamed with her or anyone else," Fred declared. "I did not go into pictures with the thought of becoming part of a team, and if that's what RKO has in mind for me, we'd better end the contract right now. I've just managed to live down one partnership. I'm not going to jump right into another. Besides, Ginger's not English."

Berman explained that the female lead in *Gay Divorce* could be changed to an American. Fred agreed, but he remained adamant about any teaming. How many times had he grumbled to reporters about himself and Adele: "Don't call us a team; it makes us sound like a couple of horses!"

Berman bought the rights to *Gay Divorce* for RKO at the bargain price of $35,000—no other studio wanted it. There was competition for *Roberta*, but Berman was able to outbid Paramount and MGM and purchase the musical for $70,000.

Despite the glowing reports about *Flying Down to Rio* from the studio, Fred remained unconvinced that he had a future in films. He was encouraged when the movie opened at the Radio City Music Hall in New York at Christmas, receiving an excellent critical and audience response. Filmgoers applauded at the fadeout of *Rio*, which focused on Fred and Ginger, and RKO officials considered that an omen.

Since *Flying Down to Rio* was not scheduled to open in London until after Fred closed in *Gay Divorce*, RKO arranged a private screening for him. Fred was agreeably surprised. He found the movie "novel and charming," though he felt the "Carioca" number was too long and came too soon after "Orchids in the Moonlight."

Now he was eager to start work on the next film, in which, he firmly believed, he could do much better work. He remained distressed about the possibility of a teaming with Ginger Rogers and urged Leland Hayward to squelch any such rumors. If he succeeded in films, Fred declared, "it will be as one, not as two."

He was also rankled about his RKO salary. It was laughably low, he argued; he could earn more on the stage. In fact, Howard Dietz and Arthur Schwartz wanted him for another revue in the *Band Wagon* vein, and he was considering it for the fall. Fred suggested to Leland Hayward that a revision of the RKO contract was in order.

Pandro Berman agreed. Realizing that Fred needed convincing to overcome his opposition to the Rogers teaming, Berman persuaded RKO to give him a sizable raise in salary.

Berman made two other proposals that he knew would appeal to Fred: a percentage of his films' profits, something extremely rare in actors' contracts; and complete autonomy over how the dances would be presented.

Fred closed in *Gay Divorce* on April 7, 1933, and he and Phyllis and Peter sailed four days later on the *Bremen*. After two weeks at her family's place in Aiken, the Astaires left for California and the June 15 start of the new movie.

It was now called *The Gay Divorcée*. Partly that was because RKO executives believed the new title had more titillation than *Gay Divorce;* partly the change placated the Production Code Authority, which performed the bidding of the Catholic Church. Divorce was not a proper subject for Catholic audiences.

Joseph Breen, the industry's chief censor, retained his misgivings about the proposed film, deducing that the play concerned divorce by collusion. Also, many of the play's lines were too risqué ever to pass the Production Code. Pandro Berman persuaded Breen that the lines would be laundered, the story would be treated as a broad farce comedy, and the attempts at collusion would fail. Breen gave his consent for *The Gay Divorcée* to proceed.

Producer Berman realized the need for a corps of expert farceurs to bolster the featherweight plot. Three became important fixtures in the Astaire-Rogers films:

Edward Everett Horton, genius of the double and triple take, played the London lawyer whose sense of decorum was shocked at the outrageous goings-on (Charles Ruggles was considered for the role, but Fred didn't think he could seem British). A native of Brooklyn, Horton had perfected his character of the amiable ditherer in countless stage farces.

Eric Blore learned in English music halls how to milk laughs from straight lines by hunching his shoulders and contorting his pie-like face. He proved invaluable as the waiter or valet without an ounce of servility. He had made his movie debut in *Flying Down to Rio*.

Erik Rhodes, with his waxen mustache, store-dummy face and tortured accent, seemed the ideal continental gigolo. He was a student at the University of Oklahoma when he won a scholarship to study drama in New York. Cast as Rodolfo Tonetti in *Gay Divorce*, Rhodes, who was a language major and expert mimic, devised a comical accent. He was type-cast for the rest of his career. Both he and Blore played in the New York and London companies of *Gay Divorce.*

Helen Broderick, a veteran of Broadway revues, was Fred's first choice for the self-explanatory role of Hortense Ditherwell. But she was committed to *As Thousands Cheer* on Broadway, and Alice Brady, an expert in fluttery females, was cast. Miss Broderick, with her blank-eyed delivery of sly wisecracks, would join Astaire and Rogers later.

For director, Pandro Berman chose another Astaire-Rogers stalwart: Mark Sandrich.

He did not fit the usual pattern of a Hollywood director. He was quiet-spoken, neatly dressed, a pipe-smoking, contemplative man who directed analytically, not from raw instinct. He had studied mathematics at Columbia University, and he applied his knowledge to the making of movies, charting the scripts until each page was timed to the sixth of a minute.

Mark Rex Sandrich entered the movie business by accident, he said. Vacationing from his college studies in 1922, he visited Century Studio and found an old-time director, Al Herman, puzzling over a gag sequence for a two-reel comedy. The young math student solved the problem with a diagram and was offered a job on the spot.

He became prop man, cutter, gag man, still photographer, assistant director—ideal training for a director. In 1930 RKO hired him to direct two-reel comedies for Lou Brock's short units. He tried to inject music into the comedies wherever possible.

"In those early talkie days, they were shooting musical numbers the way they were performed on the stage," he recalled later. "The musicians were either in the scene or playing alongside the set. That made the songs static and dull."

Sandrich thought there had to be a better way. He helped develop the playback, by which the music was pre-recorded and played back while the number was filmed, the actors and musicians synchronizing their movements to the recording.

Assigned to a three-reeler starring the bandleader Phil Harris, Sandrich decided to test the new method. Shooting on a golf-course location, he filmed four bars of a song in one spot, four bars in another, moving eight times as the song continued. The technique was so startlingly new that *So This Is Harris* won the 1932–1933 Academy Award as best comedy short.

Mark Sandrich was considered a comer at RKO. He was assigned to a pair of comedy features starring the studio's comedy team, Bert Wheeler and Robert Woolsey. Then *The Gay Divorcée.*

Sandrich worked closely with Dave Gould to ensure a smooth flow of the dance numbers. Gould remained the dance director, but in the day-to-day preparation of the numbers, Fred relied increasingly on Hermes Pan.

> FRED: Pan was full of ideas, and he was exceptionally good with the girls, working up a routine and teaching it to them.
>
> I always like to work with a choreographer. He can be a lot of help in doing your thinking and making suggestions. Pan worked with me on a lot of pictures, then I had a whole lot of others, almost every [film choreographer] you can think of. On a couple of films, I had to do the choreography myself, because somebody wasn't available.
>
> In the end, I had to do most of my stuff, anyway. It wasn't just a matter of staying there and learning a lot of steps from somebody.

Hermes Pan reflects: "Working with Fred Astaire was the greatest thing that ever happened in my career. I found that not only did we look alike—we *thought* alike in our ideas of dance. We had the same feelings of rhythm. He would do things that just knocked me out. It pleased me so much, because he expressed things that I had always felt.

"I always loved after-beats and broken rhythm. And he was the master of the broken rhythm. The first thing I showed him was a broken-rhythm thing, and that appealed to him. It's a black tradition, and I learned it from the blacks in Tennessee. There was such a difference between that kind

The first great romantic duet, "Night and Day" (RKO)

of tap and the kind I learned from dancers in New York. I used to dance on my flat foot and heel, which Fred does. Most tap dancers do it on their toes; it's the orthodox style: tip-tap. It's more mechanical, but very intricate.

"Fred and I used to call it 'gutbucket.' He and I would work up terms so we could understand each other. Like, 'a whip,' or 'right-now beat.' He'd do something and say, 'What do you think?' I'd say, 'Great.' He'd say, 'I don't like the way you say "Great." If you said, "Knocked-out," I'd believe you.'"

Now more confident in his relations with the studio, Fred demanded more time to prepare for *The Gay Divorcée*. While he could easily reproduce the "Night and Day" dance from the stage version, it would be entirely new to Ginger. She needed to dance with the same smoothness that Claire Luce had exhibited in New York and London.

The rest of the songs were new. Except for the hit song, Berman discarded the entire Cole Porter score and commissioned Hollywood songwriters to supply new songs. Harry Revel and Mack Gordon contributed "Don't Let It Bother You" and "Let's K-nock K-nees." Con Conrad and Herb Magidson wrote "A Needle in a Haystack" and the final production number, "The Continental."

Sandrich hoped "The Continental" would repeat the success of "The Carioca," and he devoted more than seventeen minutes of the film's 107 minutes to the song, which was danced in the motifs of various nations. While the dance itself never became a craze, the song won an Academy award and became another of the Astaire-introduced hits.

> Beautiful music . . .
> Dangerous rhythm . . .
> It's something daring, The Continental,
> A way of dancing that's really ultra-new.
> It's very subtle, The Continental,
> Because it does what you want it to do.
> It has a passion, The Continental,
> An invitation to moonlight and romance.
> It's quite the fashion, The Continental,
> Because you tell of your love while you dance.

The Gay Divorcée was released in the fall of 1934, with results that RKO executives had been praying for. Suddenly the specter of receivership faded with the emergence of a new team that entranced American film audiences. Astaire and Rogers offered a new kind of romance, supremely sophisticated yet accessible to everyone. Their mutual attraction avoided outward displays of affection—on the "Continental" line "you kiss while you're dancing," he kisses her hand. They expressed their feelings as they glided over the polished floor, she at first rejecting his advance, then submitting to his embrace.

"We always figured that Ginger gave Fred sex appeal," says Irene Dunne. Indeed, Ginger's fascination for the man with the inverted-pear head gave him unexpected allure. But his polished manner and uncommon grace—many filmgoers thought he was English—also muted the brassiness that had been part of her screen image since her debut in *Young Man of Manhattan* with the deathless line, "Cigarette me, big boy." He made her a lady.

Fred Astaire, movie star.

It was a role he hadn't really anticipated. Celebrity had come to Fred early in life, and he had learned to deal with it. Being recognized in New York or London was discomforting, a jar to his innate shyness. That was nothing compared to what happened after his stardom in films. He was spotlighted wherever he went.

After the release of *The Gay Divorcée,* the RKO publicity department was flooded with requests for interviews with Fred Astaire. Fred complained to the publicity chief, Perry Lieber: "Why do I have do all these interviews? I've done interviews all my life, in every city I've played. I've said everything I have to say."

"Fred, did you ever play Tacoma?" Lieber asked.

"Tacoma? No."

"Well, your movies play Tacoma. And Boise, and Altoona, and Shreveport. They want to know all about you in all those towns, all over. That's why you gotta do interviews."

The Astaire grace also showed on the tennis court (RKO).

Fred sufferingly endured interview after interview, striving for spontaneous replies to the same dreary questions. He even submitted to fan-magazine interviewers, who turned out such breathless articles as "Why Fame Can't Spoil Fred Astaire," and "My Companion Said, 'I'd Just *Love* to Dance with Fred Astaire.'"

Every aspect of Fred's life was considered fair game. Sidney Skolsky wrote a column packed with Astaire information, including:

"He is five feet, nine inches and weighs 138 pounds dressed. Has brown eyes, thinning brown hair, and a mole not brown under his left eye.

"He wears two-piece underwear, running trunks and a shirt, when not working. When doing a dance number he wears a union suit.

"He is a plain food eater. He likes to have a bowl of ice cream about once a day. His favorite dish, of all dishes, is a large bowl of chicken noodle soup.

"He is a mild person, pleasant, generally trying to

please. He has a bad temper, and when he gets angry he breaks furniture and throws handy objects.

"He has his monogram on his shirts, underwear, pajamas and dressing gowns. He has over a hundred neckties and will put on and take off fifteen before he finally decides which one to wear. He stands in front of a mirror and makes faces at himself while dressing.

"He sleeps in a twin bed, and sleeps on his stomach. He wears pajamas, trousers and jacket. The pajamas are always silk, and the color is generally blue. He often wiggles his toes while sleeping."

While Fred could force himself to tolerate such an incursion on his private life, Phyllis could not. She detested the publicity that attended Fred's new movie career. It was inimical to her own upbringing amid the polite reserve of Long Island society. She was repelled by many with whom Fred worked in films; she found them loud, coarse and unmannered. She preferred to stay aloof from his studio life and rarely visited him while he was working. Nor did the Astaires attend the big Hollywood parties, which both of them abhorred. Phyllis chose their friends with care, preferring those with genteel backgrounds like her own. Many were from Hollywood's colony of Britishers.

> FRED: Phyllis and I had just been married when we came out here, and I had to go straight to work. I didn't get a chance to see her much while I was working. Phyllis didn't know whether she liked Hollywood very much. It was very difficult because she didn't know anything about show business. She began to like it somewhat, and we made a good many friends here. But in the beginning she was a little bit reluctant about wanting to socialize. All her friends were in the East, and none of them was connected with show business.

One of the friends that Fred made in Hollywood was Douglas Fairbanks, Sr., who had starred at Proctor's Fifth Avenue when the Astaires were fired from the bill. Fairbanks helped answer some of Fred's perplexities about his movie career.

FRED: He was an extraordinary man. When I got to Hollywood, he was through [in films]. He simply had no more interest in it at all.

He was fascinated by the fact that I was making a hit. He used to say, "You're really doing something unusual." And I would say, "How long can you keep up? What do I do? This picture is good, and maybe the next one will be good. What happens after that?"

"Well," he said, "the way I worked it, I just did the best I could, then I went away and got some fresh ideas and came back. I did that for so long that I can't remember how I did it, but that's what I did."

Anyone who has any creative art necessary in his career does the same thing. Some people just sit around and wait for a good part to come along. They don't create things, and for them it's a little tougher.

Roberta, the third pairing of Fred Astaire and Ginger Rogers, was shrewdly planned by Pandro Berman. Instead of making Fred and Ginger carry the load, the producer supplied two other stars and a hit Broadway show with one of Jerome Kern's best scores. Even with "Yesterdays" and "Smoke Gets in Your Eyes," Berman thought more songs were needed.

Kern came to Hollywood and collaborated for the first time with Dorothy Fields, daughter of Lew (Weber and) Fields. The movie required a song that could be used both for a fashion show and a love scene, and they produced "Lovely to Look At." When RKO officials complained the song was too short at sixteen bars, Kern replied, "That's all I had to say."

Fred Astaire suggested the other Kern tune. Before leaving London, Fred had seen a new Kern musical, *Three Sisters.* The show was a failure, but Fred admired the score, especially one song that seemed ideal for *Roberta.* Dorothy Fields and Jimmy McHugh augmented the original lyrics of Oscar Hammerstein II, and "I Won't Dance" provided one of Astaire's wittiest numbers.

RKO's foremost star, Irene Dunne, was cast in the role

Their looks told the story, Roberta (RKO).

"Smoke Gets in Your Eyes," Roberta (RKO)

of the Russian princess. Randolph Scott, who became a golf partner and enduring friend of Fred Astaire, played the American football player. They carried the somewhat tedious burden of the plot, and the entertainment sections focused on the studio's new team, Astaire and Rogers.

Gaining confidence after two films, Astaire took credit as dance director, with Hermes Pan listed as assistant. Fred's talent was in full flower. He played accordion with his Wabash Indianians dance band, pounded some "feelthy piano" to "I Won't Dance," devised a tap duet with Ginger on "I'll Be Hard to Handle," as well as a thrillingly romantic dance with Ginger to "Smoke Gets in Your Eyes."

Roberta, the third Astaire-Rogers film to play the Radio City Music Hall, was their third hit, delighting audiences and critics alike. The film even drew a good review from the exacting Jerome Kern, who wired Pandro Berman: "It certainly was unique experience to find motion picture version of one of our plays something to be proud of instead of otherwise. . . . Sorry I had so little to do with it."

Since their dances could be enjoyed regardless of language, the musicals of Astaire and Rogers proved immensely popular in foreign countries. There were exceptions. The Nazi censor barred *Flying Down to Rio* from Germany as being "too frivolous." The Fascist censor refused to allow *The Gay Divorcée* to be shown in Italy because the character of the cuckolded Tonetti, as played by Eric Rhodes, was "offensive to Italian prestige."

Fred Astaire felt betrayed.

He had placed all his aspirations for the ideal film musical in the project that Pandro Berman and Mark Sandrich were preparing (a movie veteran, William A. Seiter, had directed *Roberta* so Sandrich would have more time to prepare the next film). Fred was thrilled by the promise of a score by

Irving Berlin, whose songs he and Adele had used in vaudeville. When Fred completed *Roberta,* he read the new script.

"I cannot see that my part embodies any of the necessary
elements except to *dance, dance, dance,*" Fred commented in a
furious, hand-written letter to Berman.

He added that his role cast him as a straight juvenile,
rather cocky and arrogant, that the entire script seemed a
rehash of *The Gay Divorcée,* without the latter's charm and
suspense. His comedy was virtually nil, Fred complained, and
he was forever pawing the girl or she was rushing to his
arms. At least twice she slaps him. The entire script relied too
heavily on the Berlin songs, Fred argued, adding that it
would be impossible to sell the numbers unless his role received a complete overhaul. He asked for an immediate
meeting with Berman to thrash out the problems.

All of Fred's frustrations about his movie career suddenly crowded to the fore. It had not developed as he had
hoped and planned. He had envisioned himself playing light
comedy, not romance. He had thought he would be performing one dance per film, not five or six. Most of all, he was
profoundly disappointed to find himself irretrievably paired
with another dancing partner.

Berman and Sandrich placated Fred—he was always
more emphatic in letters than in conferences, when his natural reticence took over—and assured him that a script rewrite
would give his character substance and provide more for him
to do but dance, dance, dance.

Such was the beginning of *Top Hat.*

Astaire himself had helped provide the title. During *The
Gay Divorcée,* he had suggested repeating the machine-gun
number he had done in *Smiles.* "Great idea," enthused Sandrich. "Let's save it for our next picture, so I can really spot-
light it."

> FRED: I like fooling with rhythms and beating the
> floor and making noises. I started using canes and
> props. I can't remember how many specialty tap
> dances and trick tap dances I did in the movies.
>
> I started using the cane in a thing called "High
> Hat" in *Funny Face.* It was a strutting number, the hit
> number in the show. An applause getter.

(RKO)

The machine gun number, Top Hat *(RKO)*

CHEEK TO CHEEK
Music and Lyrics by
IRVING BERLIN
from
THE RKO RADIO PICTURE
TOP HAT
starring
FRED ASTAIRE
and
GINGER ROGERS
a PANDRO S. BERMAN production
directed by
MARK SANDRICH
-25
CHEEK TO CHEEK
ISN'T THIS A LOVELY DAY
(To be caught in the rain?)
THE PICCOLINO
NO STRINGS (I'm fancy free)
Top hat, white tie and tails
IRVING BERLIN Inc.
Music Publishers
799 SEVENTH AVE., NEW YORK, N.Y.
MADE IN USA

Irving Berlin came to Hollywood to write songs for the Astaire-Rogers film, and he worked closely with Mark Sandrich, who wanted the songs to advance the plot, not interrupt it. "Top Hat" was the only song that was not plot-related. It was sung and danced on a London stage by Astaire, establishing him in the film as an entertainer of rare talent and sophistication. One of Fred's most indelible numbers, it also established forevermore the Fred Astaire uniform in the minds of the American public.

> I just got an invitation through the mails:
> "Your presence is requested this evening,
> It's formal—top hat, white tie and tails."
> Nothing now can take the wind out of my sails,
> Because I'm invited to step out this evening,
> Top hat, white tie and tails.
> Oh, I'm puttin' on my top hat,
> Tiein' up my white tie,
> Brushin' off my tails.
> I'm dudin' up my shirt front,
> Puttin' in my shirt studs,
> Polishin' my nails.

Berlin composed some of the songs to fit the script, or the script was altered to accommodate his songs. After he presented "Isn't This a Lovely Day to Be Caught in the Rain," Sandrich devised a scene in a London park where Astaire and Rogers dance during a rainstorm.

Fred and Hermes Pan contributed the ideal Astaire-Rogers duet. Fred and Ginger have an entire park bandstand as their stage. The number begins with Ginger still piqued at his effrontery. Slowly she begins to melt as he points out the circumstances they find themselves in.

> Isn't this a lovely day to be caught in the rain?
> You were going on your way, now you've got to remain.
> Just as you were going, leaving me all at sea,
> The clouds broke,
> They broke, and oh what a break for me.

Her resistance melts, and he begins challenging her to repeat the tap steps he offers. She accepts the challenge and copies his steps with equal zest but with feminine style. Their delight builds as the challenge continues until they climax by whirling around the bandstand, embracing in a mutual ecstasy.

Fred was not overly impressed when Irving Berlin played "Cheek to Cheek" for him on the famed Berlin upright, key-shifting piano. For one thing, the tune climbed to notes that strained the reedy Berlin voice. Fred realized he would be hard put to achieve such heights with his own limited range. But it seemed like a good song to depict the depth of feeling between the warring lovers.

The stage on which the "Cheek to Cheek" number was filmed became the site of the famous Battle of the Feathers.

RKO hands believed Lela Rogers was the culprit. With Ginger's star ascending, her mother took a commanding role. She read all of Ginger's scripts and made detailed analyses which she presented to studio executives. She attended the rushes and registered her approval or disapproval. She reviewed the publicity photographs and killed those she considered unflattering to Ginger. Lela also supervised all of Ginger's costumes and hence helped perpetrate the feathers.

The tale has been told many times, but never better than by Hermes Pan in an interview with Bill Davidson:

"We were ready to go with the 'Cheek to Cheek' number when Ginger arrived in this dress. It was covered with ostrich feathers from neck to hem. It was late in the afternoon, and we were to shoot the number early the next morning. They began to rehearse, and the feathers flew all over the place. They blinded Fred and got in his nose and made him sneeze. After about an hour, he gave up.

"The next morning we had a meeting, and the dress designer assured us it would be okay. But the feathers kept flying, and late in the afternoon, Fred threw up his hands. He was white with anger. He yelled something at Ginger. She burst into tears, and Lela came charging at Fred like a mother rhinoceros protecting her young.

"After a lot of hollering, Fred retired to one side of the sound stage, and Ginger and Lela settled down on the other. For a whole day, there was stony silence. Finally, the designer

Ginger, Fred and feathers, "Cheek to Cheek" (RKO)

agreed to spend all night sewing each feather into place. On the third day, though a few feathers still flew, we were able to shoot the dance."

Afterward, Fred and Hermes serenaded Ginger with their own parody of the song:

> Feathers—I hate feathers—
> And I hate them so that I can hardly speak,
> And I never find the happiness I seek
> With those chicken feathers dancing
> Cheek to cheek.

Fred learned his lesson and throughout his film career he insisted on inspecting his dance partners' costumes before filming. He was wary of wide skirts that would tangle his feet, weighted sleeves that would whack his face, feathers, sequins and beads that would fly over the dance floor.

The antagonism over the feathers didn't appear on the screen. "Cheek to Cheek," with its lyrical romanticism and adroit change of rhythms, provided the perfect Astaire-Rogers number. Nothing the pair ever danced, before or after, could match its grace.

> Heaven,
> I'm in heaven,
> And my heart beats so that I can hardly speak.
> And I seem to find the happiness I seek
> When we're out together dancing cheek to cheek.
> Heaven,
> I'm in heaven,
> And the cares that hung around me through the week
> Seem to vanish like a gambler's lucky streak
> When we're out together dancing cheek to cheek.

The amazing Berlin also provided "No Strings (I'm Fancy Free)" and the obligatory production number, "The Piccolino," a light-hearted spoof of "The Carioca" and "The Continental."

The release of *Top Hat* in late summer of 1935 created a sensation. Records were broken at the Radio Music Hall. Theaters that normally played a movie for one week held *Top*

Top Hat *(RKO)*

Mark Sandrich,
Ginger, Fred,
Irving Berlin,
1935 (RKO)

Hat for three or four or more. All five of the Berlin songs became hits, and "Cheek to Cheek" set a new record for the number of weeks a song remained number one on the "Hit Parade" radio show. Filmed at a cost of $620,000, *Top Hat* collected more than $3 million at the nation's box offices, enriching Fred Astaire and Irving Berlin, both of whom collected a percentage of the profits.

The critical reaction to *Top Hat* was near-ecstatic. The New York *Daily News* announced in an editorial that it was revising its list of all-time all-American movies to include *Top Hat* along with *Birth of a Nation, Broken Blossoms, The Four Horsemen of the Apocalypse, The Kid, The Big Parade, Cavalcade,* et cetera.

Declared the *Daily News:* "*Top Hat* is the best thing yet done in a movie musical comedy. The music is Berlin at his best; the settings are gorgeous; the lines are among the funniest we have heard; and the dancing and comedy by Fred Astaire and Ginger Rogers are something to go back and see again.

"Especially the dancing. Astaire has long been known as the man who made over the humble buck-and-wing into an art; and in Ginger Rogers he has found a lovely and agile dance partner—a worthy successor to his sister Adele, now Lady Charles Cavendish."

The impact on movie audiences of the Astaire personality, especially when complemented by the sunshiny Ginger, was enormous. There had never been a star quite like him. Marilyn Miller, Harry Richman, Helen Morgan, Fanny Brice, Dennis King and other Broadway stars had appeared in early talkies but hadn't caught on. Astaire succeeded, not merely because he was a divine dancer and a likable singer. He won the American public because his personality was new, fresh and engaging.

His on-screen persona had been self-created. He borrowed the elegance and style of Britain's aristocracy and America's wealthy and added the raffishness of vaudeville and the racetrack. Beneath it all were his native shyness, his eagerness to succeed and please.

Top Hat was equally adored by the English, who had long considered Fred Astaire one of their own. The *Observer*'s

The RKO stock company: Edward Everett Horton, Helen Broderick, Eric Blore, Ginger, Fred, Erik Rhodes, Top Hat *(RKO)*

critic commented: "The tonic appearances of young Mr. Fred Astaire are amongst the greatest joys of the modern cinema. Watching him, you are suddenly aware that the lower half of the cinema screen has been wasted all these years. I know of no screen stars except Chaplin and Fred Astaire who have really learned to act volubly from the knees down."

Fred and Phyllis Astaire decided to make a quick trip to Europe before he reported for work on a second Berlin musical, *Follow the Fleet.* They visited the Cavendishes at Lismore Castle and shared Adele's happiness over her second pregnancy. Her doctors had told her to expect twins. In London, Phyllis had joyous news for Fred: She was pregnant with their first child. No more touring for her, Fred decreed. They would return to America immediately.

Back in New York, Fred began the first of six musical hours on radio for Lucky Strike cigarettes. On the first program he sang three songs from *Top Hat* and did some tap dancing, accompanied by Lennie Hayton's orchestra. Always unsure about his vocal talent, Fred was delighted by a rave from *Variety:* "It was to be expected that he would be a smash hit with his tapping, and he was. But it was Astaire's singing that really connected and surprised."

Only on radio and on phonograph records could the Astaire voice be appreciated fully. In the films, his songs acted as preludes to the dance, the lyrics neatly delivered, the melody unwavering. His adroitness was often overlooked in anticipation of the excitement of his dancing.

By hearing the voice without the image, the listener can understand Astaire's mastery of the show tune. The voice lacks resonance, but it is lyrical and persuasive as it tells of the happiness and sorrows of being in love. Astaire was blessed with top-notch lyricists—Cole Porter, Otto Harbach, Dorothy Fields, Irving Berlin, Ira Gershwin, Johnny Mercer—and he respected their words. But Astaire probably could have been convincing with the most banal of lyrics.

Even though the Astaire shows were broadcast by NBC, with which RKO was affiliated, the studio protested that Astaire's radio appearances were in breach of contract. Fred was furious. He accused the RKO bosses of ingratitude. After all, hadn't he and Ginger virtually saved the studio from bankruptcy?

Leland Hayward informed RKO that his client deserved a new contract. Astaire wanted a salary of $4,000 a week, payable fifty-two weeks a year, as well as his percentages of his films' profits. He wanted to appear on radio shows and make phonograph records on Sundays or at others times when he wasn't needed by RKO.

Importantly, Astaire sought relief from the screen partnership with Ginger Rogers. He wanted assurance that she would not appear in more than three of his next five motion pictures—unless he consented in writing.

RKO, unwilling to anger Fred further, agreed to the terms. The studio provided added evidence of his value by insuring him for a million dollars. Ginger Rogers and Katharine Hepburn were insured for half a million each.

When the theater owners of America voted for the stars who sold the most tickets in 1935, Fred Astaire and Ginger Rogers placed fourth, behind Shirley Temple, Will Rogers and Clark Gable and ahead of Robert Taylor, Joe E. Brown, Dick Powell, Joan Crawford, Claudette Colbert, Jeanette MacDonald and Gary Cooper.

Despite the new contract and his box-office stature, Fred found things to moan about. There was a *Pictorial Review* article about which he complained to the studio brass. Excerpts:

"Having very little to say at any time, he is unusually fearful of the press. Fred's thinning hair is a source of considerable sadness. Unless he is wearing his spurious top-piece, only his perfect manners make him uncover.

"Astaire's marriage has undoubtedly colored his personal and professional career. I have the feeling that he not only loves his wife devotedly but stands a bit in awe of her. . . . Mrs. Astaire carefully stays out of the way of photographers, and sees to it that her daughter [sic] by her first marriage is not caught by snooping lens-snappers."

Even on radio Fred wore tails, at least for publicity photos (NBC).

Fred's shyness was often mistaken for aloofness. At the studio he sometimes seemed aloof because of his intense concentration on his work. Even in social situations, his conversation was fragmentary and surface, partly because he was aware of his lack of formal education, partly because he abhorred controversy. "I don't get drawn into arguments very easily," he admitted, "because I refuse to discuss politics, religion, dancing, movies, et cetera. There is only one subject on which I could talk for hours and hours, and that's a certain sport."

Fred took golf as seriously as dancing. He became a member of the Bel Air Country Club, one of the first performers to be admitted, and played every day when he wasn't working. If he hadn't been a dancer, he would like to have been a professional golfer, he told interviewers.

"The only time I have ever sulked," he claimed, "was when I thought I had won a golf tournament, only to find that I had been disqualified because I unwittingly drove two balls off the first tee. I am still sulking."

His friends were surprised by certain things about Fred that seemed so un-Astaire-like. His fascination with bellhops, for example. "Whenever I check into a hotel, I make friends with the bellhops," he remarked. "If you want to know what's going on in a city, ask a bellhop."

Friends were startled to discover that not everything about Fred was pure elegance. When angered or frustrated he could resort to language employed in backstage crap games and racing-stable conversations. His friend and admirer James Cagney once remarked, "You know, Freddie, you've got a touch of the hoodlum in you."

> FRED (laughing): I used to shock him sometimes
> when I would come out with some sleazy language.

The most surprising aspect of the private Fred Astaire was his fascination with crime and criminals.

In Los Angeles and New York, observers at the scene of a robbery or a shooting were sometimes startled to see Fred Astaire step out of a police car along with the officers. He was introduced to the practice of observing police work by his friend Douglas Fairbanks, Sr.

FRED: Doug liked to do it, and he took me out a couple of times. We'd go down to the morgue, go out on a police calls.

Police work has always fascinated me. I used to explore prisons on visits when I was a kid; I just wondered what it would be like to be in prison. I can tell you one thing: I never once wanted to stay.

Later on, I attended the police lineup in New York at eight o'clock in the morning. My wife Phyllis liked to go, too. We watched as all the previous day's prisoners stood up. That was the real thing.

On October 27, 1935, in London, Adele Astaire Cavendish gave birth to twin sons. Like a daughter two years before, the babies died a few hours after birth. The mother's condition was reported as "very satisfactory," but it was the beginning of many months of deep sorrow for Adele.

On January 21, 1936, in Los Angeles, Phyllis Astaire gave birth to a six-and-a-half-pound baby boy. Both mother and son were said to be in excellent health. The boy was named Fred Astaire, Jr.

"We did two Astaire-Rogers pictures a year at RKO," recalls Pandro Berman, "one with Fred and Ginger alone, one with another couple. *Follow the Fleet* was one with another couple."

The secondary romantic plot was carried by Fred's pal Randolph Scott and Harriet Hilliard, popular singer and wife of the bandleader Ozzie Nelson. Irving Berlin provided another of his hit-filled scores, and for the first time, Astaire and Rogers were not placed in an atmosphere of ultra-sophistication. RKO executives reasoned that their most popular actor might lose his appeal to the common folk if he was repeatedly seen in white tie and tails. In *Follow the Fleet* he played a gob.

The Astaire-Rogers films had acquired a visual style that was as distinctive as the stars' dancing. Partly that was due to

Fred proved as appealing in a sailor suit as in tails—"Let Yourself Go," Follow the Fleet *(RKO).*

Fred and Randolph Scott gag it up for the publicity photographer (RKO).

economics. As Mark Sandrich, Jr., points out: "RKO had limited budgets, so the Astaire-Rogers films had to be carefully planned. The cast was small—usually six people. The production was built around one large set, where the finale dance number was staged. The rest of the sets were small— hotel rooms, apartments, business offices. The sets were very contrasted: the whites were gleaming white, the blacks were shiny black." The art-deco look was the work of the art directors, Van Nest Polglase and Carroll Clark. "They established that look in *Flying Down to Rio*," says Berman, "and it proved so effective and so different from other musicals that we kept it. I don't think the pictures would have been any better if we'd had more money to spend, except for one thing: color. But then, color films were still in their infancy."

Fred had now systemized his making of the musicals. Two months before the start of filming, he began rehearsals. They took place on an empty stage with only two others present: Hermes Pan and Hal Borne.

Borne had become part of the Astaire team on *Flying Down to Rio*. He had studied classical piano in Chicago and had come to Los Angeles with his family during the Depression. Borne was playing piano in the Colony Club, an elegant gambling spot on the Sunset Strip, when Max Steiner came in one night. Steiner offered Borne a job in the RKO music department as sideline player (playing before the camera but not recording) until he was eligible to join the musicians' union.

Fred heard Borne play during the "Orchids in the Moonlight" number. "That's the guy I want for rehearsal pianist," Fred told Steiner.

Hal Borne did more than accompany Astaire and Pan as they concocted dances. "I did all the dance arrangements and then gave them to the orchestrators," he says. "I added my own melodies to the songs because it was impossible to do a dance number with just thirty-two or forty bars. The numbers could last five, seven, even ten minutes. A lot of music had to be filled in."

Borne sometimes worked with composers, especially Irving Berlin, in converting their songs to dance arrangements. For "Cheek to Cheek," Berlin was stuck for bridges to punctuate the lyric "Heaven . . . I'm in heaven. . . ." Borne supplied the now familiar "la-da-da" after each "heaven." For the "Fancy Free" sandman dance, in which Fred lulled Ginger to sleep in the apartment below, Borne interspersed the song with snatches of "Rockabye Baby."

Recalling the rehearsal sessions, Hal Borne says, "Hermes' contribution was always great. Hermes was a very good dancer, also a singer—he started out as a singer. His rapport with Fred was sensational, because they both thought alike. When they danced, you thought you were watching two Fred Astaires. Sometimes they'd walk around in circles, scratching their heads. No one would talk and I wouldn't play. I just let them figure out what they were trying to figure out. Fred would say, 'Let's try this: You go over there and you'll be the Ginger part.' And he would start. It was hard to figure who contributed what to the choreography. In the production numbers it was mainly Hermes, because he had to set up all the steps for the chorus. If Fred didn't like something, he would make suggestions. It was always pleasant. Never a hint of unpleasantness."

Fred began rehearsing promptly at 10 A.M.—his vaudeville training had made him a stickler for punctuality, as Pan and Borne learned early. Fred started the session with ten minutes of warm-up movement, like a fighter shadowboxing. Then he ad-libbed dance steps for another ten minutes, roaming through his repertoire. Pan recalled watching Fred ad-lib for twenty minutes without repeating a step.

Getting down to work, Fred danced to a song as Borne played, a few bars at a time. Fred tried steps, Pan offered suggestions, Borne jotted down music notes to fit their ideas. Slowly the dance developed. Fred usually lunched on the stage with his customary noodle soup. He avoided the studio commissary, where he would be stared at as he ate.

The rehearsal usually lasted into mid-afternoon, sometimes later if Fred was on a streak. If he faced a deadline, he worked on Saturday and Sunday. Hal Borne recalls a session with Fred on the Fourth of July.

At the end of rehearsal, Fred seemed as fresh as when he started. He sweated little, though he dropped five pounds during the weeks of rehearsal. He stopped the sessions a week before filming so he could regain his normal weight of

Fred and Hermes Pan demonstrate the phony dance diagram (RKO).

140 pounds. Otherwise his face would photograph even thinner than it did.

Rehearsals were not all work. The three men played gags on each other, and Fred succumbed to occasional fits of silliness, as when he pirouetted wildly and cried, "Help! I can't stop!" Once he telephoned Pandro Berman and said,

"Come down right away—I've got a great new finish for the dance!" When Berman arrived, Fred showed him the step: an old-style shuffle-off-to-Buffalo. One morning Fred convulsed Pan and Borne with an amazingly accurate impression of Shirley Temple singing and dancing "On the Good Ship Lollipop."

At the behest of the RKO publicity department, Astaire and Pan posed for a photograph in front of a blackboard on which was chalked a diagram that resembled an intricate football play. This was purportedly how Astaire and Pan plotted the dances. It was, of course, nonsense, because the Astaire-Pan inventions were impossible to diagram. Fred went along with it, and he added a few chalk marks of his own. "What's that?" Pan asked. "That's the horse shit," Fred replied.

From the rehearsal sessions came a revolution in film dance. Before Astaire, most dances were photographed as numbers on a stage, within the confines of the proscenium arch. Movie dances were equated with the bizarre spectacles of Busby Berkeley.

The Astaire-Rogers films demonstrated that dances could be convincingly staged in hotel rooms, offices or gardens. Fred, who had been furious over the editing of the "Carioca" number, had firm notions about how the dances should be photographed, as he explained to an interviewer:

"In the old days, they used to cut up all the dances on the screen. In the middle of a sequence, they would show you a close-up of the actor's face, or of his feet, insert trick angles taken from the floor, the ceiling, through lattice work or a maze of fancy shadows. The result was the dance had no continuity. The audience was far more conscious of the camera than of the dance. And no matter how effective the trick angles and cockeyed shots might have been in themselves, they destroyed the flow of the dance—a factor which is just as important on the screen as on the stage.

"I have always tried to run a dance straight in the movies, keeping the full figure of the dancer, or dancers, in view and retaining the flow of the movements intact. In every kind of dancing, even tap, the movement of the upper body is as important as that of the legs. Keeping the whole body always in action before the camera, there are certain advantages that the screen has over the stage.

"You can concentrate your action on the dancer; the audience can follow intricate steps that were all but lost behind the footlights, and each person in the audience sees the dance from the same perspective. . . .

"Chorus numbers should be used only when you have a definite idea of something for the chorus to do that will heighten the whole dance number. On the stage, you can bring them close to the audience and get a visible emotional reaction. In the movies, the chorus should be used largely as background, because you cannot recreate the same kind of reaction. By the time you line up thirty girls in the forefront of the screen, they are so small their individuality is lost."

Astaire decried the studio thinking that every musical needed a splashy production number as a closer. His first four musicals had them. Starting with *Follow the Fleet,* they were dropped.

He preferred to film a dance without interruption, at eye level and with three cameras—straight-on, left and right. Often the camera at one side captured the most interesting composition, he found. Planning was everything: "If the dance is right, there shouldn't be a single superfluous movement."

He added, "It is extremely important for a dance cue to flow naturally in and out of the story. I think the audience always slumps—even more in the movies than on the stage—when they hear an obvious dance cue, and both the picture *and the dance* seem to lose some of their continuity.

"Each dance ought to spring somehow out of the character or situation, otherwise it is simply a vaudeville act. Also you have to be able to sense the moment when the audience reaches its peak of exhilaration and feels like applauding. Then it's over." All those years of performing the runaround with Adele had given Fred a precise feel for when the audience felt like applauding.

Fred broke his own rule with the "Let's Face the Music and Dance" number in *Follow the Fleet.* It tells a story that is unrelated to the movie's plot and is danced onstage during a musical performance.

"Let's Face the Music," Follow the Fleet *(RKO)*

Once again in white tie and tails, Astaire plays a gambler who loses his stake in Monte Carlo, goes outside the casino and finds he is shunned by his onetime friends. As he puts a pistol to his head, he sees the gorgeously gowned Rogers, ready to take a suicide leap. He rescues her, throws away his pistol and empty wallet and sings one of Berlin's loveliest lyrics.

> There may be trouble ahead,
> But while there's music and moonlight
>   and love and romance,
> Let's face the music and dance.
> Before the fiddlers have fled,
> Before they ask us to pay the bill,
> And while we still have the chance,
> Let's face the music and dance.

In his *Spectator* review of *Follow the Fleet,* Graham Greene continued his Mickey Mouse analogy:

"If one needs to assign human qualities to this light, quick, humorous cartoon, they are the same as the early Mickey's: a touch of pathos, the sense of a courageous and impromptu intelligence, a capacity for getting into awkward situations. Something has to be done, and Mickey without a moment's hesitation will fling his own tail across an abyss and tread the furry, unattached tightrope with superb in-

On top of the world—the RKO trademark (RKO)

souciance. Something has to be done, and Mr. Astaire bursts into a dance which in its speed and unselfconsciousness seems equally to break the laws of nature. They are both defending Minnie, though Miss Ginger Rogers will never quite attain Minnie's significance (she is too brazen and self-sufficing for the part), and there is no villain type, no black Pasha cat continually to threaten her with ravishment; the plots of Mr. Astaire's plots are more everyday; one might almost say more decent, more 'family.'"

The Astaire-Rogers films had become RKO's most valuable property. Too valuable to entrust to a single director. Although Mark Sandrich's three films had proved enormously successful, Pandro Berman decided to alternate him with another talented RKO hand, George Stevens.

The two directors had similar backgrounds. Both started in two-reel comedies; Stevens had been a camera-man, then director for Laurel and Hardy. Both joined the Lou Brock shorts unit at RKO and directed Wheeler and Woolsey. Both were active in the Screen Directors' Guild, then struggling for recognition, and both would serve as president.

Mark Sandrich, with his background in science, was a methodical director. Every camera angle, every movement of the actors was planned before he came on the set. He never consulted the script, instructing the actors from memory in a quiet, businesslike voice. He never acted out a scene, nor did he print the first take. Like most graduates of two-reel comedies, he sought ideas wherever he could find them. During a boat trip with his family from New York to Los Angeles via the Panama Canal, he paid a visit to the boiler room. When Fred, hearing the rhythmic counterbeat of a cement mixer on the RKO lot, suggested a dance with machines, Sandrich remembered his boat trip. The result was the "Slap That Bass" number in a ship's engine room in *Shall We Dance?*

George Stevens, who came from a theatrical family, was an instinctive director. He had a keen sense of comedy, realizing from his Hal Roach training that it must come out of

"Pick Yourself Up,"
Swing Time *(RKO)*

character. He directed meticulously, lavishing time with his actors until they were comfortably assured in their scenes. His deliberateness caused fits in the production office, but he would not be hurried. If pressured to step up his tempo of filming, he would dismiss the company for the day. Stevens always won. He had proved the value of his methods with *Alice Adams* and *Quality Street,* both starring Katharine Hepburn.

The new film was originally titled *I Won't Dance,* then *Never Gonna Dance,* a new song Jerome Kern and Dorothy Fields had written. Kern suggested that both titles might confuse the film with *Roberta.* He proposed *Swing Time.* He had written a number called "The Waltz in Swing Time," which he hadn't planned to publish. But he would publish it if the title was changed. It was, and Fred Astaire was pleased. He much preferred the reference to the nation's music craze, with which he himself was enamored.

Jerome Kern wrote his most varied score for *Swing Time,* as if to prove that he was capable of more than melodic ballads. Each song fit perfectly into the plot. "A Fine Romance," which was subtitled "A Sarcastic Love Long," provided the perfect vehicle for the Astaire-Rogers romantic byplay.

> A fine romance, with no kisses.
> A fine romance, my friend, this is.
> You're calmer than the seals in the Arctic Ocean.
> At least they flap their fins to express emotion.

"Bojangles of Harlem," a song totally unlike any previous Kern, provided Astaire with one of his most electric numbers, especially when he danced with three immense shadows of himself. An homage to Bill Robinson, whom Fred had admired in vaudeville, it was the only time in Fred's career that he donned blackface. The dance is totally devoid of racial stereotype and scarcely related to Robinson's style.

"The Way You Look Tonight" was the hit of *Swing Time,* and Academy Award winner as best song of 1936. Remembered from Dorothy Fields' lyrics as a poignant love song, it actually was sung by Fred to Ginger as her hair was covered with shampoo.

Some day, when I'm awfully low,
And the world is cold,
I will feel a thrill just thinking of you,
And the way you look tonight.

After he finished *Swing Time*, Fred and Phyllis left California for a European vacation. In New York he wrote Pandro Berman that the "Bojangles" number seemed to have been worth all the effort they put into it. Fred added: "I think my taps were O.K. for sync and all in all I'm nuts about the number and will be terribly disappointed if it doesn't get a hell of a reaction from the audience." Fred made a pitch for special screen credit for his collaborators, Hermes Pan and Hal Borne. Then: "I'm off on the Normandie tomorrow (Wed.) and will be anxiously awaiting news of the picture."

The Astaires visited Adele, still bereaved over the loss of the twins, renewed old friendships in London, then took off for a week incognito in Paris. After another week in London, they sailed back to New York.

Swing Time drew the audience reaction Fred had hoped for, and reviewers acclaimed the "Bojangles" number as a new high in the Astaire art. Though praising the film, *Variety* commented that it fell below the previous standards for Astaire-Rogers movies. *The New York Times* agreed. Other critics hinted that after six films, the cycle was showing signs of fatigue.

RKO executives detected disturbing signs in theater receipts for *Swing Time*. While opening weeks were excellent, business fell off sooner than with the previous Astaire-Rogers musicals.

Fred had little time to worry. He returned to California to start preparations for a new movie, this time a happy reunion with the Gershwins. He had also committed himself to thirty-nine weeks of a radio hour for the Packard Motor Company. He had forgotten about the contract during the European trip and tried to bow out. But the Packard people insisted they wanted Fred Astaire as radio salesman to the wealthy who bought their cars.

The orchestra leader for the Packard Hour was Johnny Green, an old friend. At the age of twelve, Green had first seen Fred and Adele in *Apple Blossoms* in New York and had insisted that his mother take him backstage to meet Fred. Their friendship began after Green became a composer, pianist and conductor in the Broadway theater, as well as an associate of George and Ira Gershwin.

On the Packard Hour, Fred ad-libbed tap steps on a small wooden floor, a challenge for a dancer who liked to be unlimited in his movement. He exchanged patter with Charles Butterworth and sang tunes from his Broadway shows and movies. On occasion he introduced a song written by Fred Astaire.

Songwriting has been a lifetime passion for Fred, as well as a source of occasional frustration.

> FRED: I have had a couple of fair songs. The nearest thing I've had to a hit potential was a thing I did in the past few years called "Life Is Beautiful." I had some before that: "It's Like Taking Candy from a Baby" and one I wrote with Johnny Mercer called "I'm Building Up to an Awful Letdown."
>
> I've got about forty to fifty songs, and maybe half a dozen aren't too bad. When a song isn't a hit you don't love it too much. But there were two or three of them that were noticed and played. And I got a nice low rating on ASCAP.
>
> I'd love to have been able to do more with my music, but I never had the time. I was always working on dance numbers. Year after year I kept doing that. Somehow or other I always blame myself, because I say, "Well, I could have found the time; why the hell didn't I do it?"
>
> But I had a lot of family, and between pictures I didn't sit around playing the piano.

When the theater grosses of *Swing Time* indicated the first weakening of the Astaire-Rogers cycle, Fred began to worry more than usual about his future in Hollywood. He retained fresh and painful memory of reviews from his first appearance without Adele in *Gay Divorce*—"not for the general good is he sisterless." Could he expect the same when he was Gingerless? Without doubt.

Fred decided the time had come to exercise his option

Fred's only blackface number, "Bojangles of Harlem," Swing Time (RKO)

for a film without Ginger. He told RKO that after *Stepping Toes,* the title of the scheduled film with a Gershwin score, he wanted to dance with a different partner. It would be better for him to make the break, he reasoned, before the public became fed up with the Astaire-Rogers films. Otherwise he might have to start all over again, as he did when Adele married Charlie Cavendish.

Ginger faced no such danger. Between the musicals with Fred, her acting career had been carefully nurtured by RKO with such films as *Romance in Manhattan,* with Francis Lederer; *Star of Midnight,* with William Powell; *In Person,* with George Brent; and *Stage Door,* with Katharine Hepburn. If the studio officialdom showed any hint of neglecting Ginger, her mother was nearby to correct them. In 1935, Lela Rogers was appointed head of the newly established department to develop acting talent.

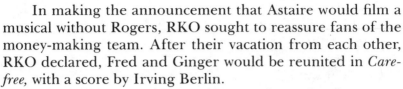

In making the announcement that Astaire would film a musical without Rogers, RKO sought to reassure fans of the money-making team. After their vacation from each other, RKO declared, Fred and Ginger would be reunited in *Carefree,* with a score by Irving Berlin.

The announcement seemed to confirm what fan magazines and gossip columnists had been buzzing about for a year: that Fred and Ginger were feuding.

The rumors became so persistent that Fred felt compelled to issue a statement: "There has never been one single second of dissension between Ginger and me." Ginger also dismissed the reports.

Pandro Berman, who was closer to the Astaire-Rogers films than any other person, comments:

"It was always believed through the press that there was real friction between these two people. but there wasn't. I was well aware of what happened. Fred, as a result of the team breaking up when his sister got married and having had a deal of difficulty getting work on his own, had been wary.

"In *Flying Down to Rio,* which I had nothing to do with, Fred and Ginger seemed to me an instantaneous success, even though they played minor roles in a not-very-good picture. The last thing in the world Fred wanted to do was make another picture with her. Not because she was Ginger, not because she wasn't good, but because it was another teaming. He had been through a bitter experience.

"He didn't mind Adele's success. What he minded was that when the team broke up he was on his ass. Nobody paid any attention to him because Adele was gone. He went sort of dry; nobody was after him.

"When he came to RKO and the success of *Rio* indicated that it was pretty obvious that they should be put together again, Fred began inwardly resisting the idea even before it was ever brought up."

That inward resistance continued through six co-starring films even though, feathers aside, they avoided any show of contention. Ginger was put to the test when she endured forty-seven takes of "Never Gonna Dance" in *Swing Time,* bloodying her feet before Fred was satisfied with the

number. He absorbed without complaint a beating in the face
from the flying sleeve of the heavily beaded gown she had
chosen for the "Let's Face the Music and Dance" number in
Follow the Fleet.

Ginger was not given to fits of temperament. She let Lela
do the fighting for her, and Lela performed ably. Fred rarely
allowed his considerable temper to burst forth. He reserved
his outbursts for private moments, and often they were directed at himself.

By the accident of circumstance, Fred and Ginger practiced what long-performing teams from Smith and Dale to
Laurel and Hardy had learned by experience: The best way
to preserve the partnership was by keeping their personal
lives separate.

In 1934, Ginger married Lew Ayres, and they became
principal figures in Hollywood's vital young tennis-playing
society. The Astaires were more sedate. Their friends were
society figures from the East, the Whitneys and the Vander-
bilts, or the more established members of Hollywood's
fragile social structure, the David Selznicks, the Samuel
Goldwyns. Fred and Phyllis played golf at a country club
frequented by the rich of Los Angeles—he bragged that she
could hit a ball as far as a man. She was also a good shot, and
they hunted duck and coyote at the ranch of Douglas Fairbanks, Sr., in San Diego County.

Fred and Ginger lived in separate, non-competitive
worlds, and that, plus a mutual respect, allowed their professional partnership to continue.

At last, a Gershwin score for an Astaire-Rogers movie.

Both Fred and Ginger were delighted. The Gershwins
had written songs for two of Fred's most successful stage
musicals, *Lady, Be Good!* and *Funny Face.* They had also scored
with *Girl Crazy,* which brought Ginger to prominence.
George Gershwin had dated Ginger in New York. No romance developed, and he once remarked to Oscar Levant
about Ginger, "She has a little love for everybody, but not a
lot for anybody."

Shall We Dance *was the first Gershwin score for Astaire-Rogers (RKO).*

The Gershwins had not been part of the gold rush that had brought most of Broadway's top songwriters to Hollywood for the musical cycle. They had contributed songs to *Delicious,* a Fox musical starring Janet Gaynor in 1931, and had received few other offers for films. Because of George's ventures into more serious music, film producers considered the Gershwins too highbrow to write the snappy hit tunes to sell movies. When George heard about such talk, he wired his Hollywood agent:

RUMORS ABOUT HIGHBROW MUSIC RIDICULOUS STOP AM OUT TO WRITE HITS.

The Gershwins had sought $100,000 for the Astaire-Rogers movie, but Pandro Berman offered $55,000 for sixteen weeks' work, with an option for another film at $70,000. The brothers accepted. Irving Berlin had received $100,000 for *Top Hat*, plus a percentage clause that earned him $285,000.

Stepping Toes, which later took the title of a Gershwin song, "Shall We Dance?," was the fifth Astaire-Rogers film co-written by Allan Scott, and it followed the same pattern: a gossamer plot interwoven with musical numbers.

The script ran into immediate problems with the newly vigilant Production Code Administration. The industry's censor, Joseph I. Breen, labeled the script "enormously dangerous from the standpoint of [government] censorship, both in this country and in England."

Breen continued: "The attempt to make comedy out of the suggestion—even though such suggestion is quite untrue—of an unmarried woman who is pregnant, is, in our judgment, highly offensive. . . . This element will have to be completely and entirely removed before the picture can be approved by this office."

The Breen message indicates the restraints under which filmmakers toiled in the 1930s. He cited nineteen specific deletions that would have to be made, including the line, "But Cleopatra had an asp." Breen added a final warning:

"Throughout this production, greatest possible care will have to be exercised in shooting dancing scenes, especially where dancers are shown in costume. Please keep in mind that the Code ordains that 'the intimate parts of the body *must* be fully clothed at all times.' This applies, in particular, to shots of the breasts of women."

The script underwent several overhauls, hence the Gershwin songs were not as astutely integrated as had been the case in previous Astaire-Rogers vehicles. The brothers had rented a house in Beverly Hills, and Fred often dropped in to hear the new songs. He was delighted, as were Pan Berman and Mark Sandrich, with the sophistication and inventiveness of both music and lyrics.

Fred was especially wary of love songs. He was disdainful of the hackneyed June-moon lyrics, and he detested any-

"They All Laughed," Shall We Dance *(RKO)*

thing mushy. Writing a love song for Fred Astaire always challenged a lyricist, but Ira Gershwin succeeded in *Shall We Dance?* He drew his inspiration from the famous ad that offered piano lessons by mail: "They all laughed when I sat down to the piano." The words stuck in Ira's mind for years, and he recalled writing a postcard from Paris: "They all laughed at the Tour d'Argent last night when I said I would order in French." Finally the phrase became a song for Fred and Ginger, to the sprightly melody by George.

> They all laughed at Christopher Columbus
> When he said the world was round;
> They all laughed when Edison recorded sound.

The film also needed a contentious love song, and the Gershwins provided the brilliant "Let's Call the Whole Thing Off." Ever seeking new ideas for duets with Ginger, Fred suggested a number on roller skates. He had had plenty of practice on his midnight skates up Park Avenue, and the athletic Ginger could match him on wheels. The result was one of their most memorable numbers.

You say "eether" and I say "eyether,"
You say "neether" and I say "neyether."
"Eether"—"eyether," "neether"—"neyether,"
Let's call the whole thing off.

Shall We Dance? also required a rueful love song which Fred could sing to Ginger and then dance with Harriet Hoctor, a popular acrobatic toe dancer. The movie cast Astaire as an American ballet star masquerading as a Russian, and some ballet was called for in the script. Fred didn't want much. He had toyed with doing some serious dances and contemplated a version of Gershwin's "An American in Paris." But although he had learned ballet as a boy in New York, it wasn't his style.

Both Leonide Massine and George Balanchine were sought to direct the ballet sequences in *Shall We Dance?*, but neither was available.

The song the Gershwins provided was "They Can't Take That Away from Me." It proved the biggest hit of *Shall We Dance?* and was the only song by George and Ira to be nominated for an Academy award. It lost to "Sweet Leilani."

The way you wear your hat,
The way you sip your tea,
The memory of all that,
No, no, they can't take that away from me.

On December 3, 1936, George Gershwin wrote a friend in New York:

"The Astaire picture is practically finished and so far everybody is happy. The studio, realizing Gershwin can be lowbrow, has taken up their option on our contract for the next movie which, incidentally, will be minus Rogers. Fred has wanted to go it alone for a long time and he'll get his chance in the next picture."

The film was *A Damsel in Distress,* and it was George Stevens' turn to direct. RKO didn't want Fred Astaire to go it entirely alone, and the studio announced that Carole Lombard would play opposite him. Her salary would be $200,000, a figure that infuriated Lela Rogers. Ginger, still under contract at a weekly salary, had been paid $61,193.28

for *Swing Time*. Fred's salary for *A Damsel in Distress* was said to be $250,000, but he was paid $119,000 plus his usual percentage.

Carole Lombard dropped out, reasoning that she couldn't win as successor to Ginger. Alice Faye was considered, also Ida Lupino. Pandro Berman finally agreed to Joan Fontaine, who had the advantage of being under contract to RKO. She was also English and could fit the role of Lady Alyce of Totleigh Castle. Could she dance? A little.

Fred accepted the casting with some trepidation. His fears grew when he tried a few steps with the eighteen-year-old actress. But she had studied ballet as a girl, and Fred and Hermes Pan believed they could fashion a duet or two with her modest talent.

"Before the film began," Miss Fontaine later recalled, "I took tap-dancing lessons from Ruby Keeler's brother, who came to the house each day with a portable wooden dance floor. Why these tap lessons, I never knew. I didn't have to do any tap steps in the film."

Fred was eager for his first starring movie without Ginger to succeed, and he poured all of his creative force into the numbers. He was helped by another engaging score by the Gershwins. One song had its inception when George returned from a party early one morning and found Ira reading.

Ira recalled that his brother removed his dinner jacket, sat down at the piano and said, "How about some work? Got any ideas?"

"Well, there's one spot we might do something about a fog," said Ira. "How about 'a foggy day in London,' or maybe 'foggy day in London Town'?"

"Sounds good—I like it better with 'town,'" said George, starting to pick out a melody. Within an hour they had written the melody and the refrain for one of Fred Astaire's most evocative numbers.

> A foggy day in London Town
> Had me low and had me down.
> I viewed the morning with alarm.
> The British Museum had lost its charm.

Pandro Berman realized the *Damsel in Distress* cast would need bolstering, and he wanted George Burns and Gracie Allen to provide comedy as well as join Fred in musical numbers.

"The deciding factor was whether we could dance with Fred," George Burns recalls. "Gracie was a good Irish-clog dancer, and I could get by, but I was a right-footed dancer. My left leg is a washout. I was afraid to dance in front of Fred Astaire, but the money was good—sixty thousand dollars— and I decided what the hell.

"I remembered an act in vaudeville, a couple of guys who were part of a dancing act, not even billed. They did an unusual dance with a couple of whisk brooms. One of the guys had died, but the other one was alive, and I sent for him. Paid his fare to Hollywood and his room and board while he was here. I also paid him to teach me and Gracie the whisk-broom dance.

"I took Gracie, our teacher and a pianist to RKO, and we did the dance for Fred and Hermes Pan. 'I love it!' Fred told us. 'We'll do it in the picture just as it is.'"

Hermes Pan devised another number for Fred to dance with George and Gracie, and he won an Academy Award for it. The action took place within an amusement-park fun house, and Pan devised intricate patterns, making use of all the devices: crazy mirrors, revolving cylinders, chutes and trick staircases. Fred contributed the old "Oompah" runaround, with Gracie trotting on a spinning disc.

For his climactic solo, Astaire performed a dynamic number that presaged his later feats. Dancing within a confined space, he punctuated his taps with assaults on a wide variety of drums. The Gershwins provided an ideal song for the joyous routine. The title, Ira recalled dimly, came from an English cartoon he had once seen, in which two charwomen were discussing the daughter of a third who had turned to whoring.

> Holding hands at midnight
> 'Neath a starry sky . . .
> Nice work if you can get it,
> And you can get it, if you try.

George Stevens had been uncertain about the casting of Joan Fontaine. She had performed well for him in a small part in *Quality Street*, but he doubted that she was capable of a dancing role opposite Fred Astaire. Once Miss Fontaine had been cast, Stevens accepted the fact, and he lavished extra care on her performance.

Late in life, George Stevens reminisced about *A Damsel in Distress:*

"Freddie's a great worrier, and he started worrying about Joan Fontaine. After I'd been shooting for about four weeks, Freddie and Pan Berman came down on the set and said, 'We're disturbed about Joan Fontaine. It seems to us we've got to make a change.'

"I said, 'If we take this girl out of this picture, she'll kill herself.' They said, 'Well, now, that's an exaggeration.' I said, 'It probably is. I'm not going to say, "You can do it, but I'll be elsewhere." I'll just say one thing: "I'm going to stay here, and you're not going to do it." We've got to put her through this picture.'

"I can understand Freddie; he's a great artist. But Joan was a girl with problems; she cried and all that. So they went back and thought it over, and they came back with a plea for Ruby Keeler, somebody who could dance. I said, 'I'm not going to take this girl out of the picture.'

"Freddie said, 'Go ahead, let's make the goddamned picture.' They were right: She was the wrong girl in the wrong spot. She never knew they wanted her out of the picture, or she would have collapsed."

Astaire danced three solos in *A Damsel in Distress.* Miss Fontaine's dancing was reduced to a few whirls with Fred in a park to the music of "Things Are Looking Up."

During the filming, Fred noticed that George Gershwin had not been visiting the set, as he had during *Shall We Dance?* Fred telephoned George, who explained that he had been doing a lot of painting at home. Actually, he was dying.

Oscar Levant detected something was wrong when he heard George play his Concerto in F at a Los Angeles concert. Gershwin's playing was always letter-perfect, but he missed one of four successive slow notes in the last bar of the second movement. Gershwin himself was surprised by the error. At a concert the next night he complained about a burning smell in his nose.

Fierce headaches beset him. He withdrew to his house in Beverly Hills and continued working on songs for *Goldwyn Follies* even though, as Ben Hecht described it, an ice pick was pressing into his brain. After an operation for a brain tumor, he died July 11, 1937, at the age of thirty-nine.

Fred Astaire was among the first to arrive at the Gershwin house on North Roxbury Drive to console Ira and his wife Leonore. For Fred it was a heartbreaking and incomprehensible blow, the second close tragedy to befall his lifetime. With George Gershwin, Fred had felt a closeness that went beyond the collaboration of artists. From their first meeting in Remick's when George was demonstrating songs, they were drawn to each other. Creatively they thought alike, had the same instinct for erratic rhythms.

Thirty-five years later, Fred reminisced about Gershwin:

"He used to sit and play piano for my rehearsals. I'd be dancing, and he'd get up and say, 'Why don't you try this step?' And he'd do a little dance. I'd say, 'Oh, that again! I can use that!' Then he used to like having me play the piano for him. He'd run up to the keyboard and ask, 'Now what was it you just did there?' I could play a pretty good jazz piano while he, of course, was the great concert man. But little things I did amused him like that. And little things he did in *my* racket amused *me*. So we had a good little game going with each other. He was a marvelous fellow."

When a new dance partner was sought for Fred Astaire in *A Damsel in Distress,* one of those mentioned was—Adele Astaire. Obviously she couldn't have played the romantic lead, but RKO executives theorized that the reunion of Fred and Adele in dance numbers would attract wide publicity, thus minimizing the risk of Fred's first Gingerless musical. *The New York Times* reported that an offer had been made to Lady Cavendish and she was seriously considering it.

Fred quickly put an end to the reports. Much as he loved his sister, he had no intention of resuming their partnership.

Recovered from the grief of losing the twins, Adele became once more the gay spirit who enlivened the British aristocracy with her unexpected comments, garnished with the four-letter words she had learned in the backstages of America. In 1936, she and Charlie came to America for the first visit since their wedding. Ship-arrival reporters were charmed by her remarks. She disclosed that her pet name for Lord Cavendish was "Cheffy-Weffy" and that she fed him raw cabbage for his liver condition. She denied having said that Lismore Castle had two hundred rooms and one bath.

"Since that report got out," she said, "we've received a million letters asking us what we do Saturday night." As to

appearing with her brother in films or returning to the stage: "I'm much too happy and too lazy even to consider that." For news photographers she happily displayed the famous Astaire legs.

After ten days in New York, the Cavendishes went on to Hollywood for a happy reunion with Fred and Phyllis. David Selznick was entranced with Adele and convinced her to make a screen test at his studio. He offered her a role, and Fred urged her to take it. But Adele concluded that she no longer had the ambition to be a performer.

She relented in 1937, accepting a comedy and dancing role opposite Jack Buchanan in an English film directed by René Clair. After a week of filming, Adele realized it was a mistake, and she withdrew. The film was never completed.

Adele never performed again. She seemed content in her role as a nobleman's wife, spending the season in the Cavendish town house in Carlton Gardens and the rest of the year at Lismore Castle, where she learned to garden, ride to hounds and fish for salmon in the Blackwater River, which ran under the castle walls.

"I'm Getting What I Want Out of Life" was the title of an article that carried her name in *Hearst's International Cosmopolitan*. She offered her observations of English society, at least in the upper levels:

"Englishmen do make thrilling husbands. Perhaps it is because they are not *too* attentive. They have a certain mystery, a whimsical quality that American women find irresistible. They are charming—and a little cold, sometimes impersonal, and they expect to be kept amused. Englishwomen take infinite trouble with them, no matter what they may look like, especially if they are in the 'Dowagers' Handicap,' which means they are rich and titled.

"There are more ambitious mothers with marriageable daughters over here than in America, I can assure you, so there is more matchmaking. Certainly the women do all the running. Maybe that is due to the fact that there are over a million surplus women.

"If a husband and wife can't get on in married life, they make the best of a bad job, live under the same roof and do as they please. Love and its manifestations are discussed less in England than elsewhere. I think the English are really secretly a little ashamed, or perhaps shy, of love. But I am beginning to suspect that a great deal of love-making goes on, especially in the country."

"Being a father is the best thing that ever happened to me in my life," Fred Astaire told a reporter with uncharacteristic lack of reserve. "It kind of makes any success I have on the stage or screen very unimportant by comparison."

Fred was a devoted father. He gave young Fred swimming lessons, took him along on fishing trips. Every evening when he returned from the studio, Fred devoted time to playing with the boy. Fred's home life was everything that he could desire.

He never ceased to be delighted and astonished by Phyllis. He was amazed when she assumed total responsibility for their dream house, buying four acres of hilltop property on Summit Drive, between Pickfair and Charlie Chaplin's house. She studied blueprints with the architect, conferred with the contractor, planned the swimming pool and tennis court, kept ledgers of expenses.

Phyllis also took charge of all financial matters. That pleased Fred, who had an appreciation of money but detested the boredom of managing it.

The Astaires made frequent trips to Arizona, where Peter went to school, and the boy came to Beverly Hills for holidays. Peter's onetime nanny, Enid Dickens Hawksley, granddaughter of Charles Dickens, had come from England to serve as governess for Fred, Jr.

While Fred deferred to Phyllis in most matters, he could not be pushed too far. Hermes Pan recalled visiting the Astaires at their ranch in the San Fernando valley, where Phyllis performed the chores of cooking and cleaning up. One evening after dinner, she told Fred, "*You* do the dishes." He said "Okay," and disappeared into the kitchen.

"A moment later, we heard a terrible clatter," Pan related. "We rushed into the kitchen and found Fred breaking the dishes, one at a time. He said, 'Never ask me to do dishes again.' Ninety-nine wives out of a hundred would have

Charlie and Adele Cavendish visit her famous brother (RKO).

Together again: Rogers, Berlin, Astaire, Carefree *(RKO)*

blown their tops over that, but Phyllis just burst out laughing. Then she pitched in and helped break the rest of the dishes."

To all appearances, Fred Astaire seemed singularly blessed. His family life was serene, his fortune ensured, his talent acclaimed throughout the world. The honors were unceasing. The nation's tailor designers named him the number-two male fashion leader, second only to President Franklin D. Roosevelt. A poll of women patrons of a New York beauty salon chain chose Fred Astaire among the five handsomest men, along with Anthony Eden, Gary Cooper, the Duke of Windsor and Leopold Stokowski.

But, of course, Fred found things to worry about. He and Ginger placed seventh in the *Motion Picture Herald*'s poll of money-making stars of 1937, dropping from third the year before. Fred's hopes for a successful screen divorce from Ginger Rogers were dashed when *Damsel in Distress* failed to match the business of the Astaire-Rogers films.

Fred was disturbed by an interview Mark Sandrich gave to the London *Daily Express,* which had been sent to Fred by Adele. Sandrich had been asked how much longer the Astaire-Rogers series could continue.

"I don't think very much longer," the director replied. "You see the snag we're up against is that we have to keep to the same story formula. Not because we want to, but because the public squawks at the slightest deviation."

What about the recurrent rumors that Astaire and Rogers detested each other?

"Just this much. They're scared of losing their identities. Every time they see that group of letters 'Astaire-Rogers' in a headline it makes them sick in their stomachs with the thought that there's another shred of their claims to be individual entities gone with the wind."

Asked to describe the pair, Sandrich observed: "Astaire is a genius, and an ole worryguts. The only difference between his worrying in a stage show and his worrying in a film studio is that with films, he's only got his dancing to fret over. The rest is none of his darned business. Ginger Rogers is a darling. She's just a hard-working little girl, as genuine as they come. Her only fault is an inferiority complex. She doesn't know how good she is."

Fred passed the article along to RKO executives, who chastised Sandrich for talking so loosely about the studio's major assets. The studio didn't need any more trouble. With the Astaire-Rogers musicals slipping at the box office, so were RKO's fortunes, and bankruptcy was once again beckoning.

One day at RKO, Pandro Berman encountered Fred Astaire on a studio street. "I want to thank you," Fred remarked.

"What for?" the producer asked.

"I've been thinking. Sam Goldwyn, Jack Warner and David Selznick are good friends of mine, but they don't hire me. You've made pictures with me, and they've been good. So I want to thank you."

As Fred sauntered down the street, Berman stared after him in astonishment. Theirs had been strictly a professional relationship, and it was the first time Fred had ever said anything personal. And the last.

*C*arefree reunited Fred Astaire and Ginger Rogers after fifteen months apart. Pandro Berman produced, Mark Sandrich directed, and Irving Berlin wrote the score. But unlike the songs in *Top Hat*, only one became a hit—"Change Partners."

Fred plunged into the dance rehearsals with Hermes Pan and Hal Borne. Determined more than ever to produce something new, he concocted a routine from his favorite sport. With furious energy, he danced in mock Scottish style over crossed golf clubs, then whacked golf balls down a fairway with his lightning feet. The Berlin song was "When They Turned 'Loch Lomond' into Swing."

> FRED: I always said [to a choreographer], "Don't repeat anything. Use some excerpts of something, get some offshoots from it, perhaps." One thing suggests another, and the first thing you know, you're doing a whole new routine. I always made it a point to say, "Oh, I can't do that; I did that in the last picture. But let's see how we could twist it around a bit." Then we'd start working on it. There was any amount of days going by when you didn't *get* anything, you just go there and look for something. All of a sudden [snapping fingers] you get it.

For an added attraction for *Carefree,* Fred proposed something new for Astaire and Rogers: a kiss.

Columnists and fan magazine writers for years had exploited the fact that Fred and Ginger had never kissed on the screen. Partly that was due to the nature of the scripts, always the chase, hampered by roadblocks of misunderstandings. Fred, who never considered himself a romantic figure, vetoed any display of affection in the films, fearing he would be laughable if he murmured "I love you," except in song. Most importantly, Phyllis didn't want him to make love on the screen.

For the duet to "I Used to Be Color Blind," Fred and Hermes devised another novelty, a dance in slow motion. Fred wanted Ginger to appear floating in air, so he included a series of lifts. This was also new. Fred had always whirled Ginger about, but rarely into the air, lifts being a strenuous

"The Yam" provided a lively number but never caught on as a dance craze (RKO).

feat for any male dancer. To maintain the dreamy quality of the dance, Fred at the conclusion gave Ginger a kiss, also in slow motion.

Phyllis Astaire made a rare visit to the studio to see the kiss in the rushes. Sandrich had purposely kept the camera operating so the kiss would seem endless. "Did you say you were going to make up for all the kisses you missed?" Phyllis remarked to her husband. "Well, you certainly did!"

The kiss created a flurry of publicity, but the most affecting expression of romance between Fred and Ginger remained their dances together. Never were they more lyrically persuasive than in the climactic number, with Irving Berlin's words providing the perfect scenario.

> Must you dance/every dance
> With the same/fortunate man?
> You have danced with him since the music began.
> Won't you change partners and dance with me?
> Must you dance/quite so close
> With your lips/touching his face?
> Can't you see I'm longing to be in his place?
> Won't you change partners and dance with me?

Carefree provided $1,731,000 in rentals for RKO, resulting in a loss of $68,000. It was the first time an Astaire-Rogers musical had failed to earn a profit.

WAKE UP, HOLLYWOOD PRODUCERS!

The red-bordered advertisement in the *Hollywood Reporter* could hardly be ignored. It had been taken by Harry Brandt, New York theater owner and president of the smallish (three hundred members) Independent Theater Owners' Association. His message: Many of Hollywood's high-paid stars were obsolete.

Brandt proclaimed: "Among those players whose dramatic ability is unquestioned but whose box-office draw is nil, can be numbered Mae West, Edward Arnold, Garbo, Joan Crawford, Katharine Hepburn and many, many others." The ad also listed Marlene Dietrich and Kay Francis as box-office poison and advised producers to concentrate on making good pictures because "sound judgment and good business are valuable assets in an industry that is far from being an art."

The broadside drew wide attention in the press. Glorying in his notoriety, Brandt called a news conference in New York and pilloried other Hollywood stars: Lily Pons, Grace Moore, Joe Penner, Fred Astaire.

Time magazine published a photograph of Astaire and indicated that he had been included in Brandt's original ad. RKO induced Jimmy Fidler to point out the error on his popular radio broadcast. In fact, Fidler declared, records indicated that Astaire was one of the top ten box-office stars. The gossip broadcaster concluded: "At a late hour tonight, Fred could not be reached for a statement, but his representatives said he would probably demand a complete retraction, pending further action."

RKO officials held lengthy meetings about possible action, legal or otherwise. Fred fretted and fretted until Phyllis finally told him to stop worrying about it.

The Astaire-Rogers alliance was coming to an end.

Fred was more than ever convinced that he had to conclude the divorce from Ginger in order to ensure his future in films. Lela Rogers believed the partnership was hindering her daughter's future as one of Hollywood's top dramatic stars. RKO, acutely conscious of the falling grosses of the Astaire-Rogers musicals, realized that Ginger offered more value in non-musicals.

The Story of Vernon and Irene Castle was announced as the final film starring Fred Astaire and Ginger Rogers.

Pandro Berman had bought the rights to the Castle saga with some trepidation. Irene Castle was a woman of strong opinions and fierce will who continued preserving the memory of her celebrated marriage twenty years after her husband's death. She would sign over rights to the Castle story only if she was granted final approval of casting, script and costumes. Berman reluctantly agreed.

Trouble started immediately. Mrs. Castle agreed that Fred Astaire was the ideal dancer to portray her husband, but decreed that Ginger Rogers was all wrong to play Irene Castle. She insisted on a nationwide search for an unknown to appear opposite Fred. Berman humored her, but he had no intention of casting anyone but Ginger.

"Irene was a pain in the ass," recalled H. C. ("Hank") Potter, a former Broadway director who was assigned to *Castle*. She insisted that all of her dancing costumes be reproduced in precise detail, including the same material. She protested that Ginger's hair was not as short as she had worn hers in the famous bob. Irene approved the first script by Oscar Hammerstein II, then complained about the many rewrites by other hands. She wanted a scene reshot because Ginger returned bareheaded from horseback riding— "I wouldn't be caught dead riding without a hat."

Pandro Berman, who had handed over production matters to George Haight, finally found a solution to the Irene problem.

"Irene was driving me crazy until a very lucky thing happened," Berman says. "My secretary, Eleanor Heineke, came in to see me one day and told me she had just heard about an important meeting of the Humane Society concerning an anti-vivisection bill that was going on the state ballot. She had mentioned it to Mrs. Castle, who was an ardent anti-vivisectionist.

"I told my secretary to follow it up, and she took Mrs. Castle to the meeting. That was the last we saw of her. Mrs. Castle took over the Southern California Humane Society and became so involved in the political campaign that she forgot about the movie."

The Story of Vernon and Irene Castle was a departure for Fred and Ginger. For the first time they played real-life characters; for the first time they were husband and wife. The songs were not fitted to them and the script by the nation's best songwriters; except for one new tune, the score was comprised of oldies like "By the Light of the Silvery Moon" and "Waiting for the Robert E. Lee." Furthermore, Fred had no opportunity to create new and original dances. Although Fred was determined not to give an imitation of Vernon Castle, he was limited to the kinds of dances the Castles had made popular: the Bunny Hug, the Turkey Trot, the Castle Walk. Fred and Ginger gave the dances freshness

The Castle Walk—Ginger's costume matched Irene Castle's, including the Dutch cap (RKO).

and vivacity, but they unavoidably seemed like period pieces in the jitterbug era.

The serious nature of the story and its tragic ending helped contribute to the most disappointing box-office returns of the Astaire-Rogers series. Everyone agreed it was time to stop.

When *The Story of Vernon and Irene Castle* was released on March 31, 1939, Fred Astaire was a month shy of being forty. An advanced age for a dancer, especially one of Fred's intensity. Now he was faced with the same struggle he had known when Adele retired: building a new career. Was it worth it? Fred had flirted with retirement at times when he was depressed by his film career. His mother encouraged him. She argued that since Fred had started work at such an early age, he deserved to retire when he was thirty-five. But every time he grumbled about quitting, Phyllis cajoled him out of it.

He decided to continue, vowing never again to trap himself with a single partner.

What if Fred had stopped after *Castle?* His position in the pantheon of dance would have been ensured. The impact of his dozen films was immeasurable. Not only did he become the god of young men like Patrick Dennis, he inspired a whole generation of male dancers to pursue an art that he had made both exciting and manly.

Tracing the history of dance, Margot Fonteyn wrote:

"From the Charleston it was an easy step to the emergence of a male superstar dancer, and he was ready and waiting at the right moment. He was the great Fred Astaire, with his magic of magic, who made dancing look easier than walking, more natural than breathing, and indisputably masculine. Perhaps no one thought of it at the time, certainly not Fred, but in retrospect it is clear that he, more than anyone else, led men back to their rightful place in the world of dance."

5

On His Own

Fred Astaire once worked so hard
He often lost his breath.
And now he taps all other chaps to death.

—Lorenz Hart, "Do It the Hard Way," Pal Joey

Eleanor Powell reminisced about how she came to meet and work with Fred Astaire:

"When I was doing stage shows in New York, I had many opportunities to be introduced to Mr. Astaire by Al Jolson, by Fanny Brice and others at social functions. I always refused, because I wanted to talk hoofers' language with him: What do you wear on your shoes? et cetera. So I didn't meet him, but I adored him, like every dancer.

"After I had been in films at MGM, Mr. Mayer called me in his office and said, 'How would you like to make a picture with Fred Astaire?' I thought it was impossible, because I was at MGM and he was at RKO, and in those days studios were jealous of their stars and didn't loan them. But Mr. Mayer said, 'He has read the script and likes it, the money is fine, it all looks good except for one thing: You may be too tall. You be in Mervyn LeRoy's office at ten tomorrow morning, and you'll meet Mr. Astaire.'

"The next morning I got to Mervyn's office early, about nine-fifteen, and we talked for a while. Then Leland Hayward and his client, Fred Astaire, were announced. To this day I don't know why I did it, but Mervyn said, 'Ellie, go hide behind the door.' Ordinarily my reflexes would make me say, 'Why?' but I was so nervous that I went ahead and hid behind the door.

"Leland and Mr. Astaire came in and there was some small talk about the racetrack and so forth, then Mr. Astaire said, 'Oh boy, I hear she's a perfectionist, I hear she works hour after hour. So do I. I just hope I'm tall enough for her.' In the midst of this, Mervyn said, 'Ellie, you can come out now." Well, I was so embarrassed my face was beet-red.

"I sat down, and there was a lot of chitchat. One by one, the executives came in and stood behind the desk. Finally, the moment of truth. Mervyn said, "Would you please stand up, the two of you?' Ohhhh. We stood up, back to back, and he was taller than I was, about two inches!"

The movie was *Broadway Melody of 1940,* the fourth and last MGM musical to bear that title. The project seemed promising to Fred. Cole Porter was writing the songs, and Fred would be dancing with Eleanor Powell, a dynamic tap dancer whose style was totally different from Ginger Rogers'.

The dynamic "Begin the Beguine" with Eleanor Powell in Broadway Melody of 1940 *(MGM)*

Fred's first dance partner after Ginger: Eleanor Powell, Broadway Melody of 1940 *(MGM)*

One thing concerned Fred: George Murphy, a friend since the days when George and Julie Murphy were a dance team at the Central Park Casino, was MGM's leading male dancer.

"I won't do the picture if George's position at the studio will be hurt in any way," Fred declared. The astonished studio executives assured Fred that Murphy's position with MGM would not be endangered. In fact, George Murphy would co-star with Astaire and Powell in *Broadway Melody of 1940.*

Fred felt the need to get away before launching the new phase of his career. He and Phyllis sailed for Europe and enjoyed a happy reunion with the Cavendishes in Ireland.

The visits to London and Paris in that spring of 1939 were somber. Fear of war hung over both capitals with an aching melancholy.

Fred reported to MGM to begin rehearsals for *Broadway Melody of 1940*. Everything was new. No more the practice sessions with Hermes Pan and Hal Borne. Fred had to accustom himself to new surroundings, new collaborators.

At first the rehearsals, Fred and Eleanor Powell were excessively polite. It was "Mr. Astaire" and "Miss Powell." They listened to the pianist play "Begin the Beguine" and neither dancer made a move.

"She a 'put 'em down' like a man, no ricky-ticky-sissy stuff with Ellie," Fred commented (MGM).

Finally Miss Powell said, "Mr. Astaire, I have a number I would like to do for you; there's something wrong with the middle of it. I can't put my finger on it, but maybe you can help me."

"Fine," said Astaire. She performed the routine and he started to make suggestions, then backed off.

"Look," she said, "I don't know what we're going to do. You're not going to tell me how to dance, and I'm certainly not going to tell you. I've got an idea, if it meets your approval. I'll go over in the corner and you go over there, and let's just noodle around to eight bars of 'Begin the Beguine.' If you see or hear something you like, stop and I'll try to find what it is. I'll do the same, and maybe we can start that way."

The system worked. By dancing independently, then combining their steps, they produced a counter-rhythm that was stunningly effective. Their challenge dance to "Begin the Beguine" proved the highlight of the film.

Fred at last had found a partner who would work as hard as he did. The formality continued until one day when she delighted him with a dance invention. He lifted her into the air exultantly, then blushed in embarrassment.

"We cannot go on like this," she declared. "I'm Ellie and you're Fred. We're just two hoofers. Remember how we started way back there on Broadway? Let's just be ourselves."

The rehearsals with George Murphy were warm and cordial from the beginning. After thirty-five years of conducting female dancers over the dance floor, Fred found it refreshing to dance side-by-side with another man. He had never been so loose in rehearsals. One day he demonstrated for Murphy how James Cagney would do the dance step they were rehearsing—a series of machine-gun taps. Then George Raft—a sinuous movement of the hips. He also gave his impression of a dance in the style of Adolf Hitler.

Both Astaire and Murphy ganged up on Eleanor Powell, whose sense of rhythm was infallible. Fred danced slightly out of rhythm, then accused Eleanor of losing the beat. "Fred's absolutely right," Murphy claimed.

Murphy found Fred was capable of surprise, as when he stared in the mirror and commented, "Do I look as much like Stan Laurel to you as I do to myself?"

Largely because of working with Eleanor Powell and George Murphy, *Broadway Melody of 1940* proved a happy transition for Astaire, and the film's success in theaters encouraged him to believe that he might be able to continue his movie career without Ginger.

*S*econd Chorus seemed like a step down in the Astaire career. It was not made by a major studio but by an enterprising, independent producer, Boris Morros, later to be famed as a counterspy. The budget was not lavish, though the cast was good. Fred and Burgess Meredith played musicians, both in love with Paulette Goddard. Fred was attracted to the project because it included the swing band of Artie Shaw. Fred adored the irregular rhythms of swing music and dreamed up a solo in which he led Shaw's band with his tapping feet.

Hank Potter of *Castle* was director, and Fred was able to work with his old team of Hermes Pan and Hal Borne. *Second Chorus* provided Pan with his first and only opportunity to appear with Fred on the screen. He danced as a ghost in a number with Fred, "The Ghost Upstairs." The number was cut from the final movie.

Paulette Goddard was no more of a dancer than Joan Fontaine had been. But she worked hard, and Fred managed to lead her through a single duet, "I Ain't Hep to That Step But I'll Dig It," written by Hal Borne and Johnny Mercer.

Second Chorus was released by Paramount to little audience enthusiasm, and it seemed to signal an abrupt decline in the Astaire career. Was he box-office poison, after all? Producers may have thought so, because for the first time in a lifetime of performing, Fred had no offers. The Astaire style, with its high-gloss elegance and airy sophistication, seemed out of sync with a nation mobilizing for war.

> FRED: I saw *Second Chorus* recently, and it looked good. I hadn't seen the whole picture, because while we were doing it, I didn't think it was going to be too good. It was a small-budget picture, didn't amount to very much. But when I finally saw it, there was a

Just for laughs: Burgess Meredith and Charles Butterworth make bookends for Paulette Goddard and Fred, Second Chorus *(Paramount).*

lot of entertaining stuff in it. One of the reasons I liked doing the picture was Artie Shaw and his orchestra.

The "Ghost" number was cut out of the picture for some reason or other. It wasn't much of a number, didn't mean anything. The idea was all right, but something didn't work out. You wouldn't have seen Hermes, anyway. He had a veil over his head throughout the number.

Fred didn't want to wait around Hollywood until another movie turned up. Nor was he interested in the many offers to return to the theater or appear on radio or in movie-theater stage shows. He liked film work best of all, and he decided to wait out the slump.

The Astaires traveled to Aiken, where Phyllis visited with her family and Fred worked out his frustrations on the golf course. As his game improved, his worries grew. Finally, good news from Hollywood. With the nation under conscription and defense plants gearing for full production, Americans wanted entertaining, trouble-free movies. Musicals were once more in vogue.

Fred suddenly found himself with an embarrassment of riches: two films with Rita Hayworth, one scored by Cole Porter, the other by Jerome Kern; a film with Bing Crosby, songs by Irving Berlin. Fred decided to do all three.

The meeting with Rita was ceremonial. She was exceptionally nervous, he was shy. He remarked about knowing her father in vaudeville. He made cautious inquiries about her height—she was safely five feet six. He led her in a few twirls around the rehearsal-room floor, studying their movement in the wall mirror. Yes, he decided they looked good together.

Rehearsals for *You'll Never Get Rich* began. Fred found ways to penetrate Rita's awe about dancing with Fred Astaire. He joked with her, played tricks. Before starting practice steps, he dipped his hands in ice water, and she squealed at his touch. Fred found her totally responsive, the fastest learner he had ever danced with.

"I'd show her a routine before lunch," Fred once remarked. "She'd be back right after lunch and have it down to perfection. She apparently figured it out in her mind while she was eating. But she was better when she was 'on' than at rehearsal."

Whenever the camera started turning, something remarkable happened to Rita, transforming her from a frightened introvert into a vividly sensuous woman. It was a quality that Columbia Pictures' bombastic boss, Harry Cohn, had recognized and the reason he was devoting the studio's resources to making her a top star.

The songs for *You'll Never Get Rich* were strangely hitless for a Cole Porter score. Partly this was due to a strike by

ASCAP that prevented their being played on radio. The ultra-sophisticated Porter seemed uninspired in writing songs about the draftee army. He found working conditions primitive at Columbia, which still bore evidence of its Poverty Row beginnings. Porter was amused but also irritated when his songs were tested on studio workers by Cohn to determine their acceptability by average listeners.

Cohn, who had been a Broadway song-plugger when Astaire was starring in musicals, was thrilled to have the dancer working for Columbia and treated him with uncharacteristic civility.

> FRED: I didn't have many words with him. I did two pictures there, and I met him a couple of times. I think he might have come down on the set once or twice. He certainly didn't treat me anything but nice.

Columbia staged a big buildup for Rita Hayworth's first musical, culminating in a *Time* cover story that proclaimed her the best partner Fred Astaire ever had. *You'll Never Get Rich* seemed to be exactly what American audiences needed in the autumn of 1941, and the film attracted crowds at the Radio City Music Hall and elsewhere in the nation. Fred Astaire's viability at the box office was restored.

*H*oliday Inn proved an even bigger hit. Fred was delighted to be co-starred with his golfing friend, Bing Crosby. The pair blended ideally, on the screen and off. Both were intensely private men, wary of strangers. Each bore the unassuming confidence of being premier in his field, Fred as a dancer, Bing as a singer, and there was never a hint of competition between them. Neither was noted for being a conversationist, but Fred and Bing always had something to talk about: golf and horses.

Irving Berlin had originated the idea for *Holiday Inn*, about a fellow so lazy he wanted to work only on holidays. Berlin had a half-serious motive. Having established "Easter Parade" as a perennial hit, he wanted to lock in the rest of the

In You'll Never Get Rich, *Fred danced with Rita Hayworth, daughter of an old vaudeville friend (Columbia).*

Marjorie Reynolds, Bing Crosby, Virginia Dale, Astaire, Holiday Inn
(Paramount)

Phyllis and Fred at Santa Anita, 1940 (Wide World Photos)

*Fred leaped for publicity
shots atop a Columbia roof (Columbia).*

holidays. He succeeded beyond even his own ambitions with a song for Bing, "White Christmas."

Astaire had his own standout number, "Let's Say It with Firecrackers." It was a solo in which Fred punctuated his own taps with the blasts of firecrackers and torpedoes.

> FRED: I liked that, because I had to have a lot of explosives in my pocket—torpedoes. The whole stage was electrified with explosive flashes, and a fellow would work all those things. When I threw the torpedoes, they'd explode themselves. But at the end I'd throw a bunch of firecrackers in the air and they were supposed to drop on the floor and explode all over the place. It was a very good effect. I loved that number because there's a certain amount of satisfaction when you want to fill in a break. Like da-da-da-da-da pow! pow! Then spin off and do something else and pow! Just like the Fourth of July!

Encore with Rita: You Were Never Lovelier *(Columbia)*

Mark Sandrich was the director of *Holiday Inn,* having moved to Paramount after the end of the Astaire-Rogers cycle. With his scientific skill, he helped engineer an electric console which a dance assistant played like an organ to detonate the firecracker blasts. The sequence required two days of filming, thirty-eight complete takes before Sandrich announced the number was over. Fred was still not satisfied. He was willing to continue despite the expenditure of energy and weight. During the filming of *Holiday Inn* he dropped from 140 to 128 pounds.

> FRED: It's a very funny thing—the first time I met Gene Kelly was when I was rehearsing the firecracker number. Gene was going through the Paramount studio a day or two after he had arrived. I hadn't seen his work, but I had heard about him

because of some show [*Pal Joey*] he had been doing in New York.

Jerome Kern died before the release of *You Were Never Lovelier,* Astaire's second Columbia film with Rita Hayworth. Kern had collaborated with Johnny Mercer as lyricist, producing one of his most melodic scores: "You Were Never Lovelier," "I'm Old Fashioned," "Dearly Beloved," as well as dance numbers, "Wedding in the Spring" and "Shorty George."

It was a pleasant film for Fred, a reunion with Bill Seiter, who had directed *Roberta.* The movie had a foolish script, but with the country now at war, it filled the growing need for light entertainment.

You Were Never Lovelier *(Columbia)*

Fred had hoped for a girl, and on March 19, 1942, Phyllis gave birth to their second child, a daughter weighing six pounds. She was named Ava, after one of Phyllis' friends. Since the friend was known as "Ah-va," so was the Astaires' daughter.

When the Selective Service lottery was held in March, the draft number assigned to Fred Astaire was 156. This was duly noted in the press, but it seemed unlikely that the star would be drafted. He was forty-two years old and the father of three children.

Fred was willing to serve his country in any way possible. As an American, he was dedicated to the war effort. As an Anglophile, he had been gravely concerned for England's survival. He was proud of Adele's contribution to the war effort.

After the war broke out, Adele converted the Lismore property into a farming project. Charles was in failing health because of a liver ailment complicated by excessive drinking. After the United States entered the war, Adele left her mother in charge of Lismore Castle and went to London. She worked seven days a week at the Red Cross's Rainbow Corner canteen. She danced with the homesick GIs, shopped for them, but mostly she wrote letters, eight thousand of them.

She later described how she operated:

"I had a desk in the basement with a big sign over my head reading, 'Let Adele write letters home for you.' My desk was right next to the little boys' room and I'd get the GIs as they came out and ask them, 'Don't you want me to write your mom?' They couldn't write letters from London unless they went to the post office and had them censored. But I knew what could be said. I'd take their messages down on a stenographer's pad, and then when I got home I'd spend hours writing the letters. There was one time I knocked off one hundred and thirty letters a week. That's how I lost my eyesight." She always signed the letters "Adele Astaire, Fred's sister."

Rehearsing for the Hollywood Bond Cavalcade: Jose Iturbi, Lucille Ball, Harpo Marx, Astaire

Fred volunteered to serve wherever he was needed, and he was sent to California bases to entertain troops. He and Adele had done the same thing in New York during the First World War. In September of 1942, the Treasury Department launched a billion-dollar War Bond drive, and Hollywood stars were sent around the country to promote sales. Fred and Phyllis Astaire, along with Ilona Massey and Hugh Herbert, traveled by train and car throughout Ohio, making twenty to thirty appearances daily.

The camp appearances continued throughout the war, whenever Fred wasn't involved with a movie. In 1943, he took part in the Hollywood Bond Cavalcade, which carried a trainload of film celebrities across the country for a massive bond-selling campaign. James Cagney, Judy Garland, Mickey Rooney, Greer Garson, Harpo Marx, Kathryn Grayson, Betty Hutton, José Iturbi, Paul Henreid, Dick Powell, and Kay Kyser and his band were among the travelers.

Shy of crowds and never gregarious, Fred nevertheless enjoyed himself immensely during the two-week tour. Traveling by train across the country, he was reminded of the happy times he and Adele had known when they moved from city to city with vaudeville units. The Cavalcade stars were transported by special train, and in each city were paraded down the main street in Jeeps. They made individual appearances during the day at war plants, civic gatherings and theaters, then gathered at night to perform before huge audiences in football stadiums. Then back to the train and on to the next city.

The stars unwound in the lounge car each night and entertained each other. Mickey Rooney played the drums and sang with Judy Garland. José Iturbi accompanied Kathryn Grayson on the piano. James Cagney displayed some of his old-style hoofing. Fred was merely a fascinated spectator. He was especially impressed by the multiple talents and boundless energy of Mickey Rooney.

Lena Horne joined the Cavalcade in Washington, D.C. Fred admired her greatly, and he was disturbed when she didn't stay with the troupe at the Washington hotel. Was it because Lena was black and the nation's capital was segregated? Dick Powell suggested that perhaps she had a date in Washington, and no one, including Lena, made an issue of the fact that she did not stay at the hotel.

Fred had been wanting to entertain troops overseas, and in 1944 the opportunity came. Allied armies were still liberating France when he flew in a bucket-seated C-54 cargo plane from New York to Scotland, nursing a sprained back from carrying his heavy bags. Fred was flown to London and a reunion with Adele, again bereaved. Charlie had died in

*On the road: Judy Garland,
Dick Powell, Betty Hutton, Astaire*

*Fred was fascinated by the extroverted
Mickey Rooney (with MGM
aide Les Peterson).*

*Joyous reunion with Adele
in London (Wide World Photos)*

March following a long illness. He was thirty-nine years old. Adele found the best way to assuage her grief was to continue working at the Rainbow Corner, writing letters from the homesick GIs. Fred did a show at the Rainbow Center and served as master of ceremonies for a theater benefit featuring English stars.

In France, Fred teamed with a comic, an accordionist and four dancing girls for shows wherever the fast-moving troops could be found. The entertainers passed through Paris, its streets still littered with burned-out cars and trucks, and continued by Jeep into Belgium and Holland. In Maastricht, Fred at last played the Palace. He found the boarded-up theater and convinced the manager, who recognized Fred, to open it up. The show played to four tiers of cheering army engineers. The entertainers spent that night in cots on the Palace stage, and Fred slept through a German air raid.

Fred was pulled out of the combat zone and transported by weapons carrier to Paris to appear with Free French performers at the Olympia Theater, the first entertainment by an American since the liberation. He was billeted at the Ritz, then a military hotel, and he luxuriated in his second bath in five weeks. The Astaire troupe appeared in nearby hospitals and was summoned for a warm evening with General Eisenhower and his staff at the Supreme Command headquarters.

In France Fred appeared in shows with Dinah Shore and Bing Crosby, who were also touring for the USO. Fred and Bing returned to New York on the *Queen Mary*, along with thousands of soldiers and fliers, many of them destined for the Pacific.

Phyllis had arrived in New York to welcome Fred, and he poured out tales of his adventures.

"Those GIs are wonderful," Fred told the press at USO Camp Shows headquarters. "The way they go right back in there time and again to hit the Germans is something it's impossible to forget. They make wonderful audiences, too. After the show they'd swarm around me and shout, 'Gee whiz! You're the lucky guy that danced with them girls! How does it feel to hold Ginger Rogers or Rita Hayworth in your arms?' I'd answer, 'Fine—they're beautiful dancers.'"

Entertaining at Versailles

Fred told of dancing before audiences of 200–12,000 three or four times a day, using a six-by-twelve-foot dance mat when possible. Otherwise he improvised with hastily built platforms or the back of trucks. In hospitals he jumped from the floor to beds to tabletops, making noises with any props available. During a blackout, he was almost blinded when hundreds of soldiers shone their flashlights onto his makeshift stage. "The GIs liked it," he said, "they like to see you in trouble." Before leaving for California, Fred made hundreds of telephone calls to the families of servicemen he had met in Europe.

Another movie for RKO.

It was called *Handful of Heaven, Look Out Below* and *This Time It's Love* before the studio decided on *The Sky's the Limit*. Fred was accorded his usual terms: top billing, choice of co-star and director. But his salary was $100,000, less than he had received for the films with Ginger. He did get a better percentage, a graduated scale rising to 10 percent after the film had earned back its cost plus the overhead fee of 27½ percent and distribution cost of 25 percent domestic, 30 percent foreign. Because Hermes Pan had left RKO to choreograph Betty Grable musicals at Fox, Fred himself directed the dances.

Fred and Robert Ryan were cast as Flying Tigers pilots, with Robert Benchley and Eric Blore to provide the comedy. For leading lady, Fred had Joan Leslie, the young Warner Brothers actress who had appeared opposite Gary Cooper in *Sergeant York* and James Cagney in *Yankee Doodle Dandy*, Academy Award performances for both stars.

Miss Leslie had met Fred before.

"I tried out for *Holiday Inn*," she recalls. "I went over to Paramount to meet Fred and Bing, and I sang and danced for them, and we talked for a while. Then Fred did something unusual. He put his arm around my waist and started to dance. Of course he was marvelously easy to dance with. I guess he satisfied himself that I could follow his steps."

Though he had some reservations about her age—she was seventeen—Fred asked that Joan Leslie appear with him

Joan Leslie was seventeen when she danced with Fred in The Sky's The Limit *(RKO).*

in *The Sky's the Limit.* He laid down the rules with her at the outset: no feathers on her costumes; no high heels that might bruise his feet; no arm makeup that could smudge his suits.

Joan learned her co-star had other quirks. He disliked visitors on the set, especially studio big shots. One day Charles Koerner, head of production, was scheduled to visit the set. Knowing that Joan was trained in acrobatics, he proposed, "When Mr. Koerner gets here, you stand on your head between us."

Although he often deprecated his singing voice, he also had a certain pride. "Did you know," he said to Joan, "that I can sing higher than Bing Crosby?" Just before a scene began, Fred sometimes mused irrelevantly. Once he remarked, "You know, sometime I would like to go out a door in a bow tie and gray suit and appear on the other side in a checkered coat and four-in-hand and see if the script girl would notice."

The Sky's the Limit had two splendid Harold Arlen-Johnny Mercer songs, "My Shining Hour" and "One for My Baby," and was moderately successful with wartime audiences. Some of the reviews were unkind. Fred was perplexed by Bosley Crowther's critique in *The New York Times* that stated, "Mr. Astaire does one solo which is good, but a bit woe-begone and the rest of the time he acts foolish—and rather looks it—in his quick-fitting clothes." It was perhaps the first and only time that the Astaire wardrobe was deprecated in a review.

James Agee in *The Nation* cited the film's shortcomings, but he was more complimentary about its star: "Fred Astaire has a lot, besides his Mozartian abilities as a tap-dancer, which is as great, in its own way, as the best of Chaplin. It is the walk, the stance, the face, the voice, the cool, bright yet shadowless temper, and it would require the invention of a new character, the crystallization of a new manner, probably the development of a new cinematic form, to be adequately realized."

Just when Fred was despairing that he had no movie offers, Arthur Freed called.

Louis B. Mayer had transformed MGM into a musical factory, hiring the best songwriters, choreographers, music arrangers, vocal coaches and orchestra conductors that money could buy. The musicals were made by three producers: Joe Pasternak, a Hungarian who had produced the Deanna Durbin films at Universal and knew how to entertain the masses *(Thousands Cheer, Two Girls and a Sailor);* Jack Cummings, a Mayer nephew with a showmanly flair *(Bathing Beauty, Broadway Melody of 1940);* and Arthur Freed, a songwriter whose taste and perfectionism made his musical unit the Cadillac of MGM.

Freed had been a fourteen-year-old singer on the same vaudeville bill with Fred and Adele. He turned to songwriting and became MGM's resident lyricist beginning in 1929 with *The Broadway Melody.* Ten years later he became a producer with *Babes in Arms,* and he began surrounding himself with the best of musical talent. Naturally he wanted Fred Astaire to become an MGM star, beginning with an all-star extravaganza, *Ziegfeld Follies of 1944.* Fred agreed.

The entire MGM contract list was mobilized for *Ziegfeld Follies.* Vincente Minnelli, acclaimed for *Meet Me in St. Louis,* would direct. The cost would mount to more than $3 million, MGM's biggest outlay since *Gone with the Wind.* Despite three years of trying, Arthur Freed never did get *Ziegfeld Follies* right. Plotless revues hadn't succeeded since the late 1920s, when sound was a novelty.

Fred Astaire carried the heaviest load in the film. He was pleased to be doing a number based on "Limehouse Blues," a song he had liked since Gertrude Lawrence introduced it in *Charlot's Revue* in 1924. Minnelli devised an elaborate production that ran thirteen minutes and cost $230,000. Fred also enjoyed another story number, "This Heart of Mine," in which he played a jewel thief, with Lucille Bremer as his victim.

Fred appeared in the opening number, "Here's to the Girls," with Lucille Ball, Lucille Bremer and, briefly, Cyd Charisse; and in the finale, "There's Beauty Everywhere." The latter is still remembered by participants for the time when the bubble machine went mad. Robert Alton, the choreographer, had wanted to fill the stage with bubbles to

The statue aged, along with Fred and Gene, in "The Babbitt and the Bromide" (MGM).

create a dreamy phantasmagoria. The machine would not shut off, and it spewed foam that engulfed the set and threatened to swallow dancers and crew alike. Panic resulted, and chorus girls ran out the stage door screaming.

A solo number, "If Swings Goes, I Go Too," displeased Fred, and after the preview he requested that it be deleted. What *Ziegfeld Follies* is most remembered for is the classic confrontation of Fred Astaire and Gene Kelly in "The Babbitt and the Bromide."

Fred liked the idea of repeating his number from *Funny Face,* this time with a male partner. And what a partner. After three short years in films, Gene Kelly had found himself compared to the incomparable Astaire.

Kelly's approach to the master was respectful without being overly deferential. Gene, after all, was an achiever himself, both on Broadway and in films, and he was ambitious as well as competitive.

Minnelli recalled what happened when the two dancers started to work together:

"Each was hesitant to make the first suggestion. Neither wanted to be accused of foisting his quite different dancing style on the other. Everything was put in the form of a suggestion: 'What if we did so-and-so?' No reaction. 'Well, maybe that isn't a good idea.' 'Oh, no,' the other would protest, 'it's fine. Maybe we can take a bit of it, and then we can . . .' No reaction from the other to that suggestion. The same protests repeated, the compromises finally worked out."

Minnelli planned for the two friends to meet as young men, then ten years later and finally in heaven, repeating their endless platitudes, with a tap number after each refrain.

> FRED: In back of us was a statue that grew older with each chorus. That was Vincente Minnelli's idea. "Ten years went quickly by," then Gene and I had a little older makeup on, and the horse statue and the guy on it got older. I don't know how many people actually saw it, because they weren't looking at the background as much as what we were doing. It always amuses me whenever I see it.
>
> Gene and I never made a complete picture together, though we wanted to. We were going to do one once, but he was tied up and I was tied up, and we couldn't make the dates right.

The Ziegfeld Follies of 1944 never made it that year. Preview reaction was so devastating that Freed was forced to postpone the film's release and make wholesale revisions and additions. A prologue with Flo Ziegfeld producing his last *Follies* from heaven was filmed with William Powell repeating his role as the showman. In 1945, *Ziegfeld Follies of 1946* was released as a road show in Boston, then hastily withdrawn.

"Is it really going to be released?" Fred wrote Arthur Freed. "It is a most extraordinary experience for me to have performed something *years* before the public sees it. Dancing and entertaining in the musical line *dates so rapidly* it really worries me. . . ."

Freed assured Fred that *Ziegfeld Follies* (final title) would be released on April 8, 1946. It finally reached theaters in January of 1948.

Years later, Gene Kelly remarked that he thought "The Babbitt and the Bromide" had been a weak number; he would have preferred "Pass That Peace Pipe," a song that turned up in the 1947 *Good News*. He admitted he had been uncomfortable because his and Fred's styles were so different and thought he himself "looked like a klutz" in the third section. Kelly told Minnelli that he wished his one dance with Fred Astaire had not been so light and unchallenging.

When Minnelli relayed Gene's remark, Fred replied, "What does he mean by 'unchallenging'? Didn't we beat the hell out of that floor together? We were supposed to be a popular team. We weren't trying, after all, to do *L'Après-Midi d'un Faun!*"

The second Astaire film under his new MGM contract was *Yolanda and the Thief.* The film had become an obsession for Arthur Freed, as was Lucille Bremer, who would play Yolanda. She was a lithe dancer with a pale beauty but no apparent charisma. Everyone at Metro wondered why Freed was promoting her stardom with such determination. But then it became clear that his interest in her was more than professional.

The producer had been hypnotized by a Ludwig Bemelmans magazine story about a rich beauty in a mythical kingdom who is visited in her sumptuous palace by a swindler who purports to be her guardian angel. A fragile tale, but Freed was convinced it would work, with the proper embellishment. Irene Sharaff's costumes and the sets by Jack Martin Smith and Cedric Gibbons were lavish beyond even MGM's standards. Minnelli made his own contributions to

Yolanda and the Thief
*with Lucille Bremer
proved an artistic failure
(MGM).*

*Astaire twirls Lucille
Bremer,* Yolanda and
the Thief *(MGM).*

the design. Freed himself wrote the lyrics to Harry Warren's music.

Eugene Loring was assigned to create the dances. Fred Astaire arrived for their first meeting with a can of film under his arm. It was a five-hour compendium of all the dances he had done in films. "Look at this first, and then we'll go to work," Astaire said. "I don't like to repeat myself."

Astaire and Loring struggled to concoct dances in keeping with the fantasy of *Yolanda and the Thief.* Everyone labored hard on the film and brought forth a pretentious failure. MGM suffered a $1.6 million loss, Arthur Freed lost faith in the career of his protegée, and Fred Astaire once more pondered the possibility of retirement.

Horse racing had never lost its fascination for Fred. A decade in films had made him a wealthy man, and he decided there had to be more to life than work, work, work. Years before, he had told a trainer friend, Clyde Phillips, he would some day send him a wire to buy a pair of horses for him. In early 1944, Fred sent the wire.

Phillips shopped around for promising horses and almost bought a future champion named Busher, but on a whim changed his mind. Then the trainer found a colt by Reigh Count out of Fairday. The name was Triplicate.

> FRED: I bought him as a three-year-old after Clyde Phillips found him for me. He was eliminated from the barn he was born into, Widener, when they decided they had to cut down on the stock. I paid six thousand dollars for him.
>
> Triplicate had had a little leg trouble and hadn't shown much promise as a two-year-old, so the owners let him go. He came into his good form after I acquired him.

Phillips located other promising horses for the Astaire stable, and Fred was finding much greater pleasure at the racetrack than in a movie studio. MGM wanted him to star in another musical, *The Belle of New York,* but Fred thought the script was weak. He didn't want to risk another flop after *Yolanda and the Thief.*

The prospect of ending his dancing career grew more appealing to Fred. His mother, who continued living in Ireland with Adele, still encouraged it. Phyllis, who had never been comfortable with the Hollywood life, welcomed it. Now past forty-five, Fred himself wondered how long he could fulfill his own standards of performance. The experiences on *Ziegfeld Follies* and *Yolanda and the Thief* depressed him. He had put forth his best effort, to no avail. Why not become a stable owner and country gentleman?

But he couldn't stop dancing on a failure. Like Adele, he needed a success to retire on. Paul Draper unwittingly supplied it.

Draper had earned a reputation in New York as a high-brow tap dancer, performing ballet-style numbers to classical and popular music. Paramount cast him opposite Bing Crosby in *Blue Skies,* another compilation of old Irving Berlin songs, from "Heat Wave" to "A Pretty Girl Is Like a Melody."

Draper made the mistake of picking on his dance partner, Joan Caulfield, a young beauty with whom Crosby was enamored. Her dancing did not meet Draper's standards, and he constantly belittled her in rehearsals.

"He made me walk four feet behind him because he said I was such an inferior dancer," she recalls. "Then one Saturday afternoon, Bing and Paul and I were doing a scene with a big crowd on the set, including a lot of servicemen. I blew a few lines, and Paul, who stuttered, said, 'If you're h-h-h-h-having so much trouble, w-w-w-why don't you clear the set?' That did it. Bing said, 'I'm going swimming,' and he left the set. The next Monday I learned that Fred Astaire was on the picture."

Paramount had sent a hurry call to Astaire, and he was pleased to work with Crosby and Berlin again. Berlin wrote one new song for the film, "A Couple of Song and Dance Men," and the Astaire-Crosby duet was one of the highlights of *Blue Skies.* Also "Puttin' on the Ritz," a solo in which Fred danced with eight Fred Astaires in top hat and tails. Typically, Fred would not allow eight duplications of himself on film. He was photographed eight times in the same routine.

Astaire made it official: He was retiring after *Blue Skies.*

"A Couple of Song and Dance Men"—*Fred announced* Blue Skies *would be his last film (Paramount).*

"I've tried to fashion something new in each picture," he explained to a reporter, "but after all, there is a limit. I never found it easy to perform routines thought up by others. Lately the feeling that people might be saying, 'Jeepers, there's that Astaire again!' keeps creeping in.

"I'll look around and perhaps I'll go into production.

Maybe I'll do dramas. After all, several of my dancing partners went dramatic, and two—Ginger Rogers and Joan Fontaine—won Academy Awards. I don't blame any of them for
turning to dramatic roles. The physical strain is terrific, take
my word for it. It may look like a lot of fun to audiences, but
those long, long hours of rehearsal and take after take in
front of cameras require a lot a stamina."

When I visited Fred on the *Blue Skies* set, he was in the
midst of his last number, "Puttin' on the Ritz." He wore the
customary top hat, white tie, striped trousers, tails and spats,
and he tapped his cane nervously as he waited for Mark
Sandrich to prepare the next shot.

"People can't seem to believe that I'm really retiring," he
said. "They think I must be kidding." I asked if he would
ever dance for his own amusement. "Naw, the only time I
really feel like dancing is when I hear some really hot swing
music."

The number involved mirrors and split screens, and
Fred was required to repeat his dance again and again. Each
time he did it flawlessly. At five-thirty, Sandrich dismissed the
company, and Fred plodded wearily back to his dressing
room. He grumbled, "Forty-one years of this! Do you wonder that I'm quitting?"

A day later it came—the final scene of the last dance of
Fred Astaire. What happened was a replay of the time,
twenty years before, when he rid himself of the hated white
wig at the closing of *The Bunch and Judy* in Chicago.

Before the entire *Blue Skies* company, Fred removed his
toupee, flung it on the stage and stamped on it.

"Never, never, never," he cried, "never will I have to
wear this blasted rug again!"

6

Retirement and Return

*He's not just a great dancer; he's a
great singer of songs. He's as good as
any of them—as good as Jolson or
Crosby or Sinatra. He's just as good a
singer as he is a dancer, not necessarily
because of his voice, but by his conception
of projecting a song.*

—*Irving Berlin,* The New York Times *interview*

Phyllis and Fred had more time to hunt and travel after his retirement.

"This is positively and definitely *the* life," Fred wrote to Arthur Freed. "I feel as if I've got my head out of an olive press now that the hoofing career is behind me."

Fred Astaire felt liberated for the first time in his life. No more worry about finding another movie. No more fretting over how to avoid repeating himself. No more toupee.

MGM had released Astaire from his contract on the condition that it would have first call on his services if he returned to films. No chance of that, Fred declared.

He was busier than ever. With Charles Casanave, a film executive he had known at RKO, Fred scouted the possibility of opening a dance studio. The prospects seemed good, and in 1947 the first Fred Astaire Dance Studio was opened at 487 Park Avenue in Manhattan. The place had twenty-eight rehearsal rooms and a large ballroom which Fred named after Adele.

Fred gave the enterprise the same thoroughness he had applied to performing. He personally instructed one hundred and fifty dance teachers in the Astaire theory of dance. He was encouraged in the venture by Phyllis, whose business sense told her that fans of the Fred Astaire movies would want to learn how to dance from the master.

The Fred Astaire Dance Studio was not an immediate success, despite the burst of publicity that attended its opening. Fred was required to pour more money into it, and Phyllis feared she had misled him. But the dance studio improved with the postwar boom, and soon there were others in twenty-six cities. To counter the Latin dances, Fred invented an American number that could be danced in a small area. He called it the Swing Trot.

Horse racing became Fred's passion. He had sold his ranch in San Diego County and bought one that Phyllis had found in Chatsworth, at the far end of the San Fernando valley. It was only a half hour's drive from the Beverly Hills house, and the Astaires went almost daily to oversee the progress of their growing stable.

Triplicate was proving to be a dream horse. He had won its first race at Santa Anita on June 7, 1945, a shining day for Fred Astaire. In twenty years of dabbling in thoroughbreds, he had never seen one of his horses win a race. Triplicate ran fourth in the Santa Anita Handicap that year, and Clyde Phillips told the owner, "There's no tellin' just how good this horse might be."

In 1946, a beaming Fred Astaire stepped into the winner's circle to claim the $50,000 prize Triplicate won in the San Juan Capistrano Handicap at Santa Anita. Phillips now was aiming the horse for the $100,000 Gold Cup at Hollywood Park. The trainer scouted the country for a leading jockey, deciding on Basil James. But James was in the East, and weather conditions made it doubtful that he could fly to California in time. Howard Hughes told Fred he could arrange air travel for the jockey if necessary.

James arrived, and Triplicate won the Gold Cup, beating a horse owned by Fred's recent boss, Louis B. Mayer. Fred and Phyllis were jubilant, and Fred was pleased that Clyde Phillips had lived to witness the triumph. The trainer was dying of lung cancer.

Triplicate continued winning, amassing $240,000 in purses. In 1948, ankle trouble ended the horse's racing career. Triplicate remained at stud for a few years; then Astaire sold him to a Japanese stable.

In *The Moon's a Balloon*, David Niven wrote of Astaire's pride in his racing stable. Niven termed his friend "a pixie, timid, always warm-hearted, a sentimentalist with a Lefty Flynn-type penchant for schoolboy jokes," and he told of an early-morning telephone call from Astaire: "I've done a terrible thing. I don't know what possessed me, but at four o'clock this morning, I got out of bed and drove all over Beverly Hills, painting the city mailboxes with my racing colors."

> FRED: David loved to tell a story, and his stories got better with each telling. Imagine me going around painting mailboxes! I could have been arrested! What happened was this: I must have been bored one night, and I was thinking that mailboxes were colored the same blue as my racing colors, which were blue and yellow with a red cap. I added a strip of yellow adhesive tape to a couple of mailboxes, that was all.

Fred with his champion, Triplicate (Wide World Photos)

Fred continued buying and breeding horses, and a few produced modest winnings. But never did he find another champion like Triplicate.

Unlike some Hollywood children, Fred Astaire., Jr., remembers his childhood as a happy one: "I never felt neglected or left out. Dad used to take me to Mexico for hunting and fishing, and the family spent a lot of time at the ranch in Escondido. When we were in town, he was working most of the time. He was not a disciplinarian; the discipline I got came my mother and the help. I have a few memories of my grandmother when I was young, especially how she took me for walks down to the Beverly Hills Hotel.

"I sometimes visited Dad's movie sets. My most vivid memory was how boring it was. It seemed to me ten percent work and ninety percent wait. Especially the way Dad worked; he was so meticulous, such a perfectionist. I did a little work in movies on the business end, especially for *On the Beach,* but I was never terribly interested. It seems too self-centered to me. It's either in your blood or it isn't." Having flown from the age of sixteen, young Fred became a flight instructor and charter pilot, and now operates a ranch near San Luis Obispo.

"It's so wonderful to see all the lovely girdles. You know, our posteriors have spread quite a bit over there."

Adele Astaire, widow of Lord Charles Cavendish, had returned to the United States after a ten-year absence, and was giving interviews with her customary lack of reserve. After the privations of the war years, she was reveling in food.

"I've been eating soft-shell crabs every day," she said. "I like the idea of eating their legs and their little faces. They must look sweet underneath the rocks. And succotash! I practically bathe in it. Lima beans won't grow in Ireland, you know. I've also had plenty of hamburgers and Concord grapes. I love Concord grapes and you can't get them on Fifth Avenue. They're not a smart grape.

"Then for breakfast I've been having eggs and sausages and two Shredded Wheat biscuits. How do you like that? Oh, I eat a hell of a breakfast. And I've been guzzling ice cream sodas and eating avocado pears despite my middle-age spread. I weigh one hundred and fifteen pounds now and I should only weigh one hundred and ten. But I don't care. I'll give up eating as soon as I get used to it."

Adele talked proudly of her brother and told of attending the London premiere of *Top Hat:* "Let's see, that was the year I lost the twins. That would have been in 1935. I remember the old witch in the audience who said afterward, 'I think it was a very good film except for the dancing.' I'll think of her name in a minute. Oh, yes, the Countess of Oxford and Asquith. That's who it was."

She talked about her service at the Rainbow Corner during the war and how one boy from Omaha recalled hearing his family talk about the Astaires. "Your mother?" she asked. "No, my grandmother," he replied.

Would she return to performing?

"Never. I'm naturally lazy and I used to hate all the worry of opening nights, the indigestion and everything. I fooled the public for years. It was never me. It was always Fred. He pushed me forward. The minute I left the stage, all the Astaire talent came out with a bang. I was never good at dancing, really."

Adele talked about Lismore Castle, which her mother managed in her absence. Seventy workers raised crops and cattle, cut timber and fished the river.

"We used to sell enormous quantities of salmon," she said, "But since the war they haven't been coming up the river like they used to. You trap them and hit them over the head. It sounds like a vaudeville act, but that's the way you do it."

Somewhat wistfully, she added: "Ireland is a fine country if you do not stay there too long at a time. Lismore is a dream place. But if Charlie ever knew how lonely it is there with no children."

During the Rainbow Corner days, Adele had met an officer who was chief of intelligence for the Eighth Air Force, Kingman Douglass. The acquaintance was renewed in New York, where he worked as an investment banker. On April 28, 1947, Douglass, fifty-one, married Lady Charles Cavendish in the Presbyterian church of Warrentown, Virginia. It was the second marriage for both. Adele gave her age as forty-seven, although she was two years older.

A quiet morning in Beverly Hills. Fred Astaire was loafing in his den, taking a few pool shots, leafing through his phonograph records. He picked out a Lionel Hampton number, "Jack the Bellboy," and put it on the player. He listened for a few moments to the pounding rhythm of Hampton's vibraphone.

"The music started to send me," Fred recalled. "I jumped to my feet and started dancing."

To resume a dancing career at the age of forty-eight seemed unthinkable. Yet Astaire had remained remarkably limber, and he had none of the stiffness and pain that most retired dancers suffer. Despite his athleticism, he had escaped serious injury.

> FRED: I have a back that through various phases of my career got injured; I don't know any dancer who doesn't. I turned my ankle a couple of times, and I broke my arm when I was a child, doing a cartwheel. Sometimes I fell during a dance, but I could usually get away with making it seem part of the routine.

Fred was ready to return to dancing. All he needed was the opportunity, and that was supplied unwittingly by Gene Kelly.

In 1917, Irving Berlin wrote a song called "Smile and Show Your Dimple." To his surprise, it proved a flop. Berlin never lost faith in the melody, and in 1933 he brought it back with a new lyric for the revue *As Thousands Cheer.* He called it "Easter Parade."

Twentieth Century–Fox, which had enjoyed huge success with a Berlin musical, *Alexander's Ragtime Band,* proposed another one, to be titled *Easter Parade.* Berlin was willing, but, as always, he drove a hard bargain. He wanted a percentage of the profits, and that was something Fox would not grant.

Louis B. Mayer was so eager to acquire *Easter Parade* that

he agreed to give Berlin the percentage he wanted, as well as a purchase fee of $500,000. Arthur Freed was assigned to be the producer.

Freed cast Gene Kelly, Judy Garland, Ann Miller and Peter Lawford in *Easter Parade,* with Garland's husband, Vincente Minnelli, to direct. Minnelli had just directed Kelly and Garland in *The Pirate,* a difficult film made harder by Judy's erratic behavior. She was jealous of the time her husband and Kelly spent together in devising the intricate dances. Judy suffered a mental breakdown after filming was completed and spent time in a psychiatric sanitarium.

She seemed recovered, and she began rehearsals for *Easter Parade* in high spirits. After five days, Freed broke the news to Minnelli: "Judy's psychiatrist thinks it would be better all around if you didn't direct the picture. . . . He feels Judy doesn't really want you as director, that you symbolize all her troubles with the studio."

Charles Walters took over as director.

Gene Kelly rehearsed for a month on his numbers, including "Drum Crazy" and the tramp song with Judy, "A Couple of Swells." On Sundays, Kelly always gathered chums for an athletic afternoon in the backyard. Their games were not social sports, but hard-fought contests led by Kelly, who loved to win. During a touch football match, Kelly crashed to the ground. He couldn't stand up. His ankle was broken.

"What are we going to do, Arthur?" Irving Berlin asked.

"Don't worry, I'll handle it," the producer said confidently.

Fred Astaire read about the accident in the newspaper, and he telephoned his sympathy to Kelly. The two dancers were not close friends, but they admired each other's work. Fred had always sent a telegram of appreciation whenever he saw a Kelly dance he liked.

An hour later, MGM called Astaire. Would he be willing to come out of retirement and appear in *Easter Parade?*

"Gee, I don't know," Fred replied. "I'll have to think it over."

He telephoned Kelly again. Just as he had with George Murphy, Fred wanted to make sure that he wouldn't harm Gene Kelly's career in any way.

"First of all, do you think I can do the dances, Gene?" Fred asked. "We have different styles, you know."

"Of course," Kelly replied. "But there's no reason they couldn't be adapted to your style."

"Is there any chance you could do the picture?"

"Not possible. I won't be able to dance for at least five months. The studio has everything ready to go. They can't wait for me. I wish you'd do it, Fred. As one hoofer to another, I'd like to see you back in pictures."

The prospect of working with Judy Garland and another Irving Berlin score was irresistible. Three days after Gene's accident, Fred started rehearsals with Robert Alton, the choreographer. Except to demonstrate ballroom steps for his dance studios, Fred hadn't danced in two years, and he began warily. Within a few days he was hoofing as rigorously as ever.

Judy Garland was equally pleased to be co-starring with Fred, and she remained on her best behavior throughout the filming, even though she was doing retakes for *The Pirate* at the same time. Fred was amazed at the facility with which Judy learned dance routines. Although not primarily a dancer, she could repeat steps after watching them twice. She was the best study Fred had known since Rita Hayworth.

Again Astaire challenged himself in the solos. For "Stepping Out with My Baby," he used slow motion, as he had in the dream sequence of *Carefree.* This time he did free-floating leaps while a chorus danced rapidly in the background.

For "Drum Crazy," Fred used a cane and drumsticks as well as his hands, feet and head to make noise on three bass drums, four snare drums, plus various toy drums, tom-toms, bells, cymbals and wood blocks. Furthermore, he reversed the usual procedure of dancing to prerecorded music, then adding the taps and sound effects later. *Everything* was prerecorded. That meant Fred had to perform the dance and make all the noises in perfect synchronization to the sound track. He did it to his satisfaction by the ninth take.

Easter Parade proved to be one of the big money-makers of 1948, and MGM was eager for a follow-up. Fred Astaire and Judy Garland were announced to star in another musical, *The Barkleys of Broadway.* Fred was delighted, but inwardly

"A couple of Swells"—Fred and Judy in his return film, Easter Parade *(MGM)*

he wondered if Judy had the stamina to start another heavy production so soon.

Betty Comden and Adolph Green wrote an original screenplay about a co-starring couple whose marriage hits the rocks when the wife decides to abandon musical comedy for drama. Comden and Green performed their script in Freed's office before the producer and the two stars. Both Judy and Fred were thrilled, and they joked that they would have difficulty equaling the Comden-Green performance.

Freed again assigned Chuck Walkers to direct Astaire and Garland. Harry Warren and Ira Gershwin wrote the songs. Fred wanted them to supply a number called "Swing Trot" to help promote the dance he invented for his dance studios. Warren and Gershwin evidenced no interest, and they submitted their eight songs for *The Barkleys of Broadway*. "Where's 'Swing Trot'?" Fred inquired. He won out, and "Swing Trot" was the opening number.

Fred began working on the dances with Hermes Pan. For "Shoes with Wings On," Pan took inspiration from Disney's version of *The Sorcerer's Apprentice,* in which Mickey Mouse is beset by an army of brooms carrying buckets of water. This time Fred would be a cobbler who tries on a dancer's shoes, then finds himself dancing amid dozens of rhythmic shoes.

> FRED: I love those mechanical things, using the medium as much as you can. You couldn't do those things on the stage if you tried. Hermes was very helpful in that number. He was taken off the picture because Judy didn't want him to choreograph. She wanted Chuck Walters, who was the director of the picture. But I finished that number before Pan had to leave. His ideas were all through it.

During the second week of rehearsals, Judy's behavior became more erratic. She had lost an alarming amount of

Judy Garland's breakdown provided the Astaire-Rogers reunion in The Barkleys of Broadway *(MGM)*.

weight, seemed excessively tired, and grew short-tempered and irrational. In the third week she collapsed.

Judy's doctor gave her sleeping pills and advised Freed that her continuance in the movie was problematical. While she might be able to perform a few days under medication, she could again suffer a collapse. "Her knowledge of having to report every morning," said the doctor, "would cause such a mental disturbance within her that the results [of a complete cure] would be in jeopardy."

Freed was forced to remove Judy from *The Barkleys of Broadway*. Again the producer was faced with the need to replace a star. What about a reunion of Fred and Ginger? Fred liked the idea. He had talked about doing another picture with Ginger. Freed called Ginger at her ranch in Oregon. "Sure—I'd like it," she said.

Ginger made her entrance in grand style. Fred was rehearsing "Shoes with Wings On" in a theater set when Ginger arrived, striding down the aisle. Fred and Ginger had rarely seen each other since *The Story of Vernon and Irene Castle,* and when she walked onstage, they embraced warmly. Chuck Walters observed the scene and broke into tears. Like everyone of his generation, he had grown up with Astaire-Rogers movies, and he could scarcely believe his luck in directing them.

Ten years had passed since *The Story of Vernon and Irene Castle.* Fred was nearing fifty, but he seemed little changed. He was still a bone-thin one hundred and forty pounds, still the worrier, still the restless seeker of perfection. Ginger was thirty-eight, and although she continued a clean, athletic life, her figure was not as delicate and slender as it had been ten years before. She had done virtually no musicals since she and Fred had parted. The Academy Award and a series of dramatic and comedy successes had provided additional sureness. She no longer relied on Mother Lela to fight her battles.

The script was rewritten to accommodate Ginger, and songs that had been designed for belting by Judy Garland were eliminated. For old times' sake, "They Can't Take That Away from Me" was brought back for a reprise. Harry Warren was not pleased by the inclusion of a twelve-year-old tune by George Gershwin.

Filming proceeded smoothly except for a nightmarish incident provoked by Judy Garland.

One day Judy appeared on the *Barkleys* set unannounced. She wore one of the costumes intended for her to use in the film, and the significance was apparent to every-

Barkleys *featured an Astaire classic, "Shoes with Wings On" (MGM).*

one. Most of the crew had worked with her on *Easter Parade,* and she greeted each one effusively. Her voice grew louder and more manic.

Ginger Rogers had been watching the scene with clenched teeth. Finally she flounced off the set and disappeared into her dressing room, slamming the door behind.

Judy continued playing her scene. Chuck Walters realized Ginger would not return as long as Judy was there. "I think you'd better go now so we can get back to work," the director said with a calm firmness.

"I will not!" Judy proclaimed.

Walters grabbed her arm and escorted her to the stage door. "I know why I'm being kicked off," Judy screamed. "It's because of the great Ginger Rogers! Well, fuck you, Ginger!"

The Barkleys of Broadway possessed none of the airy brilliance of the Astaire-Rogers musicals at RKO, but the musical numbers were clever. Aided by a wealth of publicity about the Astaire-Rogers reunion, the film performed well, though not spectacularly, in theaters. Even Bosley Crowther of *The New York Times* was complimentary:

"Ginger and Fred are a couple with incorruptible style. They also have that gift of mutual timing in absolute union, so that they're always clicking together, when dancing or trifling with the plot. . . . Watching them spin in rapturous rhythm to the lilt of 'They Can't Take That Away from Me,' the old Gershwin hit, renews one's fervor for the magic they create. Age cannot wither the enchantment of Ginger and Fred."

At the Pantages Theater on March 23, 1950, the Academy of Motion Picture Arts and Sciences presented a special award to Fred Astaire "for his unique artistry and his contributions to the technique of musical pictures." The Oscar was handed to him by Ginger Rogers.

Fred's relations with Ginger have remained ambivalent. In later years she has complained privately that Fred received all the tributes and honors despite the fact that she had been a fifty-percent member of the team. In an interview she was quoted as saying, "I've danced with doctors who were better dancers than Fred." Ginger tried to explain that she had meant there were better *social* dancers than Astaire.

Still, the bond of history between them has been too strong to be broken by occasional misunderstandings.

Whenever they met in public, such as for the presentation of the RKO archives to UCLA in 1982, the affection between them was unmistakable. In 1983, Ginger and her secretary joined Fred and Robyn at Hermes Pan's house for an evening of warm reminiscences.

Portrait of the artist at fifty—

He rarely referred to his dance partner by name. When he discussed a routine with a choreographer, his partner was always "the Lady." He'd say, "Now the Lady will go into a spin." Or, "This is where the Lady slides into my arms."

Rehearsals were conducted with utmost security. No one was admitted into the hall unless he or she was directly involved with the dance. During filming of a musical number, he had no objection to visitors.

Once rehearsals began, nothing interfered. If all the rehearsal halls were occupied with other productions, he hired a place outside the studio.

"How do I keep going? What do I do?" he once challenged an interviewer. "Nothing. Absolutely nothing. I don't eat health foods. I never dance unless I have to. I don't work out in a gym. Vitamin pills? Never! Who needs 'em? Oh, sure, when I start a picture I have to get myself in shape. I'm usually up to 138 pounds between pictures and down to 133 by the time we start shooting. So I run around the rehearsal hall if I feel like it, tap if I feel like it—anything I think might knock off those five pounds."

The rehearsal was everything. He worked almost continuously five or six hours a day, seven days a week, perfecting each turn, each arm motion, until the dance became a free-flowing whole. When performed, it seemed effortless and airy, belying the ordeal of toil and sweat that went into its creation. By performance time, the routine was so thoroughly ingrained in his mind and reflexes "that I never have to worry about the next step." If anything happened to disturb that concentration, the Astaire temper made one of its occasional appearances.

As he had at RKO, he maintained control over how his dances were photographed. Long takes, no cutaways, sta-

Fred in rehearsal (MGM)

tionary camera. "Either the camera will dance or I will. But both of us at the same time—that won't work. A moving camera makes the dancer look as if he's standing still."

The musical arrangements had to be fitted to his dances, not vice versa. That's where the rehearsal pianist was valuable, providing bridges and added bars of melody which were then given to the arrangers for final orchestration.

Fred was meticulous about synchronization, working long hours in a recording studio to lay down taps on a sound track as he watched his dancing image on a screen. Once he saw film and sound put together and he complained, "That's three sprocket holes out of sync."

Although he often deprecated his singing voice, he was also proud that Irving Berlin, Cole Porter, Jerome Kern and the Gershwins chose him as the best interpreter of their songs. Why? "I got their lyrics over, I stuck to the tune, and I phrased the way they liked," he theorized. Having written songs himself, he understood the labor involved: "I always felt that the composers approached what they did the same way I approached a dance step. I've got to work on it like mad to see whether it fits where I want it—before I feel like *showing* it to anybody. A songwriter has the same anxiety about getting it all set."

Despite years of acclaim as the screen's premier dancer, he remained Adele's Moaning Minnie.

"I'm a pessimist; I have forebodings," he admitted. But his pessimism was always self-directed. To others he was invariably cheerful and liberal with encouragement.

"I must get that from my mother. Mother is an optimist. She traveled with Adele and me in vaudeville. We got sixty dollars a week for split weeks. Out of that we paid three railroad fares, ten percent commission to the agent, five percent to the agent's agent. We ate what was left and sometimes that was the hole in the dougnut. Mother would always say comfortingly that all we needed was experience. But you can starve getting experience."

At fifty he didn't feel his age, but he was constantly reminded of it. He told Hedda Hopper: "I feel better than when I was twenty. My energy is holding up fine, and I never think about my age until I read something about it. For instance, somebody writes, 'What does a man of his age think he's doing?' That burns me up."

Destructive criticism bothered him most: "It kills me. I try to ignore it, but if there are ninety-nine good [reviews], the bad one will throw me. It's the brush-offs that slay, the implication that you think up a dance while shaving and tap it off on the way to breakfast."

More movies.

Every since *Broadway Melody of 1940,* Jack Cummings had promised to find another film for Fred. Ten years afterward, the producer sent Fred the script of *Three Little Words.* Fred took it with him on a trip to Europe and cabled: DEAR JACK, YOU'RE AS GOOD AS YOUR WORD. WHEN DO WE START? LOVE, FREDDY.

Three Little Words was a romanticized version of the lives of the songwriting team of Bert Kalmar and Harry Ruby. Fred was pleased to play Kalmar, whom he had known as a dancer in vaudeville. Fred was delighted that Red Skelton would be portraying Ruby. Skelton himself was awed at co-starring with Fred Astaire—"All that class!" But after a couple of days of excessive politeness, barriers disappeared, and the two performers worked together with total ease.

Red Skelton remembers: "Fred is not a prude by any means, but he is pretty conservative. When we were making *Three Little Words, Playboy* magazine was just becoming popular, and in those times the nude centerfolds were something new and sensational. I had the prop guy go down to the studio newsstand and buy up as many *Playboys* as he could find. While Fred was at lunch, we pinned the centerfolds all over Fred's dressing room.

"When Fred came back from lunch, he sat down at his dressing room mirror. As he always did before he went to work, he was thinking intently about what he was going to do. Then he looked up and saw the pictures on the wall. Immediately he said, 'Why, that red-headed son of a bitch!'"

Skelton recalled another incident during the finale. Singing the title song was Phil Regan, the Irish tenor who had become attached to the administration of President Tru-

Conflict of styles: Betty Hutton and Fred Astaire, Let's Dance *(Paramount)*

man. Take after take was ruined because Regan couldn't remember the lyrics. Regan explained that he was rusty "because Mr. Truman doesn't want actors around him." Astaire
muttered to Skelton, "I don't think the President has to
worry."

Astaire's dance partner was Vera-Ellen, who matched
him in training and dedication. For once he was dancing with
someone who was willing to rehearse even longer that he did.

FRED: She was a real accomplished dancer, that girl. Ballet, tap dancing, anything you wanted to do. She used to worry about the look of her cheeks, and she was doing this [fingers indenting cheeks] all day long. She'd bend over to let the blood flow to her head. She had certain ideas about how she wanted her face to look. I thought she looked pretty good. She was very thin. I liked that. I'm not too good at lifting heavy women.

Next a return to Paramount for *Let's Dance* with Betty Hutton. A mismatch. Despite some serviceable Frank Loesser songs, notably "Why Fight the Feeling," the film didn't work because of the disparity of styles. Fred and Hermes Pan tried hard with the dances, especially "Oh, Them Dudes," with the stars as a pair of low-down scroungy cowpokes. Hutton had little dancing skill, and although Fred had performed with non-dancers before, she was not as compliant as the others had been. Betty was accustomed to having her own way as queen of Paramount musicals, and she responded poorly to the Astaire discipline. In *Let's Dance,* her frenetic manner seemed out of sync with Fred's suavity.

For *Royal Wedding,* Astaire was cast opposite another star with limited dancing experience, June Allyson.

Arthur Freed had been seeking another vehicle for Fred Astaire, and he discussed his need with Alan Jay Lerner, a temporary recruit of the Freed unit at MGM. Why not a story based on the lives of Fred and Adele Astaire? Lerner devised a plot about a brother-and-sister team who play London at the time of the wedding of Princess Elizabeth to the Duke of Edinburgh. The sister falls in love with an English nobleman, the brother with a dancer, and they have a double wedding.

For the role of the English dancer, Freed wanted to cast Moira Shearer, who had created a sensation in *The Red Shoes.* Freed gave up the idea when Astaire remarked, "I know she's wonderful, but what the hell could I do with her?"

Sarah Churchill was appearing in Los Angeles in a revival of *The Philadelphia Story.* Freed liked her performance, tested her and signed her as the English dancer. She had done little dancing, but she was attractive—and she was Win-

Astaire's most astounding dance: "You're All the World to Me," Royal Wedding *(MGM)*

ston Churchill's daughter, a positive factor for the film's publicity.

Peter Lawford, an MGM contract player, was a natural for the English nobleman. Charles Walters was assigned to direct.

Astaire started rhearsing "Every Night at Seven" with June Allyson. "When I was a girl in the Bronx, I saw *The Gay Divorcée* seventeen times," she told him. "That's how I learned to dance."

At first June thought her awe of Fred Astaire was what caused her to feel weak and nauseous. Then she found out the reason. She telephoned Fred from the doctor's office: "Fred, I want you to be the first to know—I'm pregnant!" After a brief silence, he asked nervously, "Who *is* this?"

Miss Allyson retired to await the birth of her first child, Dick Powell, Jr. She was replaced in *Royal Wedding* by Judy Garland.

Church Walters, who had directed Judy in *Easter Parade* and *Summer Stock,* rebelled. "I'm terribly sorry, but I can't go through it again," he told Freed. "I've just spent a year and a half with her, and I'm ready for a mental institution." He was replaced by Stanley Donen, who was making his debut as a full director (he had co-directed *On the Town* with Gene Kelly).

Four days after Miss Allyson reported her pregnancy, Judy Garland began rehearsals with Fred. They had a joyful reunion, then settled down to work with the dance director, Nick Castle. For the first week, rehearsals went smoothly. Then Judy returned to her old habits. Her tardiness was recorded daily in the production office: one hour; three and a half hours; fifteen minutes; forty-five minutes; a half hour; forty-five minutes; two and three-quarter hours; et cetera.

By the fourth week, Judy informed Donen she could work only mornings or afternoons. When he pleaded that the final days of rehearsal were vital, she replied, "Take your choice." Freed allowed her to work only afternoons. Fred meanwhile was inwardly seething. Garland's behavior was contrary to all his principles.

On the last day before prerecording, Judy announced she was not coming to the studio. That was the end. On June 17, 1950, after fifteen years under contract to MGM, Judy Garland was dropped from the payroll. Four days later, she inflicted a wound on her neck with a broken water glass during a fit of anguish. The wound was superficial.

When Arthur Freed mentioned that Jane Powell was available for *Royal Wedding,* Astaire responded, "Grab her— please!"

For the second time, the script was revised and the Burton Lane–Alan Jay Lerner songs rearranged to fit the leading lady. Filming began July 6 with "Open Your Eyes," a number performed by Astaire and Miss Powell on a rocking ocean liner. The dance had originated with Fred, who remembered the time he and Adele had performed on the *Aquitania* during their stormy first crossing of the Atlantic.

Another *Royal Wedding* dance proved to be the most ingenious and talked-about of the Astaire career.

For some time Fred had toyed with a number in which he would climb the walls and dance on the ceiling. The opportunity came in *Royal Wedding,* for a scene in which he returns to his hotel room and realizes he is crazily in love with Sarah Churchill.

> FRED: That was an outstanding number. A lot of people don't realize how it worked. The whole room revolved, and I was on the ground the whole time, naturally. The room looks different when it turns.
>
> The camera, the cameraman and the room all turn, and I'm the one who does the climbing. Everyone asks me, "Did you turn the camera upside down?" No, *everything* turned upside down. Most people don't understand. It's too difficult to explain.
>
> It took a lot of time to rehearse and perfect. It required a special set we called the Iron Lung. At Metro they did things in a big way. When I told Arthur Freed what I wanted to do, he said, "Go ahead, it's a great idea."
>
> We did it all in one take. No cuts, no trick shots. As the set turned, I seemed to be actually climbing the wall. The first time they turned the room, everything fell down. Pictures on the wall, books, all went *clunk!* We had to lash on a lot of stuff, because the room had to stay perfectly normal.

The number, performed to the song "You're All the World to Me," was photographed in a room constructed by Bethlehem Steel. Not only did the camera and cameraman revolve 360 degrees; the light for the set revolved as well. This required a large commutator to transform power to the lights as they moved with the set. The mechanics were so well

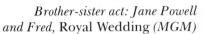

Brother-sister act: Jane Powell and Fred, Royal Wedding *(MGM)*

Jane Powell was the third star to be cast in the lead opposite Fred in Royal Wedding *(MGM).*

planned that Stanley Donen was able to film the dance in half a day.

For years people had been saying Fred Astaire could dance with a hat rack. In *Royal Wedding* he did. In his hands the hat rack seemed as pliant and responsive as Ginger or Rita.

> FRED: Hermes Pan had the idea, but he wasn't on the picture. We were discussing it a picture or two before, and I said, "I'll have to use that sometime." I thought he was going to be on *Royal Wedding,* but he was tied up somewhere else. So I got hold of him and said, "I'm going to do it."
>
> Boy, that was a tough one to get. We had an assistant who was very good at mechanical things, and we got that hall tree so I could practically tell it what to do. It had to be weighted a certain way so it would move around and I would know where to catch it. Those things take a lot of preparation.
>
> The hat rack was supposed to represent Sarah Churchill. I thought she was very good in the picture, though she was scared stiff while we were making it.

Royal Wedding, called *Wedding Bells* in England to avoid offending the royal family, cost $1,590,920, including charges of $3,334 for June Allyson and $20,604 for Judy Garland. The film grossed more than $4 million.

The Belle of New York was the project Astaire had declined before his retirement in 1946. In mid-1951 he began filming it and later wished he hadn't.

With Vera-Ellen again as co-star and Robert Alton directing the dances, Fred displayed his virtuosity, dancing on rooftops in "Seeing's Believing," through a horse-drawn trolley for "Oops" and providing a rare self-portrait with "I Wanna Be a Dancin' Man." But the creaking plot and the 1910 atmosphere weighted down his efforts, and *Belle* was a failure.

Arthur Freed redeemed himself with *The Band Wagon.* The producer had long wanted to make a musical based on the show tunes of Arthur Schwartz and Howard Dietz. The rights were not difficult to negotiate, since Dietz was advertising vice president of Loew's, MGM's parent company.

The project was first called *I Love Louisa*, from the song Fred and Adele had performed in the revue *The Band Wagon*. Betty Comden and Adolph Green were hired to write an original script. Their plot concerned the creation of a Broadway musical starring Tony Hunter, a Hollywood star in mid-career, contemplating retirement but deciding to attempt a comeback on the stage. Comden and Green worried that Fred might be offended by the similarity of Tony Hunter and Fred Astaire. But when they performed the script for them, he was delighted.

Oscar Levant and Nanette Fabray were cast as a married writing team, not dissimilar to Comden and Green. The acidic Levant found himself portraying a married man for the first time, and he later cracked that he treated Miss Fabray atrociously—"just as though she were indeed my real wife."

Clifton Webb was sought for the role of Jeffrey Cordova, a dramatic star who stages the Broadway musical and co-stars in it. Webb considered the role too secondary, and he suggested the British song-and-dance star Jack Buchanan. Freed also considered Edward G. Robinson and Vincent Price. But Buchanan arrived from London, tested for the role and seemed ideal.

Cyd Charisse had scored impressively in *Singin' in the Rain,* and Freed wanted her to play Gabrielle Gerard, the ballerina who dances with Tony Hunter. First she had to pass an important test.

"Of course I was in awe of Fred Astaire," she recalls. "I had seen all his movies with Ginger Rogers in Amarillo, Texas, where the movie theater was across the street from my father's jewelry store. I had danced around him in *Ziegfeld Follies* for the 'Bring on the Beautiful Girls' number. We were introduced, but we probably said no more than two words to each other.

"In 1954, I was rehearsing a difficult number for *Sombrero* in Rehearsal Hall C. Fred came in the center door. He was wearing a straw hat—he was *the* one who could still wear a straw hat—and he came forward with that wonderful walk,

Even the hard-working Vera Ellen couldn't help Fred save The Belle of New York *(MGM)*

hands in pockets. 'Hi, Hermes,' he said. Hermes Pan was directing the number.

"We talked, and it was a typical Fred Astaire conversation: 'How are you?' 'How's it going?' 'Doin' okay?' I noticed he was constantly looking in the mirror. He left, and twenty minutes later, the phone rang. Arthur Freed said, 'I want you to do *Band Wagon* with Fred Astaire. You know, Fred's very conscious of height, and I assured him you look taller than you are. But he had to see for himself. You passed.'"

> FRED: Cyd is a great girl, simply the most lovely-looking girl you could ever meet. She never changes, always looks the same. And the nicest-natured person. She's a fine dancer in her own way. She wasn't a tap dancer, she's just beautiful, trained, very strong in whatever we did. When we were dancing, we didn't know what time it was.

I Love Louisa became *The Band Wagon* after MGM bought rights to the title from 20th Century–Fox. Vincente Minnelli was assigned to direct, Michael Kidd to stage the dances. The Dietz-Schwartz catalog was laden with hit songs, but Freed wanted one more number, something akin to "There's No Business Like Show Business." Within half an hour, Dietz and Schwartz produced "That's Entertainment."

Dance rehearsals began, and Astaire at first was wary of Michael Kidd. It was the first film choreography for Kidd, who had been a solo dancer for the Ballet Theater and had created dances for *Finian's Rainbow, Love Life* and *Guys and Dolls*. Fred disliked the formality of ballet, and he feared that Kidd's classical training might be reflected in the dances, especially since the big production number was to be "The Girl Hunt Ballet," a satire of the Mickey Spillane detective yarns.

The Band Wagon seemed to bear out the Samuel Goldwyn theory that unhappy people make good pictures.

Buchanan was terrified of working with Astaire and in foul humor because of extensive, painful dental surgery he had been forced to undergo. Levant had suffered a heart attack six weeks before the start of production, and his hy-

"The Girl Hunt Ballet" provided the climax for The Bank Wagon *(MGM).*

pochondria helped make him more waspish than ever. Nanette Fabray, struggling in her first movie musical, found Astaire "aloof, cold, remote." She tried to be cheerful on the set, "but nobody talked to anybody; it was the coldest, unfriendliest, the most terrible experience I can remember."

FRED: I didn't think that she disliked me; I thought
we had fun, joking around the set with Oscar Levant. I think it's kinda funny if someone called me
snooty and cool. I don't think I ever had that at-
titude. I might have been very businesslike about
certain things because when I was on a show, it
meant *everything* to me. I would think about it and do
it all the time, over weekends, at midnight if I woke
up.

[Gene] Kelly is a very terrific taskmaster, too. He
works like a *son of a gun.* He doesn't kid. He also gets
so intense that you're afraid to talk to him. We
worked together a number of times, and I always
liked him for [his dedication]. Some of these guys
say, "Well, [the audience] is getting enough for their
money, anyway."

Minnelli seemed oblivious of the tensions. He continued
in his painfully methodical manner, falling so far behind
schedule that the cinematographer was fired in order to pla-
cate management.

Even Fred Astaire became exasperated by the ambigu-
ous direction of Vincente Minnelli. Fred preferred his directors to act decisively, and he found Minnelli changing his
mind from minute to minute. That happened repeatedly
during a scene with several characters on a small set. Finally
Fred exploded.

"Get me out of here!" he exclaimed, and he stomped off
the set. He started walking around the stage, his mind blank.
The others were in a panic. Stars had been known to walk off
sets, but never Fred Astaire.

Arthur Freed arrived, his bulldog face rumpled with
concern. "What's the matter, kid, what's the matter?" he
asked.

"Just give me a little time to get myself together," Fred
replied. After a few more turns around the stage, he returned.

"Gee, I'm sorry," he said earnestly to Minnelli. "I've
never walked off a set before. You know, I just had a mental
block. I couldn't think."

Minnelli smiled wanly. "I know what you mean," he said. "I drive everybody crazy."

After reading about the incident in Fred's autobiography, Minnelli responded in his own autobiography that "my reaction to his apology was automatic. I hadn't a clue to his discontent. I was too busy concentrating on the scene to even notice that he'd stormed off the set. I thought he'd left to answer nature's call, or something."

For the finale, "That's Entertainment," all of the principals were supposed to walk toward the camera, striding down a long ramp. Levant recalled, "The physical effort involved worried me, and when I told my doctor about this he said not to do it. At the next rehearsal I refused to do it, so in great disgust Fred Astaire said, 'All right, I'll carry you down.' So I did it."

All of the temper and bad humor were forgotten when *The Band Wagon* was released in July of 1953. "It is a honey," declared Bosley Crowther in *The New York Times,* adding that it "respectfully bids for recognition as one of the best musical films ever made."

Indeed, *The Band Wagon* is the most fully realized of the Astaire post-Ginger musicals. Fred at fifty-three was at the height of his powers, vocally and in dance. The melancholy "By Myself" was ideally suited for his voice, as was the upbeat "A Shine on My Shoes." "Dancing in the Dark" with Cyd Charisse was a romantic masterpiece, and "The Girl Hunt Ballet" gave both a chance at choice satire. Buchanan was near the end of his career, but he could still match Astaire in suavity on "I Guess I'll Have to Change My Plan."

Never before had Fred been afforded such a wide variety of inspired numbers. Nor would he be again.

New dancer at MGM: Bob Fosse.

He arrived at the studio in 1953; he was twenty-six and had spent half of his life as a professional dancer. At MGM he found himself preparing for a movie dance in a hall adjacent to where Fred Astaire was rehearsing *The Band Wagon.*

"Imagine working next door to God!" he remembers. "I

was so awed and overwhelmed I peeked through the key-hole—literally—so I could have a look at my idol. Stanley Donen, who was my mentor, kept telling Fred, 'You gotta see this Fosse kid.' Then one day Stanley told me, 'You're going to dance for Fred.' He took me to the hall where Fred was rehearsing 'A Shine on Your Shoes' for *Band Wagon*. 'Okay, show him, Bob,' Stanley said. And I was awful! My feet wouldn't move, I fell over myself. Fred just stood there, wearing the sweatband around his head and those great re-hearsal clothes of his. When I finished, he said, 'Very nice,' and went back to what he was doing. I was so bad!"

Another memory sticks in Fosse's mind from that pe-riod:

"One day at noontime, I was walking down a big MGM street. It was entirely empty. Then I saw a figure coming from two blocks away. I could tell immediately from the walk that it was Fred. He kept walking toward me with his head down, his hat pulled over his eyes. I didn't know what to do. I wanted to say hello, but I didn't want to disturb his concen-tration. Here I was, a kid from New York, and he was *Fred Astaire!*

"Finally we reached each other. As we passed each other, he said without looking up, 'Hi ya, Foss.' That's what he called me—Foss. He kept walking, and I turned to watch him go, because I couldn't take my eyes off him. There was a bent carpenter's nail in the street. With a flick of his foot, Fred sent it flying to the soundstage wall, where it hit with a clang and fell. It was a perfect Astaire gesture."

One day the young dancer watched Astaire rehearse a trick with a hat. Over and over again, Fred flipped the hat. Each time the trick worked perfectly, but he repeated it twenty times. It was a lesson for the future director: "I won-dered why he kept doing it over again, then I realized he wanted to make sure it worked before the camera. Whenever I'm suffering through something again and again, I remem-ber Fred Astaire and the hat trick."

It started with a fierce headache. Phyllis Astaire was sitting in a box at the Belmont racetrack in New York on a warm summer day in 1953 when her head began to throb. "I feel dizzy," she told Fred. "I think I'd better leave." Fred hurried her to the car. He was alarmed. Phyllis never complained of being ill. He wanted her to see a doctor, but she refused. "It'll pass," she assured him. And in the morning she felt perfectly normal. They went back to California and forgot about the incident.

In 1953, Fred Astaire reached another turning point in his career. His MGM contract ended with *The Band Wagon*, and the studio made no effort to sign him again. The movie business was reeling under the impact of television, and all studios were retrenching. Louis B. Mayer and other moguls were losing control of the companies they had built. Long-time stars were being dropped from contract lists.

Fred was fifty-four. Surely that was a reasonable age at which to stop performing, he believed. His dance studios were prospering; he continued his racing stable on a modest basis. Peter was finishing college, and young Fred was completing high school. With only Ava at home, the Astaires felt they didn't need the big house anymore. They were expanding the ranch house with the idea of making it their permanent home. And they wanted to travel. With Fred moving from one movie to the next, they had scarcely been out of California.

"I think I'll retire," Fred announced.

"Not again!" Phyllis replied.

"This time I'm not going to tell anyone," he assured her. "You'll be the only one who knows."

The second retirement was shorter than the first one. One night Fred and Phyllis dined at Romanoff's restaurant, a rare appearance by the Astaires in a place frequented by the movie crowd. Darryl Zanuck, production chief of 20th Century–Fox, was among the diners, and the sight of Fred Astaire prompted an idea: Why not a musical remake of *Daddy Long Legs?*

The Jean Webster novel about a young ward who falls in love with her guardian was such a surefire tearjerker that it had already been filmed three times. When Astaire's MCA

(Music Corporation of America) agent called with Zanuck's proposal, Fred was intrigued, especially when he learned that Leslie Caron was being sought as his co-star. Fred agreed to do the film, which was scheduled to start in September of 1954.

Fred and Phyllis looked forward to a half-year of leisure, watching their horses run and making some long-postponed trips. Young Fred, who had been flying since he was seventeen, had enlisted in the Air Force, and they planned to visit him in Texas. Then one day at Santa Anita, Phyllis felt dizzy again. Fred took her home and urged her to see a doctor. But she didn't like to admit to illness, and she refused.

When Phyllis decided at the last moment that she couldn't go to dinner with their good friend Cole Porter, Fred decided her condition could no longer be ignored. He drove her to the family doctor for an examination. X rays disclosed a spot on her lung that was found to be malignant. Phyllis had been a longtime smoker.

Before entering the hospital for the operation, Phyllis wanted to spend a day at the ranch, where her favorite brood mare had given birth to a filly. As they drove back to Beverly Hills, Phyllis asked Fred, "Am I going to die?" It wasn't possible, he assured her, and he was totally convinced of that himself.

On the Good Friday they had planned to spend in Texas with Fred, Jr., Phyllis underwent surgery at St. John's Hospital in Santa Monica. David Niven and Hermes Pan sat with Fred through the hours of waiting. A large section of Phyllis' lung was removed, and the operation seemed successful. But complications developed, and she was returned to surgery. Fred prayed silently, unwilling to accept the possibility that Phyllis might not survive.

It was dawn before Phyllis emerged from the second surgery. Fred was assured that the purpose of the operations had been accomplished, but Phyllis would have to undergo radiation treatment.

Five times a week, Fred drove Phyllis to downtown Los Angeles for the treatments. She responded amazingly well, and Fred was so encouraged by her recovery that he began rehearsals at Fox for *Daddy Long Legs*. On weekends the Astaires spent their days at the beloved ranch she had wondered if she would ever see again.

In July the cancer returned. Another major operation at St. John's. Again it was pronounced successful. Fred would not allow himself to believe anything else.

Phyllis came home to Summit Drive, weak and wasted. This time her strength didn't return. Fred could dance no more, and he called a halt to rehearsals. Phyllis drifted into a coma, and Fred spent hours in her bedroom, praying, always believing that she would open her eyes and be well again.

Fred wrote in his autobiography: "Phyllis slipped away from us at 10 A.M., September 13, 1954."

Fred was wild with grief. Adele, who had arrived from Virginia, couldn't console him, nor could his mother. Neither could Randolph Scott, David Niven, Hermes Pan, Samuel Goldwyn, nor the other longtime friends who arrived at the house Phyllis had planned with such taste and care.

Daddy Long Legs had been continuing in Fred's absence. Leslie Caron was filming a ballet directed by Roland Petit, but soon the production would have to stop if Fred did not return.

"You know, I don't think I can go on with the film," Fred told Adele. "I just don't feel I can do it. My heart isn't there." It was inconceivable that he could sing and dance, with Phyllis gone.

A week before, he had told Sam Engel as much. Engel was producing *Daddy Long Legs* for Fox, and he was a religious and compassionate man. He recalled that Astaire "made me an offer that was unheard of in Hollywood. He wanted to pay all the expenses of the production out of his pocket. I told him to forget it—that maybe God would intervene and Phyllis would pull through."

On the day after the funeral, Fred asked Engel to come to his house. The producer found Fred "in a bad way, sort of in a daze."

"Sam, what I told you last week still goes," Astaire said. "The kids are shattered, and I am shattered. The worst thing is that Phyllis wanted me to do this picture. But I can't. The prospect of going to the studio and smiling is just impossible."

Despite the loss of Phyllis, Fred managed to continue with Daddy Long Legs *(20th Century-Fox).*

"Don't worry about it, Fred," Engel replied. "If you feel the way you do, that's it. However, I think you'll be making the greatest mistake of your life if you don't go to work right now."

"Sam, I just can't," Fred said quietly, shaking his head. Engel drove back to the studio pondering ways to save *Daddy Long Legs.* It didn't seem possible. Fred Astaire was unique, irreplaceable. No one could provide a match for Leslie Caron in the dancing and as the foster parent with whom she falls in love.

The producer sat in his office the following morning, contemplating the loss to 20th Century–Fox by cancellation of the production. His secretary told him on the intercom: "Mr. Fred Astaire is here to see you."

Engel rushed to the outer office and found a grim-faced Astaire. "I don't know if I can make it, Sam, but I'll try," Fred told him. "I'm reporting for work."

Fred returned to the dance rehearsals with the same intensity as ever. Only during the breaks did he allow his feelings to well up. Then he had to remove himself, disappear into his dressing room or a remote corner of the stage.

"I don't know if Old Dad can make it," Fred told Engel one day. Tears began filling Fred's eyes.

"It's okay," the producer said warmly. "It's all right to cry."

Fred gazed at him helplessly. "It's rough, Sam, real rough. Especially when I go home and she's not there."

A month after his wife died, I visited Fox to interview Fred. He was working on a music stage, where he listened to a full orchestra play Johnny Mercer's "Something's Gotta Give," the hit song of *Daddy Long Legs*. Fred was dressed in trademark style: porkpie hat, sport coat, shirt with tail tied in a knot, gray flannel slacks with foulard scarf as a belt. Astaire had never been an easy interview, always reticent, careful to offend no one, willing to talk about his work but reluctant to discuss himself. But on this occasion he seemed eager to talk, especially about Phyllis.

I asked him about reports he was going to retire. "Oh, no," he said emphatically; "if I retire again, I'm not going to announce it." He had a commitment for another film at Fox and one at MGM, but he didn't know what the subjects would be.

"I'm not going to make a picture just to be making a picture," he said. "After you've been in this business as long as I have and done as many routines as I have, you don't look forward to eight or nine months of rehearsals and shooting. If I do another picture, it will have to be something really worthwhile. After my wife died, I didn't want to do this one. But they talked me into it, and I'm glad I did. I would have been a fool to pass it up. I can't really tell what I'm going to do next because I've run up against a stone wall in my personal life. Keeping busy on this picture has helped me forget my loss, but merely keeping busy won't help in the long run."

He started talking about Phyllis. How he was grateful for his retirement because it had provided two full years of traveling and being with Phyllis constantly. How he had wanted to sell all his racehorses after she died but changed his mind.

His face rumpled with perplexity.

"I've tried and tried to find a reason for her death, but I simply cannot do it. It might make sense if she had led a full life. But she hadn't. She was only forty-six, and just as beautiful as the day I met her. I just can't figure it out."

The orchestra was ready to play again, and Fred returned to the small dance floor. As the strains of "Something's Gotta Give" filled the stage, Fred glided through a routine with a dance-in for Leslie Caron. He danced with such effortless grace that few onlookers noticed that his eyes were red and damp.

Daddy Long Legs was a hit and Fred agreed to make some television appearances in New York to help publicize the movie. It was Fred's first experience in the new medium and the first time he had faced an audience since his entertaining of troops during the war. To his surprise, he enjoyed himself. He was required only to take a bow on *The Ed Sullivan Show* and to answer questions on *What's My Line* and *I've Got a Secret.* No pressure of putting on a performance.

During the summer, Fred took his mother and Ava for a visit with Adele at Lismore Castle. He returned to California and memories of Phyllis, spending long hours beside her grave. His friends urged him to work again, and he realized the need. But Fox was unable to find a second vehicle for him. He signed with Paramount for two films, a musical with Bing Crosby, and *Papa's Delicate Condition,* but neither was put into production. Finally, *Funny Face* came along.

Stanley Donen and the famed fashion photographer Richard Avedon had conceived the story of an Avedon-like character who creates a star model, then marries her. Leonard Gershe wrote a script, *Wedding Day,* which was planned as a Broadway musical. Instead, it was sold to MGM, where Roger Edens intended to produce it as *Funny Face,* with the same Gershwin score of the show Fred and Adele had done in 1928. Edens wanted Audrey Hepburn to star as the model. She agreed—*if* Fred Astaire would play the photographer. Fred was delighted.

MGM executives became wary of investing in a big-budget musical in the face of a waning market. *Funny Face* was placed on the shelf. But Audrey Hepburn was determined to dance with Fred Astaire. Roger Edens managed to transfer the entire project, including cast and creative personnel, to Hepburn's home studio, Paramount.

Astaire entered preparations for his twenty-ninth musical film without a notion of what he could do that would be new and different. But in the rehearsal hall the ideas began to flow. Arriving one stormy morning, he began improvising before the mirror. He noted that his raincoat swayed interestingly, and he whipped it around with the gestures of a toreador. It was the beginning of his bullfight dance to the music of "Let's Kiss and Make Up."

Half of *Funny Face* was filmed on the Paramount lot, then the company moved to Paris for exteriors. The rains came. Day after day the downpour continued, until Stanley Donen was forced to stage sequences in the rain. One of the important dances was a love duet Fred and Audrey had rehearsed in Hollywood. It was scheduled to be photographed at a park in Chantilly, but recurrent rains caused the sequence to be postponed. Finally the company could wait no longer, and Fred and Audrey reported to the soggy location. Now they were faced with recalling a dance they had practiced two months before and performing it with total ease on ground where they sank to their ankles.

> FRED: We were in France waiting for the weather,
> and it poured rain while we were working out in the
> field. Finally Audrey said [mock English accent]:
> "Heah I was looking forward so much to dahncing
> with Fred Ahstaire. And what do I get? *Mud!*"

Like *Daddy Long Legs, Funny Face* proved successful, and that pleased Fred, ever sensitive to the public's reception of

Fred and Audrey Hepburn brave outdoor perils for Funny Face *(Paramount).*

his efforts. He had the vaudevillian's phobia about staying on too long, failing to reach the wings before the applause died. Now approaching sixty, he had been dancing on the screen for almost a quarter century. With the preponderance of adults remaining home to watch television, the movie audience grew steadily younger. Musicals suffered another decline, this time irreversible. They were fifty percent more expensive to produce than ordinary films, and studios could no longer afford musical units such as Arthur Freed's at MGM. Popular music was shifting to the less polite sound of rock 'n' roll. The public was being satiated with musical entertainment on television variety shows.

Arthur Freed found another starring role in a musical for Fred Astaire. It was be his last.

Silk Stockings, a musicalized *Ninotchka,* had been a Broadway hit with a Cole Porter score. Since MGM had produced the Garbo film, it had first rights to the musical version. Freed saw the show and exercised the rights, paying $300,000. It would be the first production of Arthur Freed Productions, an independent company releasing through MGM.

At home with Ava

Silk Stockings. *Fred commented of Cyd Charisse: "When you've danced with her you stay danced with." (MGM)*

Astaire liked the idea of another film to follow *Funny Face,* for he had discovered work was the best refuge from the fearful depressions that afflicted him since Phyllis' death. *Silk Stockings* was especially attractive, since it meant another pairing with Cyd Charisse and a score by his dear friend Cole Porter.

Porter seemed strangely unenthusiastic about *Silk Stockings,* as he often was with film versions of shows he had already composed. When Fred tried to talk to him about *Silk Stockings,* Porter enthused about *Les Girls,* another MGM musical for which he was writing new songs.

"I want to do a rock 'n' roll number in top hat and tails," Fred told Porter. "Can you write one?"

"I don't know; I've never tried," said the composer.

Porter admitted to an associate, Alexander Steinert, that he knew nothing about rock 'n' roll. Steinert provided him with some examples on records, and Porter produced the song Fred requested, "The Ritz Roll and Rock." Fred was pleased with the song, but later fretted over how he sang it: "I overdid, overplayed it. I could have simplified it more. But you get keyed up on a certain day and maybe do something that doesn't please you. I hope nobody noticed it as much as I did, because it made me so angry." He is still displeased over how he sang "Something's Gotta Give" in *Daddy Long Legs.*

7

Television

*There never was a greater perfectionist, there never
was, or never will be, a better dancer, and I never
knew anybody more kind, more considerate, or so
completely a gentleman. . . . I love Fred, John, and I
admire and respect him. I guess it's because he's so
many things I'd like to be and am not.*

—Bing Crosby, letter to John O'Hara

FRED: The first time I saw Barrie Chase, she was an understudy, or rather a dance-in for a girl [Kay Kendall] who was doing a picture at MGM the same time I was. When I saw her dancing, she moved so well that I thought, "God, I think I could work with her."

It all started with the drums. Jack Cole, who had a passion for the primitive aspects of dance, was choreographing *Les Girls*. During rehearsal he liked to have his dancers strip to the least possible clothing—"so I can see the body move"—and to express themselves to the rhythm of a wide variety of drums and other percussion instruments. Cole's rehearsal hall vibrated with jungle sounds.

Fred Astaire was rehearsing in the next hall. Ever conscious of rhythm, he was curious about the drums and couldn't resist poking his head in the door. "There's Fred Astaire," Cole whispered to his dancers. Before they could turn to look, Fred had vanished.

The routine continued for two weeks. Fred peeked inside the door to gaze at the young bodies gyrating to the pulsing beat of the drums. "There's that man again," the Cole dancers whispered. In a moment Fred was gone.

One day Fred was emboldened to enter the hall and converse in hushed tones with Jack Cole. "Who is that struggling young girl over there?" Fred asked. He indicated a slender, long-legged dancer in tiny bra and swim shorts.

"That's Barrie Chase," said Cole. "I took her out of the chorus to be my assistant. She's dancing-in for Kay Kendall in this picture."

"She's good," Fred mused. "Damn good."

After their strenuous day in the rehearsal hall, the Cole dancers unwound over refreshments in a bar across the alley from the MGM studio. Gene Kelly, Kay Kendall and others in the *Les Girls* cast sometimes joined them. One evening Barrie Chase was surprised when Fred Astaire entered the bar and sat down beside her. They began the easy conversation of dancers after rehearsal.

"Are you serious about dancing?" Astaire asked.

"Am I serious!" she replied. "You have to be insane to work as hard as we do."

Fred grinned. "You're right. I've never seen dancers work so hard."

He did something that surprised both of them: He asked her to dinner. They seemed to have nothing in common except their profession. He was fifty-eight and was acknowledged to be the paragon of sophistication. She was twenty-one, not long out of Beverly Hills High School. Her friends were mostly other dancers struggling to earn a living, as she was.

Yet their conversation came easily, and they soon found common ground. Both were shy, uncomfortable in crowds. Although their daily work was performed amid many, both cherished solitude. Each bore a private sorrow: For Fred it was the still inexplicable loss of Phyllis; for Barrie it was the shock of her parents' divorce. Her father was Borden Chase, writer of *Red River* and other important Westerns.

Astaire asked Jack Cole to release Barrie so she could appear in *Silk Stockings.* Along with Betty Uitti and Tybee Afra, she was to dance in the "Too Bad" number as temptress of the three Russians, Peter Lorre, Jules Munshin and Joseph Buloff. Fred asked Hermes Pan to help coach Barrie in the dance. Moving from the expressionistic style of Jack Cole, she had trouble adjusting to the controlled elegance of Pan-Astaire. But she learned.

Fred observed her progress with satisfaction. He was fascinated with her natural grace, her seeming inability to move awkwardly. Although ballet-trained, she had none of the constricted formality that Fred detested in the ballet. She could do anything that was required of her.

As the "Too Bad" number approached the filming stage, Barrie Chase was subjected to the ministrations of the studio system. Her face was covered with a heavy layer of makeup, her lashes were ladened with mascara. Sidney Guillaroff, the MGM hair stylist, surveyed her short tawny locks and decided she needed a large bun on the back of her head. When Barrie presented herself before Fred Astaire, he exploded.

"What the hell have they done to you!" he shouted. "What happened to your face? What happened to your hair? It's awful. Get Sidney Guillaroff down here right away!" The

Fred's Galatea, Barrie Chase, An Evening with Fred Astaire *(NBC)*

hair stylist arrived on the set, and Fred commanded, "Take that goddamned thing off her head!"

His fellow workers had never seen Fred Astaire so angry, and they realized that he had more than a casual interest in the young dancer Barrie Chase.

After the conclusion of *Silk Stockings*, Fred occasionally asked Barrie to dinner, always in out-the-way restaurants where he could achieve a degree of anonymity. Meanwhile she had a career to pursue. She had returned to the chorus at MGM and was unhappy there. A close friend and confidant was a young filmmaker named Stanley Kubrick, who had been placed under contract to MGM as the result of his small-budget movie *The Killing*. When she complained that she couldn't get interviews for acting roles, he told her: "If you don't want to dance in the chorus, don't do it. Quit and train yourself to be an actress."

She did. She enrolled with Jeff Corey for acting lessons, living on $33 a week unemployment insurance. One day she reported to a "cattle call" at 20th Century–Fox for young actresses to appear in a Pat Boone musical, *Mardi Gras*. The producer, Jerry Wald, had discovered another Corey student, Diane Varsi, and was impressed by Barrie. "Your cheekbones are just like Joan Crawford's," he said. She was signed to a Fox contract.

Barrie's dinner dates with Fred Astaire continued. One evening she mentioned she was having trouble getting tickets for the Moiseyev Dancers, the Russian troupe that was creating a sensation on its first American tour. "I'll get you tickets," Fred volunteered, "and I'll take you."

Barrie was surprised. She knew that Fred disliked going out in public and hated ballet. But the Moiseyev was not pure ballet. It combined traditional style with folk dance and modern choreography, and Fred was overwhelmed by the vibrant energy of the Russians. He became so excited that he stood up and cheered during the curtain calls.

Barrie was fascinated by Fred and amused by his eccentricities, yet curious as to why he should devote so much time and attention to a struggling movie dancer. Something was formulating in his mind, and it had to do with television.

FRED: Barrie was the inspiration for those specials that I did. I never danced in a picture with her, although she was in *Silk Stockings* in a small bit. She has a good sense of humor, is very sensitive and very stylish. She was always putting herself down, but if *you* ever tried to put her down—look out!

She knew what she was doing, but she was just a little shy about learning this and that and the other thing. When she got up and stepped on the floor, she was effective, just fine. The age difference didn't matter. At that point I was much older than Barrie, but there was never any question about the difference in our ages, because she just carried it off so beautifully.

I wasn't going to do the specials at all. I said, "I don't know who I can do them with." Then I found myself a dancer and I knew I could do it with her. She was new, she was great with me, and she clicked. When the Chrysler Corporation offered me three shows, one a year, I said, "Yeah, I can do it."

Fred didn't take Barrie into his confidence. One night at dinner he remarked that he was thinking of accepting one of the many offers he had received for television. What he had in mind was an all-dance show, no talk. "Would you like to do it with me?" he asked casually.

"Well—yes," she said. "But how can I? I'm tied up at Fox."

"I think I can take care of that."

Fred arranged for Barrie to be released from her studio contract. He still didn't tell her she would be his partner. "I think we'll work for a while," he suggested. "No chorus, just you and Pan and me."

Barrie Chase remembers: "We just moved around in a hall for a couple of weeks. I figured they were just getting the nerves out, and I was helping them. I kept thinking, 'I'm going to crush the best feet in the world!' He never did announce that I was going to be his partner on the show."

For the first time in his long career, Fred Astaire had

complete control of his own production. On the stage and in films, he had always been a hired performer. Although he always controlled his own dances, the rest of the production was in the hands of other people. For the television special he was executive producer, and every detail had the Astaire touch.

Fred interviewed producer-directors, asking them how they envisioned Astaire on television. Bud Yorkin, who had directed Martin and Lewis, Abbott and Costello, the Ritz Brothers and George Gobel shows, came up with the right answers: "I don't see you coming up over the horizon in top hat and tails singing 'I'm Putting on My Top Hat' or 'Night and Day.' I would start the show totally unexpectedly with a jazz band like Count Basie and build from there. I think you can handle a show yourself, at least the first time, without a guest star."

Yorkin's ideas corresponded to Fred's thinking. He emphatically did not want to repeat any of the signature dances of his films. He was repelled by the guest-star cliché of television variety shows. And he wanted to interpret some jazz. He had been overwhelmed when he listened to a "Muted Jazz" album by the Jonah Jones quartet. Jones' version of "St. James Infirmary Blues" seemed an ideal vehicle for a dance duet. He played the number for Barrie one night and told her: "We're going to do a TV show together, and you're going to use that silly little walk in the 'St. James Infirmary' number." He was always teasing her about her ballet-dancer's walk.

When Yorkin told the Chrysler and advertising agency people that Fred's guests would be Barrie Chase and Jonah Jones, they panicked. "We've got to have someone like Ricky Nelson," Yorkin was told, "someone to appeal to the teenagers." They remained adamant, and Yorkin flew to Detroit to plead his case before the Chrysler board of directors.

"If we can't do fifty-four minutes of Fred Astaire with no guest stars, then everybody's in trouble—you the sponsor, the television industry, the public," Yorkin argued. When the businessmen appeared unconvinced, he remarked, "I guess the next thing is for *you* to tell Fred Astaire that he isn't able to carry a television special without Ricky Nelson." No one was willing to take that step.

Barrie listened carefully to her mentor, but had a mind of her own (NBC).

"An Evening with Fred Astaire" proceeded as the star envisioned it. That meant seven weeks of dance rehearsals before work started in the studio. Working intensely with Fred for the first time, Barrie was amazed at his energy. She had gone to ballet class every day, and before rehearsing with Fred she always did her warm-up exercises. He had done no workouts, no dancing since *Silk Stockings* a year before. He started the television rehearsal with a brief run around the hall, shadow-boxing like a prizefighter. Then he was ready to work, and he continued long after Barrie was exhausted.

> FRED: Barrie was sometimes difficult, but they were all like that, all the girls when they were learning. They were afraid of me, too. At first when I took [Barrie's] hand it was so cold and clammy in one of the rehearsals for *Silk Stockings*. I said, "What's the matter with you?" She said, "Oh—I get nervous."
>
> She was often late. "The late Miss Chase," we used to call her. She didn't even seem to know it, she didn't think about, she didn't care who thought

about it, and that was *it*. And yet if you treated her like a star, she performed like a star. I said, "Okay, she's worth it, all the trouble you may have. We'll wait until she's ready, and then we'll get it."

That happens with a lot of them. You can't just do your thing and that's *it*. She worried about her hair, she worried about everything. Usually she was more on the dot for shooting than for rehearsals. She just wouldn't get there in time. She'd have to go and get some new shoes or something. I'd say, "Why didn't you get them yesterday!"

As always, he wanted his partner to look good. But this time he seemed more concerned than ever. Barrie Chase was the first unknown to dance with him, and he wanted his choice to be justified. He approved her costumes, makeup, hair styles, shoes (flat), camera angles. He listened to her opinions. He didn't always agree, but he listened.

> FRED: Sometimes you get [partners] who say, "I don't like it!" Barrie Chase was great for that. She'd say, [mimicking] "I don't know if I like it." I'd say, "*Do* it anyway, and stop kidding around!"
>
> There's a myth about people fighting. Women have been in tears many times working with me because they're trying very hard and maybe not getting to what we want to get. And they begin to cry. I always remember their saying, "You made me cry!" Well, it's true: Everybody cries. Including myself, trying to get some jobs done.

Astaire agreed with Yorkin that the show would be telecast live before an audience. No cue cards. No retakes. It would be done just like a Broadway show. There was a single compromise. Because of the exertion for Fred and Barrie and the need to make costume changes, two of the musical numbers were pretaped. One was the show's most important number, "St. James Infirmary Blues."

It was performed at the NBC studios in a single take. "Perfect!" said Yorkin. "Ideal!" agreed Hermes Pan. Everyone confirmed that the number couldn't have been improved. "How about you?" Fred asked Barrie. She shook her head. "I didn't think it was as good as it could be."

By this time Fred had taken off his costume and had covered himself in a terry-cloth robe. Nearing sixty, he seemed totally exhausted—"like a flower that wilts," Barrie recalls.

"Let her take a look at the tape," said Fred, who never liked to look at his dances immediately afterward. The tape was replayed on the monitor, and Yorkin and Pan again declared that it was superb.

"I don't like it," Barrie declared. Pan confided to her, "I don't think Fred can do it again." Indeed, Astaire seemed to bear the weight of all his years, and more.

"Okay, I'll look at it," Fred said wearily. He stared at the tape and decreed, "She's right, it just doesn't flow. We'll do it again." Within a few minutes he was back in costume, and he performed "St. James" with even greater spirit and energy.

Barrie Chase was Fred's last dancing partner. It was easy to see why Fred was entranced with her. In the specials she combined an aloof beauty with raw sensuality. Her superb body flowed with feline grace, and she remained cloaked in mystery, a vision who appeared every time Fred needed a dance partner.

Barrie's observations about Fred:

"He is always thinking about the dance. In rehearsal of one number we were missing a connector, a way to get from one part of the dance to another. The next morning he came in and said, 'You know that area that we couldn't get? It came to me last night. I got out of bed and worked it out.' A lot of people get ideas in bed, but how many get out of bed to work on them?

"On one show there was a set of footlights on the stage. I thought they looked attractive, but Fred ordered them taken away. I asked him why. 'Because they can't see the feet,' he said.

"I wore nude-color shoes to continue the line and make my legs appear longer. When Fred asked why I didn't wear colored shoes, I told him. 'I do the opposite,' he said. 'I wear two-tone shoes or different-colored socks to call attention to my feet.'

"Fred moves like an animal—no false moves. You know

At the Emmys with his daughter and mother

how animals appear in slow-motion movies, their movements perfectly natural? That's Fred.

"No angle can be wrong, everything is planned to perfection beforehand. The hands must always be at the right level, and when your hands are supposed to join, you'd better do it at precisely the right moment.

"He's an incredible partner. He does everything exactly the way it's supposed to be done, and you can count on it. You can feel his strength. When you're let down and drained, he is very supportive. He lifts you with his energy.

"He totally inspires you. Even during a take he will talk under his breath: 'Now you're dancing!' or 'Go, girl, go!' or just a little sound, like 'Ummphh.'

"There is absolutely no ad-libbing or improvisation in the steps. The way the dance is rehearsed is the way it's performed. He always told me, 'Do it the way you're going to do it onstage,' but I always held back. He never did. Technically there was no change from his rehearsal, but the performance gave an added quality: the live orchestra, the sound surrounding you, the lights, the set, the people watching. That made it something extra."

One custom Fred could not sell Barrie on: his luncheon noodle soup. He induced her to try it, and she found it murky and forbidding. "No, thanks," she replied whenever he offered the soup again.

> FRED: She didn't like the soup, but I always did, because I didn't eat any lunch. I had soup and a cracker or something.
>
> I don't know many dancers who can eat a big meal during the day. Usually I didn't care about breakfast. I never was a big eater, and I think that's good advice to anybody: Be careful you don't eat too much all your life, and you'll be better off.
>
> I know that Leslie Caron used to eat a big lunch. A couple of steaks, somebody told me. I remember I asked her how she did it. She said, "I'm very hungry."

Often after rehearsals, Fred would invite Barrie, Pan and others in the company to his house for drinks. He'd serve the orders and make his own cocktail, a bourbon old-fashioned, which he mixed with great ceremony. For a snack, he'd open a can of macadamia nuts and shake out four or five for each guest. Finally Barrie said, "Fred, could I have a few more? I've been working all day!" He replied with a smile, "That's all you get. We don't want you to get fat."

Show time: October 17, 1958.

Bud Yorkin remembers the last moments before the broadcast: "The opening shot of the show was a close-up of his feet, then the camera was to pull back. I told the stage manager, 'Tell Fred it's ten seconds before we go on the air.' His feet were on the monitor, and I saw him move in and straighten his shoelaces. Here we were ready to go on the air live, the camera was on his feet, and he checked his shoelaces! Most people would be worried about their lines. Fred had such a sense of perfection that he was worried that his shoelaces wouldn't be right for the close-up."

The show proceeded with remarkable smoothness, not a cue missed. Toward the end of the hour, Yorkin realized that the running time was fifteen seconds too long. He instructed the orchestra leader, David Rose, to speed up the tempo for Fred's medley, the final number. "Oh, I can't do that, it'll make Fred angry," said Rose. Because Fred was so insistent on the proper tempo, Rose had timed the score down to the second. "You gotta do it," said Yorkin. Rose increased the tempo to pick up the fifteen seconds and was rewarded with an annoyed look from Fred.

The critical response to *An Evening with Fred Astaire* was overwhelming. Jack Gould in *The New York Times* wrote that Astaire "swept all before him in a tour de force of artistry and personality. The home screen was bathed in the glow of true creative theater as the dancer did one number after another for which any Broadway producer would give his eyeteeth. . . . Mr. Astaire and his colleagues have set a new standard for musical TV. By this time Western Union should be limp from delivering congratulatory telegrams." Gould also accorded the ultimate tribute to Fred's partner: in the "St. James Infirmary" number, "Miss Chase certainly held her own with the master."

Indeed, Fred was deluged with telegrams from admirers all over the country, and he was telephoned by Irving Berlin, Cole Porter, Ira Gershwin and dozens of other longtime friends. Astonishingly, the show drew a disappointing rating, causing some Detroit executives to mutter, "We shoulda got Ricky Nelson after all."

When the Television Academy Awards were presented the following May, *An Evening with Fred Astaire* received a phenomenal nine Emmys. The awards became embroiled in controversy when Ed Sullivan, whose variety show had been passed over by the Academy, demanded that the ballots be impounded and disclosed to the public. "How could Fred Astaire win as best actor over such nominees as Paul Muni, Rod Steiger, Mickey Rooney and Christopher Plummer?" demanded Sullivan.

Sullivan was accused of sour grapes by Astaire supporters, who argued that it didn't matter whether he acted or danced; he was still the best actor of the year. Astaire agreed with Sullivan that there might have been confusion over the category, and he offered to return the statuette, "as I do not wish to see the values of the Television Academy Awards impaired in any way." His offer was declined, and the controversy soon ended.

An Evening with Fred Astaire was vindicated when it was rerun on NBC in the spring. The show drew one of the biggest ratings of the 1958–59 season.

8

A New Career

If I had to pick one of [Astaire's]
virtues as the most important in his rise
to the top, I would choose his sense of
perfection. It shines through all his work;
there is never a trace of effort, and that
is because he had devoted infinite patience
to rehearsing and perfecting every detail.
His technique is astounding, yet everything
is accomplished with the air of someone
sauntering through the park on a spring
morning.

—*Margot Fonteyn,* The Magic of Dance

Noel Coward supplied the title for Fred Astaire's auto-biography. When Fred confessed that he didn't know what to name the book, Coward replied, "Call it *Steps in Time*, and don't forget that, now."

Nearing sixty and still unreconciled to the loss of Phyllis, Fred had decided to write his life story. He realized his limitations as a writer, and so he enlisted the services of Cameron Shipp, an amiable, competent veteran of magazines and studio publicity departments who had helped write the memoirs of Lionel Barrymore, Billie Burke and Mack Sennett. Shipp seemed the ideal collaborator, but, as with the dance, Fred needed to control his own destiny.

> FRED: I wrote my book with Cameron Shipp, starting out "as told to." But I didn't sound the way I wanted it to, so I said, "Let me write it myself." I wrote it and I let him edit my copy.
>
> The book was for Harper and Brothers and they always were asking, "Isn't there something we can 'spike' in this story?"
>
> But there *isn't*, you see. To me it's not a dull story, because all I was trying to do was make good all the time. And do the act, that's all.

Steps in Time was well received, even drawing praise from *The New Yorker*, customarily snooty about anything Hollywood. The book sounds like Fred: reticent, self-effacing, reluctant to criticize anyone except himself.

Hermes Pan commented: "That's the trouble with Fred: Everyone thinks of him as Mr. Nice Guy, and he tries to live up to that reputation by not saying anything bad about anybody. Some of the people in his book gave him some pretty rough times, and vice versa. If he were as nice and simple as he likes to make out he is, he'd never have been on top for so many years."

Oscar Levant: ". . . when he was on the Jack Paar show, Fred demonstrated gentlemanliness beyond the call of duty. Paar

Fred during rehearsal for a television special

asked, 'Who's older, you or your sister?' Without hesitating for a second, Fred said that he was. The truth is that Adele is his senior. I thought that was gallant."

Stanley Kramer was casting *On the Beach,* a film based on the Nevil Shute doomsday novel, which Kramer planned to photograph in Australia. Gregory Peck and Ava Gardner would play the leading couple, Anthony Perkins and a newcomer, Donna Anderson, the younger romance. For the role of the cynical British atomic scientist, Kramer had considered Alec Guinness or Ralph Richardson. Then one evening the producer-director's wife Ann was watching an old Astaire musical on television.

"There's your scientist," she told her husband.

"You're crazy," he replied. After a few moments, he shouted, "By God, you're right!"

> FRED: When Stanley Kramer spoke to me about it, I said to him, "Do you really want me to do this? Why did you pick me out?" He said, "I just could see you as this character." It was kind of a silly question on my part. But it was a big, important drama with a socko drama theme. It was the kind of thing that caused everyone to ask, "Why are you doing that?" I said, "I'm doing it because it looks like a picture that might get a lot of attention, and I love to do dramatic work anyway."

In the spring of 1959, Fred departed from California for the long flight to Australia. He found himself sitting next to Donna Anderson, Kramer's nineteen-year-old discovery, who admitted she was terrified on her first trip out of the United States. She added, "My great-grandmother told me not to worry, that Mr. Astaire would take care of me."

Fred grimaced. "Your *great*-grandmother! Couldn't you at least have said your grandmother?"

As soon as he arrived in Melbourne, Fred began work on his role. Kramer had worried about removing all indications of Astaire the dancer and even considered weighting Fred's legs to eliminate his inimitable walk. But that didn't prove necessary. Fred developed his own characterization, even mussing his toupée.

Fred had done drunk scenes before, but always in a comedic vein. *On the Beach* called for him to play a dramatic scene as a drunk, and he decided to have a few slugs of bourbon first. Since bourbon whiskey was virtually unknown in Australia, Kramer had some flown in from America.

Gregory Peck recalls working with Astaire: "He wanted every move set—the lighting of a cigarette, the body language, every gesture and movement. All good actors do. I like rehearsal myself, and Fred and I went over our scenes

The first dramatic role: with Gregory Peck in On the Beach *(United Artists)*

together in our spare time. The more rehearsal, the more effortless it seems. 'A scene must look as if it's being done for the first time,' Fred said."

Many of the Americans in the *On the Beach* company found life in Melbourne unbearably dull. A cub reporter from the Melbourne *Argus,* Jerry Pam, asked Ava Gardner what she was doing in Australia. "I'm making a picture about the end of the world, and this is the place to do it."

Astaire had no trouble keeping occupied. He planned his sixtieth birthday party at the major restaurant, Maxime's, inviting company principals for a dinner, for which he selected every course, as well as pink champagne. He visited Peck and his family at the Victorian mansion rented for them on the outskirts of the city.

"On his days off Fred often went shopping in the stores incognito," says Peck. "Once he proudly displayed a pair of brown suede shoes he had found. He could spend hours browsing through dime stores and hardware stores, buying pencil sharpeners and a variety of gadgets. All his life he had been insulated by his celebrity, and he enjoyed being among folks, unrecognized and unbothered.

"Fred and I sometimes sneaked off to the dog races. The track was a semi-shabby place where the lowlife of Melbourne congregated, and Fred enjoyed the raffishness of it. Fred wore a trenchcoat and porkpie hat, and he darted about unnoticed. I wore dark glasses, hat and trenchcoat, but eventually I was spotted. While I signed autographs, Fred disappeared. I was amazed at what a fast mover he was. After the races, he and I met at the gate and went home."

Astaire's anonymity in Australia was shattered when the *On the Beach* company was bidden to a reception on board the aircraft carrier *Melbourne,* which was being used in the movie. "I can't go," Fred complained, "I'll have to dance with four hundred officers' wives." But he did go, and he did dance with four hundred officers' wives, who lined up for a few moments in the arms of Fred Astaire. Fred, who detested social dancing, endured a simple foxtrot with each of them, surviving a three-hour ordeal.

During his visit to Australia, Fred bought a couple of racehorses. One of them showed considerable promise but lacked a name, and Fred submitted several that were rejected by the Australian track authorities. Finally, Fred told his trainer, "Call it anything." The horse Anything had a modest career on the Australian tracks.

Fred returned to the loneliness of the Summit Drive house, stirring with the ever-present memories of Phyllis. Both Peter and young Fred were married now, and Ava was in high school. Fred decided he needed to leave the place that Phyllis had planned and supervised, and in 1960 he built a new house a few blocks down the hill on San Ysidro Drive.

No longer rushing from one movie to another, Fred was able to devote time to his daughter. He attended her school functions, and on Ava's summer vacations, they traveled the world—to Hong Kong and Japan, to France and England. In London they were the house guests of Jock Whitney, United States Ambassador.

At the Goodwood racetrack, Fred and Ava were invited to join Queen Elizabeth in the royal box. Fred hadn't seen her since she was a little girl. When he remarked that he had long ago danced with the Queen's mother, Elizabeth corrected: "You mean *she* danced with *you!*"

Ann Astaire divided her time between Fred and Adele. Now in her eighties, Mrs. Astaire remained a quiet but vital presence in Fred's life. She could still voice her opinions in unmistakable terms. "I guess I got my temper from her," Fred remarked.

As Hollywood's most eligible widower, Fred was sought out by famous, attractive women. During a party at the home of David O. Selznick and Jennifer Jones, a famous star was obviously on the make for Fred. Distressed by her attentions, he asked one of the other guests to dance—Ginger Rogers. To the delight of the others, Fred and Ginger glided over the floor, chatting amiably. By the time the dance ended, Fred's pursuer had given up her chase.

The only woman in Fred's life was Barrie Chase. He continued taking her to intimate restaurants for dinner.

"During the first year or year and a half while we were dating, he never invited me for dinner at his house," she remembers. "It was always for cocktails. I could see the German maid coming in and out, and obviously dinner was ready. But Fred never asked me to stay. Why? I'll tell you why. Because he's Fred."

Fred, who had sold his share in the dance studios, continued his two major interests: horses and golf. He maintained his fascination for police work and crime, especially when he visited New York. There he'd call a friend, detective Jim McGee, and they'd go to the morgue or the daily lineup.

In New York, he often sat for hours in the quiet of St. Bartholomew's Episcopal Church on Park Avenue. He explained to interviewer Bill Davidson: "I find great comfort in that magnificent church in the midst of the hurly-burly of the city. I think of everything there—my life, my work, the hidden meaning of the good and bad things that have happened to me. I come out spiritually refreshed. It often helps me to go on." In Beverly Hills, he spent long hours of contemplation at his parish church, All Saints', on Santa Monica Boulevard.

Unlike many stars in postwar Hollywood, Fred Astaire did not become involved in politics. He was a union man; he had been a founder of the Screen Actors' Guild in the early 1930s. His political inclination was generally conservative, but he never expressed his feelings in public and rarely in private. Politics, and most politicians, bored him. Only once did he deviate from non-participation. He gave support to Dwight Eisenhower in his candidacy for President.

> FRED: I knew Ike a bit, and when he came through here on the [campaign] train I went down to see him. I knew Mamie, and I had entertained Ike, too, in France during World War II. I was on one of the things for USO. It was toward the end of the war, but they were still bombing.
>
> Later on I played golf with him, and he was a different man. He was sick and it was kinda hard for him to remember things. He was so grouchy when

he was playing golf; that meant more to him than all his service in the war. "I can't hit anything today, I don't know why," he complained.

I don't like anything to do with [politics] because too many people jump on you and use you too many ways. I'm not cut out for that. Some people can do it, I just can't. I'm not a politician.

For his second television special, Fred Astaire devoted extra care, realizing he had to meet people's expectations after the first one. He planned for three months, rehearsed seven weeks before taping. The first show was performed before an audience with an orchestra in the studio, Fred reasoning that television required such immediacy. It really didn't matter, he concluded, and the second special was taped with prerecorded music and no audience. As to cue cards: "I won't allow them on the stage; they make a performance look phony."

I interviewed him at the time of *Another Evening with Fred Astaire,* and his remarks reflected the Astaire philosophy: "I'm not trying to top myself, and I never have. I never look back, except to have an occasional regret. That's unavoidable, I'm afraid. I saw one of my pictures on television the other night, and I thought at a couple of places, 'Gee, why didn't I do that differently?'

"Performers are always talking about 'the good old days.' Well, the good old days weren't that good. With a few exceptions, the movies today are much better than they used to be. The same goes for the stage. I have never seen a better musical than *My Fair Lady.* It's simply terrific. And there are many other modern shows that top the old-time productions."

Fred admitted that the movie musical was in a slump. No studio had submitted one to him, and he doubted if he would make another musical. He was firm on one matter: "I am certainly not going to chase any girls. I'm beyond the girl-chasing stage, and I only did it in a couple of pictures, anyway. I simply won't do a movie that calls for romance.

"I'm not sure the public would accept me in a musical

anymore, because of that silly dwelling on age. It has reached the ridiculous point where every writer has to include it in his story. I think it's unfair. I never think about age, and I don't see why they should make such a big thing about it. You hear a television commentator talking about a baseball player who is 'an aging thirty-nine.' But the commentator never admits that he is fifty-six. There ought to be a rule."

Fred at sixty astounded critics and television viewers with his undiminished energy and talent. For the third and final show of the annual series for Chrysler, he realized a longtime ambition to dance to the band of Count Basie. He also learned that the swing pianist played to his own tune.

When they first discussed the show, Fred suggested, "You just play and I'll dance." Basie countered, "No, no, no, you dance and I'll play." He agreed to make the show in July on his vacation.

Fred recounted: "Comes July and I hear that Basie is on his way, his plane has landed, he's due at rehearsal. But he didn't show up. He got off the plane and went right to the racetrack. Next morning he turned up. 'Well, man,' he said, 'I'm right out o' money. Can you slip me five hundred?'

"Basie came to rehearsal three times, but we had trouble getting him to buckle down to his piano. He was always way out: 'Yeah, man!' He left to go on tour.

"Then it came time for the show. I had him in the slot for a day's rehearsal and then the final taping. Basie returns to Hollywood but doesn't show up. He went straight to the Del Mar racetrack. Next day he appeared. He needed five hundred dollars. I gave it to him so now he's in to me for a thousand. 'Don't tell my manager,' he warned me. 'Take it out of my check.' I didn't tell his manager, but he must have found out about about it when he collected what was left of Basie's fee."

Fred also discovered on the third show that his Galatea was not as malleable as he would have preferred. When he and Barrie Chase started to rehearse the "Oh, You Beautiful Doll" number, she was strangely unresponsive. He demonstrated a few steps, and she repeated them dispiritedly. Finally he exploded, "What the hell's the matter with you?"

"I can't do it!" she cried. "I don't know who I am!"

"I'll tell you who you are!" Fred shouted back. "You're Barrie Chase! Now do it!" She did it.

Barrie recalls: "Fred always listened to what you had to say and thought about it, then made up his own mind. But he could also be obstinate. When he didn't *want* to understand what you had to say, he didn't understand.

"For instance, I never talked on any of the shows. Fred didn't want me to. When we rehearsed the good-night for the last show, I said, 'I think I should say something. Why should I just stand here looking dumb?' He said, 'Because I *want* you to stand there and say nothing.' We argued, and I walked off. Herb Ross [the director] went after me and tried to reason with me. Fred never budged. I walked back."

Astaire Time, which was broadcast September 28, 1960, and won two Emmys, was the last of the Chrysler specials.

"I've had fun doing television," Fred told me at the time. "It gave me a chance to do some things I could never do in films. Like dancing to Count Basie, and doing a number on 'Miss Otis Regrets,' and a routine where I improvised seventy-five percent of the dance. I wouldn't say I have done everything I wanted to do. But I think I will let television go for a while. I'd like to devote myself to movies before I get too decrepit to do them anymore."

Fred returned to Paramount for a straight acting role in *The Pleasure of His Company.* He had only one dance, a brief spin around the floor with Lilli Palmer to the music of "Lover," by Richard Rodgers and Lorenz Hart.

The film was based on the Broadway success by Cornelia Otis Skinner and Samuel Taylor. Cyril Ritchard had created the role of the errant playboy father who returns and tries to upset his daughter's marriage. Astaire saw the play in New York, and I recall his confiding that he couldn't understand why Ritchard played the role in such a florid manner.

George Seaton directed *The Pleasure of His Company* with a cast that included Debbie Reynolds as the daughter, Lilli Palmer as the playboy's ex-wife, Gary Merrill as her second husband, and Tab Hunter as the bridegroom. Miss Palmer was terrified by the prospect of dancing with Fred Astaire, and she asked if the scene had to be played on the parquet floor of the living room.

"Yes, it must," the director replied. "We need the music, for one thing. For another, we're grateful for every chance to show Fred dancing. Surely you can do a little something. Anybody can dance with Fred Astaire!"

She recalled: "When the dreaded moment came, and Fred, according to the script, had to grab me and 'sweep me off my feet,' he certainly swept me off in a wonderfully elegant gesture, but I landed squarely on both of his feet, stopping him dead in his tracks. 'Good Lord!' said he, amazed. 'I warned you!' said I, feeling a certain satisfaction that I had been able to pin down the great Astaire, if only for a moment. The second time he swept me off, he never allowed me to land at all and I just hung suspended in his arms, trying to remember my lines while bereft of the support of terra firma."

The Pleasure of His Company was two weeks away from completion when the Screen Actors' Guild called a strike against the film companies. All production was shut down.

> FRED: The strike meant that we had to cease and pick it up six months later or something. It worried me to death, because it's very hard to get the thing back together again. Some of the people might not be available at a later time.
>
> When the strike was on, I called Ronnie [Reagan] on the phone—he was head of the Guild. I said, "Gee, Ronnie, isn't there anything we can do about this? This [film] is going well, and to break it up in halves . . ." He said, "There's absolutely nothing I can do. There's no way I can do anything about it." I've thought since then that he must have to say that to a lot of people.
>
> I used to run into Ronnie a lot when I was making my anthology show and he was on "G.E. Theater" at Universal. He's not there anymore, did you know?

The strike was settled after several weeks, then Seaton had to start *The Counterfeit Traitor* with Lilli and William Holden in Germany. When *The Pleasure of His Company* finally

Fred danced briefly with Debbie Reynolds in The Pleasure of His Company, *also with Lilli Palmer (Paramount).*

returned to production, Fred and Lilli Palmer resumed a kissing scene they had started six months before. The film was released in May of 1961 and had only a modest success.

> FRED: I think the vehicle was a good one, but I think they tried to do something to it that didn't do it any good.
> The part I played was nicknamed Polo, and his daughter is getting married, so he comes back to see her. He couldn't take it that she was going to marry this guy, no matter who he was. [Polo] was never fond of the wife that he left. They had a point of making him sorry that he left, and that weakened the thing. I can remember their asking me to do a scene in which I looked a little forlorn about having to go away from my ex-wife. Well, Polo didn't give a hoot for his ex-wife. The whole show was about that, practically.
> Another thing, Lilli Palmer was a good-looking woman. She was almost too good-looking, because on the stage [the character] was less attractive. In the play, Polo came back to make love to her more to put her down than take her on. When the same scene occurred with Lilli in the picture, they got over the idea that he wished he was back. Right there the piece began to fall apart.

In 1961, Astaire played a minor role in *The Notorious Landlady* at Columbia. The film was a disappointment to him, but making it with Jack Lemmon, Kim Novak and Richard Quine, who directed, was highly enjoyable. "Any time you work with Jack Lemmon it's a blast," says Fred.

With movie roles scarce, Astaire maintained his presence in television. From 1961 to 1963 he was the host and occasional star of "Alcoa Premiere," an anthology series of remarkable quality. Lee Marvin and Arthur Kennedy appeared in the first drama, which concerned the treatment of mentally disturbed war veterans. Other stars in the series included James Stewart, Cliff Robertson, Shelley Winters, Charlton Heston and Telly Savalas. Astaire's most memorable role came in *Mr. Lucifer* opposite Elizabeth Montgomery. He portrayed the devil in six different disguises.

Fred played a diplomat with Kim Novak in the nonmusical Notorious Landlady *(Columbia).*

Fred continued dancing with Barrie Chase. They appeared together in *Think Pretty,* a musical for "Bob Hope's Chrysler Theater," and on the "Hollywood Palace" variety show. Astaire also appeared as a pool hustler in a four-part show for "Dr. Kildare" and required no double for the trick shots on the pool table.

Finian's Rainbow had been a smash hit on Broadway from its opening on January 10, 1947. The score was packed with memorable songs: "How Are Things in Glocca Morra?" "If This Isn't Love," "Old Devil Moon," "When I'm Not Near the Girl I Love," "Look to the Rainbow." The show ran 725 performances in New York, but it was the only major musical of the postwar era that never made it to the screen. Producers were leery of its indictment of U.S. racism as well as its elements of fantasy—leprechauns, pots of gold, et cetera. Fantasy was deemed a considerable risk in movies.

Finally, in 1968, Warner Brothers decided to undertake *Finian's Rainbow*. It was a different Warner Brothers from the one that Jack L. Warner had ruled for three decades. Warner had sold out the previous year to Seven Arts Productions, which had acquired its wealth from selling old movies to television. The new administration had swept out the veteran studio retainers and brought in young talent. One of them was Francis Ford Coppola, who had directed one film, *You're a Big Boy Now,* which had been the basis for his master's degree from the film school at UCLA.

The film script was adapted by the original authors of *Finian's Rainbow,* E. Y. Harburg and Fred Saidy. The leading roles were assigned to a pair of performers from the popular music scene in England, Petula Clark and Tommy Steele. Fred Astaire was cast as Finian, the Irishman who emigrates to the Deep South with his daughter.

> FRED: [Coppola] had never done a musical before, and he was quick to tell us that. I had a good time with Francis and enjoyed him as a director, because I knew he was a talented guy. I don't believe he was quite "up" at that point to what musicals needed. Technically he was always trying to change the way the sound was being picked up and had to redo a lot of it.
>
> [*Finian's*] was a tough thing to do, and you could see why it had never been made into a picture. The Broadway musical was a big hit. Somebody should have found some way to do it, but I think they finally found out they couldn't adapt it properly. I always

thought that the daughter, Petula Clark, and I
should have been seen in Ireland for about five or
ten minutes in the early part of the show. Then they
could have seen us make the trip across. We weren't
allowed to shoot in Ireland—"We can't afford to
spend the money." I thought, "Jesus, Warner
Brother can't afford to spend the money?" I don't
think Warner Brothers ever wanted to do the damn
picture. . . .

At one point they didn't want Finian to dance,
because he hadn't danced in the stage version. That's
the kind of thinking that was going on. I said, "Wait
a minute, for God's sake. If I don't do a dance, the
people will throw rocks at this thing. They'll say,
'What's the matter with him—is he sick or what?'"

Fred's reasoning prevailed, and he took part in three
numbers, "Look to the Rainbow," "If This Isn't Love" and
"When the Idle Poor Become the Idle Rich." Hermes Pan
directed the dances, one of them a haystack number which
he described as a "gutbuster." Fred slid down ropes and
leaped about astoundingly. He was sixty-eight years old.

"Thank heaven I don't have any of those romantic numbers to do," he told me on the back lot of Warner Brothers
studio, where all of *Finian's Rainbow* was filmed. "They take
so long to rehearse, and it's murder thinking up new ideas."

Fred played Finian with an Irish brogue; but Coppola
wasn't satisfied with the disguise. He sent an emissary to
Hermes Pan to suggest, "Do you suppose you could ask Fred
to be less—uh, less like Fred Astaire?"

Warner Brothers–Seven Arts released *Finian's Ranbow* as
a road show, in first-class theaters with reserved seats and
twice-daily performances.

FRED: I think *Finian's* missed what it could have
been. They made a road show out of it, one of the
last road shows of the movies. That in itself I never
wanted them to do. I said, "God, a movie is a movie,

Fred danced at sixty-eight in Finian's Rainbow *(Warner Bros.).*

A New Career 275

don't make a reserved-seat attraction everywhere and phony it up to the point where everybody can criticize it more than it deserves." It got some favorable notices some places, but most of them found some kind of fault with it. . . .

I don't regret having done it, and I've had a lot of favorable mail about it over the years. It's the kind of thing that'll be played back again, and a certain amount of people, seeing it on television again and not realizing it's an old picture, will start writing fan mail again. . . .

I usually love every movie I'm doing. The only one I can remember being discouraged about was 'way back. The director was hard to work with—I hate to bring up his name, he's dead now. I remember saying about that picture that it was kind of a chore.

Usually I think, "This is the best thing I've ever done so far." Then you find out later that it *isn't* the best thing so far. So you say, "Jesus, you'd better make the next one better."

The final dance.

The Fred Astaire Show, the fourth of his one-hour television musicals, was presented on the NBC network on February 7, 1968. Fred was nearing sixty-nine. When I saw him in the rehearsal hall, he was drinking a mug of stout instead of his noodle soup. "Old dancers never die," he cracked wearily, "they just sweat away."

He continued: "I like to dance, but it's such damned hard work. At least it is the way I do it. I can't do things the easy way. I figure if I'm going to do something, it's got to be the best I know how. Otherwise there's no point in doing it. Oh, I know how they usually do dances on television. They say, 'Let's have a soft-shoe number here,' then they get a line of six girls and throw a routine together. That's the way it looks: thrown together.

"You may not like my show, but at least you can't say it's put on haphazardly. Everything is designed to flow together.

No flowery introductions, no idle chitchat. I hate that sort of thing, and I'm terrible at it." Barrie Chase returned to dance with him, and Fred had another band that excited him, Sergio Mendes and Brasil '68. For the first time, Fred featured guest stars, Paul Simon and Art Garfunkel.

Fred announced at the outset of *The Fred Astaire Show* that he did not plan to work as hard as he had done on the three earlier specials. He inevitably went over the time he allotted himself.

"But he didn't rehearse as much, he didn't spend as much time on the floor as he had in the previous shows," Barrie Chase recalls. "I never thought of Fred in terms of age, even though there were thirty-four years between us, and I never slowed down for him. But I knew on the last show that I had to do certain things technically to make it look good."

Again, with *The Fred Astaire Show,* he didn't dwell on nostalgia. When he performed the "Top Hat" number, it was a rock version, complete with the latest steps. The show drew the customary critical raves that greeted Astaire specials, and Fred realized it was his last.

> FRED: I worked very hard up into the age of seventy. I decided then I wasn't going to do it anymore. I didn't have any ill effects at all, but I decided I'd get sensible and tail off.

The Midas Run seemed at the outset to be a worthwhile venture. It was a caper movie, in which Fred would play a highly respectable British intelligence officer who masterminds a gold-bullion heist, then is required to capture the thieves. Raymond Stross was producing the film with a cast that included his wife, Anne Heywood, Richard Crenna, Roddy McDowall, Cesar Romero and Ralph Richardson. Locations were filmed in Venice and Florence, and Fred, Jr., and Ava were able to visit Fred. Young Fred even played a small role in the film.

The Midas Run filming was far from serene. The director, Alf Kjellin, recalls: "We had a British and Italian crew,

With Anne Heywood in the Midas Run *location*

and they were always fighting. The actors were constantly complaining about each other. The producer wanted his wife undressed as much as possible. Fred Astaire was the only one who never complained."

> FRED: It was a happy experience making [*The Midas Run*]. We were in Italy, and it's fun working in a foreign country. It's sometimes difficult if the crowds get in the street and hang around. But if you're doing a film about Paris, you ought to be in Paris, which we were for *Funny Face*. The same with *Midas* and Italy.
>
> The producer had just had a successful picture [*The Fox*] and he sort of got carried away. . . . They got the love interest into it, and there were a couple of nude bedroom scenes. At that point they were a little too new, and I got some mail saying, "How can you be in a picture like that?" Well, jeez, I wasn't even there when they shot the scenes. Nothing bores me more than that kind of thing, anyway.

In 1969 and 1970, Astaire appeared in several episodes of "It Takes a Thief," a television series starring Robert Wagner. They played father and son, elegant retired thieves who practiced their former profession in the service of a secret government agency. The Astaire-Wagner relationship proved immensely likable, the best element of the series.

The Over-the-Hill-Gang Rides Again was a 1970 television movie that cast Astaire, Walter Brennan, Andy Devine, Chill Wills and Edgar Buchanan as aging westerners saving a town from desperadoes.

> FRED: That was the first cowboy I played. Well, not a cowboy, but a westerner. I had a good drunk scene in it.
>
> Walter played my sidekick in *Castles*, so I knew him very well from those days. We always got along so well, we'd clown around, kid around. He said to me, "Is this plot any good? What's this story about?" I said, "What do you mean?" He said, "Oh, I don't read scripts." I said, "I heard that you use [cue] cards." He said, "Yes, I use cards; is this a good story?" I said, "I thought it looked fine." He said, "Good, good."
>
> He had cards all over the place. I'm seeing his

Fred appeared in a four-part TV drama for the "Dr. Kildare" series playing a pool shark, an easy role for him (NBC).

Fred's only western: **The Over-the-Hill-Gang Rides Again,** *with Walter Brennan, Chill Wills, Andy Devine, Edgar Buchanan (ABC)*

Dancing at the Oscars, 1969 (Academy of Motion Pictures Arts and Sciences)

cards and saying my lines. . . . He'd say to me the next day, "What kind of a scene have we got today?" I said, "Pretty good." He said, "Well, it had better be," and he'd look at his cards and say, "All right, ready."

He had to use cards; he was doing so many shows that it was impossible to learn all those lines. I didn't use cards on that show, but I've found it helpful since then. When you're stuck at the last minute with five pages to learn, you can't do it, unless you're a newcomer.

Fred and Gene meet again at the train shed for That's Entertainment *(MGM).*

Fred played one of the star hosts in the highly successful 1974 *That's Entertainment,* a compilation of numbers from MGM musicals. His segment offered a vivid contrast of the glory that had been MGM and the decay into which it had fallen. Fred's introduction was filmed in the old train shed on Lot 2, as he walked alongside railroads cars that were tattered and paintless. That was followed by the scene from *The Band Wagon* of twenty years before, with Fred strolling along the fresh, glistening train as he sang "By Myself."

The Astaire art dominated the many treasures of *That's Entertainment.* The classic duets were presented: with Eleanor Powell in "Begin the Beguine"; with Ginger in "They Can't Take That Away from Me"; with Cyd in "Dancing in the Dark"; with Jack Buchanan in "I Guess I'll Have to Change My Plan." Even more impressive was Fred's solo virtuosity in the gravity-defying "You're All the World to Me," the magical "Shoes with Wings On," and the hat-rack dance of *Royal Wedding.*

In *The Towering Inferno* (1975), Astaire had the most dramatic role of his film career, playing a con man trapped amid hotel guests in a high-rise holocaust. The film marked the high point in the disaster-movie cycle perfected by Irwin Allen, who produced *The Towering Inferno* as a 20th Century–Fox–Warner Brothers joint venture. The cast was impressive: Steve McQueen, Paul Newman, William Holden, Faye Dunaway, Astaire, Susan Blakely, Richard Chamberlain, Jennifer Jones, Robert Wagner, O. J. Simpson, Robert Vaughn.

> FRED: *Towering Inferno* was a good cameo. If you're going to do a cameo, that was a good one to do, because it stood out. The other guys in the picture said, "Hey, I wish I had that part."
>
> I didn't have too many things to do, but apparently the rushes were coming through pretty good. It was strong stuff, and Steve McQueen said, "What the hell are you doin'? Cut that out! I saw something good, wait a minute, hold it!" [Laughing.] That kind of thing. I said, "Was it any good?" He said, "Oh, well, yeah"—just kidding me. I knew right away there was something good, so I went to the rushes.

He was a great guy, Steve. He was a *deep* son of a gun. How unfortunate that he's no longer around, because he enjoyed himself while he was alive. He had a rough early life, I've heard. He was tough, and a bloody good actor when he was right. Just when he was blossoming right, his health went bad.

Paul [Newman] is a rock. Bill [Holden] had been away, and I hadn't seen him for a while. It was great to work with those guys, I enjoyed that. When you're in the middle of a group with good stuff going on, it's fun.

I like to get the job done and spend all my time and thoughts and throw myself into it and not be on anything else at the time. I think that's the secret of most people who are successful: They dedicate themselves to that thing and don't let anyone gnaw at them. If you're going to quarrel with somebody about something, make it be worthwhile quarreling.

The Towering Inferno was the kind of commercial film that did not evoke critical praise, but many reviewers commended Astaire's restrained performance as a scoundrel who finds his heroism in the face of death. When the Academy Award nominations for 1974 were announced, Fred Astaire was among the five named for supporting actor. Others were Jeff Bridges for *Thunderbolt and Lightfoot* and three actors from *The Godfather, Part II:* Robert De Niro, Michael V. Gazzo and Lee Strasberg. Fred thought the winner would be Jeff Bridges.

At the award ceremonies on April 8, 1975, in the Los Angeles Music Center, Fred found himself seated next to Francis Ford Coppola, director of *Finian's Rainbow.* It was a grand evening for Coppola, who won Oscars for co-writing, directing and producing the best picture, *The Godfather, Part II.*

The winner for best supporting actor: Robert De Niro. Coppola turned to Astaire and said, "I'm sorry." Fred refused to be distressed. "It's a great compliment to be one of the five," he replied.

The success of *That's Entertainment* prompted MGM to attempt a sequel. Saul Chaplin and Daniel Melnick became the producers, and Gene Kelly was engaged to direct the connective sequences. Kelly sought Fred Astaire to share the work of introducing the musical sequences. Fred was reluctant, because of his longtime phobia of repeating himself. He had, after all, done the same thing in the first *That's Entertainment.* But because Gene had asked him, he agreed.

"But no dancing," Fred said firmly.

He repeated the edict at the first meetings. Saul Chaplin recalls what happened: "I had written some connective musical material, and I was teaching it to Fred and Gene at the first rehearsal. Suddenly Fred said, 'Gene, don't you think we should do sixteen bars of dancing at this point?' Both Gene and I were astonished. And delighted."

A dance before disaster: Fred and Jennifer Jones, The Towering Inferno *(20th Century-Fox)*

Fred and Adele at the opening
of the Uris Theater in New York, 1972

Of his duet with Kelly in That's
Entertainment, Part Two,
Astaire said, "That wasn't dancing,
that was just moving around."
(MGM)

Astaire in
That's Entertainment,
Part Two (MGM)

FRED: He's a very hard worker, Gene. There was no monkeying around, like "That's good enough for them." He was very diligent about being on time and working in between shots. I used to say, "Direct me! Go ahead and direct me!" He is a darned good director.

Fred's participation in *That's Entertainment, Part II* went beyond the filming. He lent himself to the publicity hoopla at premieres in Los Angeles and New York and flew with Cyd Charisse, Kathryn Grayson, Marge Champion and other MGM stars to the openings in Paris and London. On the plane Astaire and Kelly sat next to each other and talked continuously, across the Atlantic and back.

Astaire acted in a minor 1976 film, *The Amazing Dobermans*, playing a Bible-quoting trainer of dogs employed in crime detection. "It's a family picture," he explained to a reporter, "and that's important to me. I don't like cruelty and violence." He told why he had done no acting since his Academy nomination for *The Towering Inferno:* "They kept offering me sick old men. I won't play those kinds of people. I turn down roles all the time in which the character is an old has-been crying the blues. I don't like that kind of thing. It's not me."

FRED: I enjoyed [*Dobermans*] probably more than any other picture I made, because I fell in love with those dogs. They acted as though they were looking for me, and one would come and put his neck on my knee while I was waiting for a scene. I said, "You mean this animal is going to *bite* somebody? You couldn't *make* him bite." But you could make them *act* as though they would bite. That's the thing about Dobermans: You can make them look ferocious by telling them to be that way.

In 1977, Astaire appeared in a European film, *Un Taxi Mauve*, playing an Irish doctor who counsels rich, world-weary patients. Yves Boisset directed a cast that included Charlotte Rampling, Philippe Noiret, Peter Ustinov and Edward Albert. The film never found an American distributor.

Astaire's role in a 1978 television movie, *A Family Upside Down*, was the kind he said he wouldn't play: an oldster incapable of caring for himself. The producer, Ross Hunter, had told him about the script that a young writer, Jerry Di Pego, was working on. It concerned the problems facing elderly people in an America where families entrusted their old to institutions. "Wait until you've read the script," Hunter cautioned. "The part is like nothing you've ever done."

Hunter and his partner, Jacques Mapes, waited ten months until they felt the script was ready. First they engaged Helen Hayes for the role of the wife. Then they sent the script to Fred.

"I left the script at Fred's house one afternoon, and he called me at one in the morning," Hunter recalls. "Fred told me, 'It's wonderful, but I've got dozens of questions to ask you.' We met the next day, and Fred was prepared with the script pages marked. We went over his questions, one by one. Fred seemed satisfied, but he wasn't sure he was capable of such a dramatic part. I told him to forget it— 'You'll knock the hell out of it.' We talked for four hours, and at the end Fred agreed to do the movie."

Fred insisted on a week's rehearsal before filming, a rarity in television work. When he arrived for the first rehearsal, he had no need to refer to the script. He had already memorized his lines.

"He was amazing," says Helen Hayes. "After we started filming, he once stopped a scene because I had changed one word of dialogue."

When I visited a location for *A Family Upside Down*, Miss Hayes reminisced: "I danced one time with Fred. I was appearing in *Coquette* in New York, and Leland Hayward was my agent. The Astaires were having one hit after another on Broadway, and Leland was crazy about Adele. She agreed to go out with him—if he would bring me as a date for Fred. So we went out dancing at the Palais Royale. It's peculiar, but Fred never asked me to go dancing again."

She also recalled receiving a fan letter from Fred after her film appearance in *A Farewell to Arms*. He was then appearing on Broadway in *Gay Divorce*, and he wrote: "If you ever have a part that needs filling, think of me." A few years

Fred loved working with the dogs in The Amazing Dobermans *(Golden Films).*

Mishap: A Purple Taxi *with Peter Ustinov, Agostina Belli, Charlotte Rampling, and Phillipe Noiret*

later, Miss Hayes was planning to appear with Maurice Evans in *As You Like It.* Her husband, Charles MacArthur, suggested Fred Astaire for the clown's role, reminding her of the fan letter. "But he's a movie star now!" she protested. "Charlie, being Charlie, insisted that I ask Fred," Miss Hayes says. "Fred wrote back with the expectable news that he was 'all tied up.'"

Despite its grim theme, *A Family Upside Down* was well received by the television audience. And when the Academy of Television Arts and Sciences bestowed its awards for the best achievements of the year, Fred Astaire won the Emmy for best single performance by an actor.

Ann Gelius Astaire (Austerlitz) died of a stroke in July of 1975. She was ninety-six years old and had been a widow for fifty-one years.

Until the end she remained an important presence in her son's life. Visitors at the Astaire house remember her stately appearance and how affectionately Fred introduced her. They were also amused that she called him Sonny. In her late years, Mrs. Astaire enjoyed watching soap operas on television, and whenever he was home in the afternoon, Fred watched with her. Their favorite programs were *As the World Turns* and *Guiding Light.*

Adele was a widow again. Her second husband, Kingman Douglass, a financier who had served two years as assistant director of the Central Intelligence Agency, died in 1973. After his retirement from Dillon, Read & Company in 1971, he and Adele had moved to Phoenix because of his failing health. She continued to make Phoenix her home, spending each summer at Lismore Castle, which she was privileged to use as Charlie Cavendish's widow. Adele continued to entertain at the castle in grand style. When President and Mrs. Kennedy paid a visit to Ireland, they stopped at Lismore Castle for lunch with Adele. She proudly raised the American flag for the occasion.

Adele never changed. In her seventies she still adored shocking people by tossing out four-letter expletives with the casualness of tea conversation. Fred, who never used salty

Fred won another Emmy for A Family Upside Down *with Helen Hayes (NBC).*

language on social occasions, always viewed his sister with bemused tolerance.

If Adele never changed, the times did. During the 1960s and 1970s both America and England underwent social upheavals that changed forever the kind of world that Adele had known. Although she herself had always been totally frank, she railed at the new freedom. "All this sex stuff nowadays, it's so phony," she told a young friend. "I'd just love to see everyone get impotent. I think it would be great fun."

One night over dinner at Hermes Pan's house, Adele was voicing her criticism of the Freedom Marches and other demonstrations for black rights. Barrie Chase, who had accompanied Fred to dinner, listened to her remarks with rising anger. Although no activist, Barrie was part of a generation that realized the need for social change. Finally Barrie exclaimed, "Oh, Delly, stop it! We're living in another age now!" Adele was greatly offended, and for years she wouldn't talk to Barrie.

Christmas party at Gregory and Veronique Peck's house, 1978. The Pecks had transformed their downstairs den into a disco, hiring a disc jockey to play records for dancing. After dinner, the guests congregated downstairs, and the dancing became spirited. Among the guests were Fred and Adele Astaire.

Adele was eighty-one, Fred was seventy-nine, and when they started to dance together, something magical happened. The other dancers drew back in awe, and soon Fred and Adele occupied the floor, gliding in solitary splendor. They were two kids from Omaha again, dipping, sailing, twirling in silken movement.

Then it happened.

The music quickened, and Fred and Adele instinctively took their places beside each other. They began circling the floor, slowly at first, then with faster pace, grinning broadly, hand in hand. The joyful guests, most of whom had never seen the runaround, cheered wildly as Fred and Adele Astaire raced to the final exit.

9

Robyn

*You know, you give your own performance
and receive applause and you think maybe,
just maybe, you're successful. And you
go home feeling good and turn on television
to relax and there [Fred Astaire] is,
making you nervous all over again.*

—Mikhail Baryshnikov,
American Film Institute
dinner honoring Fred Astaire

They met on New Year's Day 1973 at Santa Anita race-track, where she was racing horses for Alfred Gwynn Van-derbilt's Sagamore Farm.

When Vanderbilt said he wanted her to meet an old friend, Fred Astaire, she said, "Fine." Robyn knew that Fred Astaire was a famous star, but she had never seen him on the screen. When she was growing up, she had hated musical films.

Robyn strode out of the jockey's room and into the glaring sunlight of the paddock to claim her horse, Exciting Divorcée. Vanderbilt introduced her to Astaire, and they exchanged a few pleasantries. She remembers that Fred was "very humble, and I thought he was cute because of that; sweet, I guess is the word."

Exciting Divorcée crossed the finish line a winner, paying long-shot odds. Among the lucky betters was Fred Astaire.

At the end of the racing day, Vanderbilt said to Robyn: "I haven't seen Fred for quite a few years, and I'd like to have dinner with him. Would you like to come along?" Robyn said, "Sure."

They dined at Chasen's that night, along with a racing friend of Vanderbilt's. While Vanderbilt conversed with his friend, Robyn talked to Fred, who was amazed that such a pretty young woman could be a winning jockey. Later she told Vanderbilt, "I had a good time last night, and I thought Fred Astaire was a lot of fun." At the end of the Santa Anita season, she returned to the East, where she did most of her racing.

In 1976, Robyn Smith was again racing at Santa Anita for Sagamore Farm. She suggested to Vanderbilt: "Why don't we get together with Fred Astaire and have dinner? You haven't seen him in three years." The dinner was arranged, and Robyn was once more impressed by how humble and sweet Fred was.

The following year, Robyn flew to Los Angeles to appear in a television commercial for Shasta soft drinks. After she had returned to racing in the East, the advertising agency called in a panic. The Shasta can in the commercial looked too much like Pepsi Cola. Robyn would have to return to California for retakes.

She thought to herself: "I have to leave racing and fly to California to shoot that commercial again! How boring!" An idea came to her: Why not call Fred Astaire and go out with him? That would relieve the boredom.

"Fred, this is Robyn," she said on the telephone.

"Robyn who?"

"Robyn Smith. I'm coming out there to film a commercial, and I'd like to take you out to dinner."

"We'll go out," he replied, "but I won't let you pay for dinner."

On the night of their dinner date, Robyn called for Fred at his house, and they drove to the Bistro in Beverly Hills. As they left the car and headed for the restaurant, Fred took her hand and said, "Come on." The tiny gesture made an instant impression on her. "My God, that's authoritative," she thought. "I really like this man."

Her thoughts were racing as she drove back to her hotel after dinner. She recalls what happened:

"I thought, 'Wow, I think I've been hit by something, but I really like this man.' I knew he couldn't care less about me, other than that he respects me, as a jockey. And as a person, maybe.

"I thought, 'God, I've got to start planning how we're going to get together again without making it seem that I'm going to use him for something. But what can I do? I've got to go back to New York!' I knew I was in trouble because I had fallen for him. Just because he had grabbed my hand; there was something I liked about that.

"As I drove, I kept thinking, 'What am I going to do? I know I am going to miss this man so much. I want to get back together and go out again. But how am I going to do it? I don't want to hurt my riding career by not paying attention to it and thinking about Fred Astaire all the time.'

"I stayed at the Beverly Wilshire Hotel for a couple of days to make the commercial, and I was hoping he would call me. I didn't want to push myself on Fred, but he didn't call *me*. I was kind of hurt. I thought, 'Gee, I thought I made a better impression on Fred that that.' I'm pretty sure of myself with men. I never heard another word from Fred. I went home and found out later he tried to call me the next day. But he called the Beverly Hills Hotel.

"I got back to business, but I couldn't get Fred out of my mind. So I thought, 'Well, I know one thing I can do: I can write him a thank-you note for taking me out to dinner.' I told myself: Don't get carried away, Robyn; be discreet. So I just wrote,

"'Dear Fred, Thank you for dinner last week. I had a good time, and I miss seeing you, although I don't know why.'

"I sent the note and figured, 'That's it. That's the last I'll hear from Fred for a while, until I can think of something. That may not be for years, because I'm going to be here in New York, riding.' I was pining away for Fred in my own way, thinking that maybe I would hear from him after I wrote him the note. Two weeks later I got a letter from him. Oh, God, it was wonderful! Then I knew it was on."

Who is Robyn Smith and where did she come from?

During her riding career, her background was the subject of much conjecture, and she did little to dispel the mystery. It was better for reporters to foster inventions than for her to recount her wretched childhood.

She was born August 14, 1944, in San Francisco to a woman who allowed the baby to be adopted by a wealthy Oregon lumberman, Orville Smith, and his wife. As Robin Smith, she had a happy childhood until the age of five, when her mother regained custody on the grounds that the girl wasn't being raised in the religion she was born into—Catholicism. Soon, the mother later said, she was unable to care for her daughter because of ill health. Like Marilyn Monroe, Robin grew up in a series of foster homes, some of them pleasant, some miserable.

After graduating from high school, she turned up in Hollywood as Robyn Caroline Smith, having feminized her first name. She had a fresh, attractive face and a boyish figure that bespoke her love of games. "When I was growing up, I resented being called a tomboy," she later said. "I don't want to be a man. I like them too much. I just get along with them, period."

Her efforts to find an acting career met with no success.

When Robyn was trying to land an interview with Martin Ransohoff, president of Filmways Productions, a friend advised her: "Tell him you're a college graduate from some big school; Marty loves that." Robyn sent word that she was a graduate of Stanford University. The interview was granted.

Robyn Smith was placed under contract to Filmways, which had little work for her besides television commercials. Ransohoff enrolled Robyn in an actors' workshop at Columbia Studio. She attended a few sessions, but she was repelled by the method-acting techniques ("bark like a dog") and began skipping classes. She had found a new passion.

One day in 1968 a boyfriend took her to the races at Santa Anita. Robyn was overwhelmed by the excitement and the pulse-quickening drama of a dozen animals hurtling down the stretch to the finish line. She realized that afternoon that she wanted to be a jockey. It was no longer impossible. Early in 1968, Kathy Kusner had sued for the right to compete as a jockey in Maryland. The growing awareness of women's rights was making track owners realize they could no longer bar women riders.

Robyn, who had ridden horses only rarely before, began hanging around the Santa Anita stables in the early morning hours. She was befriended by a trainer named Bruce Headley, who allowed her to exercise some of his horses.

"The horses weren't so scared, but, boy, I was!" she said later. "Invariably, they'd run away with me, but it was dark in the morning that time of year, and Headley couldn't see. One day, when it got lighter in the morning, he said, 'Gee, you don't gallop real good, do you?'"

After several months, the presence of an exercise girl became less of a novelty. Largely because of the Kusner suit, the male domain of jockeydom was finally opened to women, with expectable condescension and ridicule. Robyn was booed when she appeared on her first mount, Swift Yorky, at Golden Gate Fields track in northern California on April 3, 1969. It was Ladies' Day, and the boos were drowned out by a crowd that rose to cheer her, as much in curiosity as in admiration.

Swift Yorky moved off to an alert start, and Robyn was between horses on the far turn when she edged to the rail for the stretch drive. She whipped Swift Yorky toward the finish line but could not catch the front runner, Thirteen Tricks, which won by seven lengths. Swift Yorky was second by three quarters of a length. "Smith did very well," said a steward. "She did not appear to get flustered when in between horses, and she helped her mount down the stretch."

A week later she raced Money Road and finished last. The Golden Gate Fields Board of Stewards conceded that the horse bled and obviously couldn't run and considered her two performances sufficiently expert to grant her an apprentice jockey's license. But the gesture seemed little more than a publicity stunt, and Robyn found herself still on the outside of an all-male fraternity.

She wouldn't give up. She sweated, exercised and starved to remove ten pounds from her already slim figure, reducing herself to one hundred and five pounds. She studied a book by Eddie Arcaro and copied his way of sitting in the saddle and whipping the horse. She was getting a few mounts in the small-time California county-fair circuit when her ambition drew the attention of a flamboyant trainer, Howard ("Buddy") Jacobson. He agreed to take her east for a try at important tracks. But Jacobson proved unreliable, and she was cut adrift, broke and friendless.

Trainers were scornful of her pleas to ride for them. One of them, Frank Wright, had once been quoted as saying he would hire a woman jockey on the day the Chicago Bears drafted a tight end from Vassar. He changed his mind on a rainy November day in 1969 at Aqueduct Racetrack in New York.

"It was a cold, driving rain," Wright later recounted. "I had chased her away from the barn once before, but I guess somebody had sent her back because I had been one of the first to use exercise girls, and my wife is a show-ring rider. Robyn just stood there outside, with the rain falling on her, and when I looked down and saw the water running out of her boots, I said, 'Well, please come inside.' I told her, all right, I would give her a chance to gallop for me, and she just smiled and thanked me and ran right off to the next barn."

Two weeks later, Wright gave Robyn her chance to race. The horse was Exotic Bird, a nag that was a consistent loser. Robyn surprised Wright by pushing Exotic Bird to the utmost, barely missing fourth place. She had more starts on eastern tracks during 1970, but she could not break the sex prejudice. Trainers and owners would not entrust their best horses to her, reasoning that they had a better chance with male jockeys. "She's a loser," they scoffed, unwilling to realize that no jockey could win with the plugs she was assigned.

"She's good out of the gate, but she can't finish." Robyn knew that was being said about her; she was accused of not being strong or adept enough to whip across a winner. To counteract the charges, she exercised until her lean muscles were steel-hard. And she learned to toss the whip from one hand to the other, without the time-waster of putting it in her teeth.

At last—a winner! It happened on October 22, 1970, at Aqueduct. The horse: Hill Cloud.

Robyn's fortunes improved when she attracted the approval of the highly respected Allen Jerkens, trainer for Hobeau Farms. Unlike other trainers, he was not concerned that she was tall for a jockey, five feet, seven inches. "She's got good hands on a horse," Jerkens observed. "She gets what there is in a horse. And she gives a horse a chance. Most horses appreciate that. They appreciate the chance to get their legs under them. . . . She cajoles a horse into giving his best. A lot of times I'd rather have Robyn on a horse than many guys. Some guys wouldn't give a horse a chance. They'd rush a horse."

In 1971, largely because of Jerkens' sponsorship, Robyn rode in more than a hundred races. That was an improvement over her sixty-seven mounts in the previous two years, but it was one fifth of the races ridden in by an average male jockey.

Her best year was 1973. It started on New Year's Day at Santa Anita, where she was the lone woman among a hundred jockeys. Among those racing against her was Bill Shoemaker, but she came in first aboard Exciting Divorcée. The horse paid $35.20 for a $2 ticket, and among the winners was Fred Astaire.

Alfred Gwynne Vanderbilt now sponsored her career, and he provided her first chance to compete in important stakes races. He admired her capacity for perceiving a horse's potential, for example, North Sea. It was considered a wild and uncontrollable horse, but Robyn learned how to handle it. On March 1, 1973, she whipped North Sea across the finish line to win the $27,450 Paumoanok Handicap at Aqueduct. The sports pages proclaimed the historic event: A woman jockey had scored the first victory in a stakes race at a major track.

A month later, she rode North Sea to win the $50,000 Westchester Handicap at Aqueduct. During the 1973 season, Robyn rode 501 times and won 51 races. She finished in the money one third of the time, earning $634,055 in purses for the owners. Her share was ten percent.

Her achievements and her fashion-model looks at-tracted magazine covers and new stories. Gossip columnists hinted at a romance between Robyn and her patrician men-tor, Alfred Vanderbilt. Both denied it. Robyn told Frank De-ford of *Sports Illustrated* that Vanderbilt's relationship with her was "more of a father-daughter thing. I mean, there's no romance. Look, I'm a whole lot closer to Mrs. Vanderbilt [his third wife] than I am to Mr. Vanderbilt. You ever heard that? No, because nobody wants to hear that."

Robyn gained a reputation among the racing crowd for being a loner who retired to her tiny apartment alone at the end of the racing day. She was a fighter, with fierce bursts of temper when she felt wronged. She was also devoid of fear.

She was racing a long shot at Saratoga one day when her horse suffered a coronary as it was leading the pack in the final sixteenth of a mile. Robyn walked away from the spill.

At Santa Anita on February 22, 1973, she was riding another long shot, her only mount of the day. She was off to a good start and felt she could win. Then, as she told a reporter, "My horse's chest hit the rail, and it threw me up around his neck. Then I lost my balance and fell. There were two or three other horses behind me, but the riders could see what was going on, so they got out of the way." When the ambulance arrived on the track, she refused to enter the back, and she rode in the front seat instead. She was racing the next day.

By 1978 Robyn Smith had been racing for nine years, and for the first time she was discouraged. She and other female jockeys had been unable to dispel the belief of most trainers that women simply didn't have the strength and stamina to compete with men. Robyn thought otherwise.

"I know I'm as good as those male jockeys up there," she

told a *New York Times* reporter. "No question. Horses run for me. But you can't ride winners if the trainers don't put you on any horses. . . . All I ever ride are long shots. The male jockeys get the Cadillacs and I get the Volkswagen—if I'm lucky. Hell, I haven't ridden a horse for some of my customers in months."

And now there was something new in her life to distract her from a single-minded pursuit of a racing career. She was in love with Fred Astaire.

"I did pursue Fred," says Robyn Smith Astaire. "I sent him flowers. I really did what he should have been doing to me. But he was interested in me or it wouldn't have worked.

"If he had pursued me, I probably wouldn't have been attracted to him. It was meant to happen, because the last thing in *my* mind was wanting to get married. I had an open mind about it; I was hoping that I wouldn't go through my whole life without getting married. But if I never married, it wouldn't have bothered me.

"My career was dwindling because I was getting older and finding it difficult to get good mounts. I had gone beyond the stage of getting a thrill by riding anything, because I had ridden good horses. The timing [for marriage] was good. It couldn't possibly have happened ten years before, when all I could think about was horses. . . .

"I was approaching my middle thirties, and that's pretty old for a woman jockey. Certain men can get away with it. I could have gone on—athletes always think they can go on. But unless you have the horse, you can't win. I said when I started my career that I didn't want to stay in the business if I couldn't maintain the top part of it. And I wasn't.

"It got so I was spending a lot of money going out to California to see Fred. I'd have to be back for riding a day later, two days at the most. I was traveling out and back, staying in the best hotels and getting first-class service, and I was doing it every other week. . . . I think we both knew it was serious, right away almost. I told Fred I liked him very, very much, and once he found that out, he started pursuing a little bit."

Her problem was her work, his was his family. Both Ava

and Adele were totally opposed to Fred's romantic attachment. A series of distressing scenes occurred.

> FRED: They were wondering about my age, and you certainly can't blame them for that. There's a rightful feeling about someone eighty marrying somebody thirty-six. I just ignored that. . . . I just wasn't questioning anything at all. "Why? What's the matter?" I said. I had been a bachelor, or a widower, for twenty-five years. I never thought I'd ever get married again. But I got the feeling, and when it happens, it happens. That's all there is to it. You don't sort of juggle it around and say, "Wait a minute, how do I do this?" You say, "This is it! Do it!" I never had that feeling before in all those other years.

In November of 1978, Fred was scheduled to receive, along with Richard Rodgers, Marian Anderson, George Balanchine and Arthur Rubinstein, the Kennedy Center Honors in Washington, D.C. He told Robyn he would then go to New York and meet her. They would visit their friend, the ailing Jock Whitney, whom Fred had known for fifty years and for whom Robyn had ridden horses.

Fred's plane arrived in New York at five-thirty in the morning. As he emerged into the terminal, he was surprised when Robyn popped out from behind a group of people. Fred and Robyn embraced, oblivious of the stares of passersby.

They visited Jock Whitney in the afternoon, and he volunteered use of his limousine. Fred and Robyn discussed where to have dinner and decided to try Tavern on the Green in Central Park. It was the first time they had met in New York City and they felt a new intimacy.

Midway through dinner, Fred said abruptly, "Let's elope!"

"What a good idea!" she answered lightheartedly.

Neither was serious. Both realized there were problems to solve: his family; her career.

"You know that we'll have to spend the rest of our lives together," he said.

"Yes, I do know that," she said. "I don't know why, but it

just happened, and let's not fight it. But let's not rush it, either." They didn't. Two years would pass before they married.

When I telephoned Fred on the eve of his eightieth birthday, May 10, 1979, he grumbled, "What's all the fuss about? It's only a round number."

He had recently played a role in "Battlestar Galactica," a space television series. It was a curious booking for Fred Astaire, but he explained: "I did it for my grandchildren." (Fred, Jr., has three children, Peter has three, and Ava has two stepsons.) He found it a tough show because of special effects that caused three days of overtime, and because of the space language, which he didn't understand.

At eighty he remained the same trim, agile Astaire. "I don't eat too much, and I don't diet," he explained. "I'm basically light, rarely over a hundred and thirty pounds. I don't go in for any physical torture: jogging, calisthenics, that sort of thing. I like to loosen up and play golf and occasionally tennis. The main thing is to keep moving around. I'm lucky to retain command of whatever athletic ability I've had."

Three years before, he had learned a lesson about doing too much. He enjoyed riding his grandson's skateboard around the driveway of the Astaire home, but one day Fred fell and broke his wrist. He was so embarrassed he wouldn't allow any photographs of the cast.

Producers continued to send scripts for Fred Astaire to International Creative Management, but Fred's agent, Michael Black, submitted only a few to his client. Fred had made it clear what he would not do. No singing, no dancing. No retired singers or retired dancers. No choreographers or fathers of entertainers. No hoboes or pathetic oldsters. Having accepted A Family Upside Down because of the strong role and the chance to act with Helen Hayes, Fred had insisted on one small touch of class in the house painter's wardrobe: a cashmere cardigan sweater. "We can say his kids gave it to him for Christmas," he reasoned.

"I would never submit a deal to Fred without a firm

offer," says ICM's Black. "Other stars may need to meet the director and audition for a part. Not Fred Astaire."

Every week Black has received offers of honorary awards and chairmanships, and each spring has brought numerous proposals for honorary degrees from universities. Fred declines all of them, partly because of his innate modesty, partly because he doesn't want to accept some and offend others.

The television networks were eager to produce specials honoring Fred's eightieth birthday. Even though his presence would be required for only half a day, he declined. "Let 'em do 'Happy Birthday, Bob' [Hope] and 'Happy Birthday, George' [Burns]," Fred told Black. "It's not for me."

Some honors, such as the one at the Kennedy Center, could not be refused. In 1973 he accepted a tribute from the Film Society of Lincoln Center in New York. He received three standing ovations from a crowd that watched thirty dance sequences from twenty-three of his films. "My gosh, I was a lucky fellow," he said. "Wow—all those gorgeous girls I worked with." Among those present were Adele and Ginger, Cyd Charisse and Joan Fontaine.

In 1978, Fred attended a dinner honoring his dance specials, given by the Academy of Television Arts and Sciences, and he accepted the National Artist Award of the American National Theater and Academy. But for two years he resisted suggestions that he accept the prestigious Life Achievement Award of the American Film Institute. He declined offers to write forewords to books, to be interviewed for an Astaire biography, or to act as consultant for a Broadway musical.

Fred agreed to an homage to his work by Public Television, as long as he didn't have to appear on it. His friends and co-workers were interviewed for the show, which was narrated by Joanne Woodward. Even Adele agreed to talk— but not on camera. Now past eighty, she was still strikingly handsome, but although she arrived for the interview in a stylish dress and a lavish amount of jewels, she allowed the crew to record sound only. She wanted to do the interview in the garden of Barrie Chase and her husband, Dr. James Kaufman. It marked the reconciliation of Barrie and Adele, who had forgiven Barrie for her remark at Hermes Pan's dinner party.

In his dance revue, *Dancin'*, Bob Fosse included a number "For Fred." A line of male dancers performed an approximation of an Astaire dance and, at a dramatic moment, swept aside their jackets to reveal foulard ties as belts. Fred didn't see the show in New York, but he attended a performance of the road company in Los Angeles. He was so pleased that he went backstage afterward and shook hands with each of the dancers, who were understandably awed.

Fred granted permission for a Jerome Robbins dance for the New York City Ballet based on "I'm Old-fashioned," which he danced with Rita Hayworth in *You Were Never Lovelier.* Robbins included a film clip from the movie at the beginning of the ballet, which was a hit of the 1983 season. Less successful was *Astaire,* an unauthorized ballet performed by Les Grands Ballets Canadiens at New York City Center. A sixty-year-old attempted to impersonate Astaire, and production numbers of the Astaire-Rogers films were duplicated.

Steve Martin and Bernadette Peters performed a "Let's Face the Music and Dance" imitation in the 1981 film failure, *Pennies from Heaven.* Tommy Tune choreographed an Astaire-Rogers number—seen from the knees down—in the Broadway musical *A Day in Hollywood/A Night in the Ukraine,* and the *New Yorker*'s dance critic, Arlene Croce, termed it "the cleverest tribute to Astaire (and Rogers) I have seen."

Fred rarely attended the theater, because he disliked being recognized. He was impressed by the shows that he did see, realizing how far the theater had advanced in technique and sophistication from the innocent era when he and Adele were starring on Broadway. A musical that impressed him was *A Chorus Line.*

> FRED: It was very good, a whole new way of doing a show. Michael Bennett hit it right on the head. I can see why they haven't made a movie of it yet. Its very charm was a certain stage treatment that it had.
>
> I liked the show because it didn't make the chorus line an unfairly treated group. They didn't say, "We never got a chance." They *do* get a chance to go beyond and make good at the game. Chorus people get a shot at showing off how talented they are.

Fred still liked the movies, and he often patronized theaters in Westwood and Beverly Hills in the afternoon, when there was less chance of his being recognized. When I interviewed him for this book in mid-1983, he was marveling over the dynamic dancing in *Flashdance,* though he was amazed that the filmmakers did little to disguise the fact that the star, Jennifer Beals, did not perform all of her dances.

Fred can be as enthusiastic as any fan about exciting new entertainers. He telephoned congratulations to Michael Jackson for the video film to promote his hit record album *Thriller.* Fred comments: "Anybody who can sing and dance at the same time, and do both well, is pretty darned good, and that's what Michael does. I've known him since he was a little kid. The Jacksons used to live near me, and they would ride past my house on their bicycles and wave at me. I've known the whole family, and Michael and I talk now and then on the telephone."

Fred danced only in private. Sometimes he sat at his drums and pounded out some rhythms, then did a few steps for his own amusement. Or he would hear a record by a new band that excited him, and he would react to it. At such times he often called Barrie Chase to say, "Gee, I just heard a swell piece of music—you'd be great doing it." She had long before quit dancing to be a wife and mother; her son was born in 1973.

Fred and Barrie remained solid friends. They often gossiped on the telephone, and he kidded her about believing her son "was the only boy in the world." The partnership of Fred Astaire and Barrie Chase had been a successful one, and their friends wondered why they never married.

FRED: There was no romance, positively not. I valued her as a partner; we used to date. There was never a matter of my asking her [to marry]. I wasn't even *thinking* about it. I was trying to get my career working on a new thing like TV. I was grateful for her, because she was perfect for me. I might never have made a television show if it weren't for the fact that I could see in her something worth working for.

Fred's close friends were few. The most enduring was William Self, a television and motion-picture executive. They had met in 1960 at Bel Air Country Club, where both were members. The caddymaster teamed them for a twosome, explaining to Self beforehand that "Mr. Astaire is very shy." For the first four holes, the two players exchanged scarcely a word. Then Fred remarked, "You're in television." Self admitted he was, and Fred added, "I've been offered a television series. I won't tell you what it is, but it's a well-known title being made by a respectable company. Right now they're trying to get a well-known producer."

"Is it 'Father of the Bride'?" Self asked. The astonished Astaire said it was, and Self disclosed that MGM was seeking him to produce the series.

"If you're the star, I'll consider it," said Self.

"If you're the producer, I'll consider it," Fred replied.

A few weeks later, Astaire spotted Self across a fairway and ran over to announce, "I'm not going to do it." ("Father of the Bride," starring Leon Ames, lasted one season.) Astaire and Self never worked together on a project. "Maybe that's why our friendship has lasted," the producer observes.

When Self was head of television production for 20th Century–Fox, an assistant wanted Fred Astaire to appear on a show about *Daddy Long Legs*. "I'll mention it to Fred, but I won't ask him," said Self. At first Fred dismissed the idea. Four weeks later, he said to Self, "What was that show you told me about?" and he agreed to do it.

For many years, Astaire and Self have engaged in a gin-rummy game almost every Sunday. They play for minor stakes and long ago gave up paying up after each session. They agreed to settle the account when either player had won a hundred dollars. To Fred's distress, he has never collected.

Self and his wife often dined in restaurants with Fred, always in places like Chasen's, La Scala, the Bistro and Adriano's, where he was a regular customer. "Fred doesn't know what to tip the maître d' and the captain," explains Self, "so to save the embarrassment he goes to places where they don't present the check but send it to him later."

Fred often referred to Bill Self as his best friend. But

Ginger and Fred remained loyal, and he appeared at the 1981 Masquers Club dinner honoring Ginger (MGM).

Self admits that he was not the recipient of confidences and intimate revelations such as best friends often exchange. The few people who saw Fred on a regular basis were concerned about his increasing isolation, the unremitting loneliness of the big white house occupied only by himself and servants.

Midafternoon in a crowded parking lot in Beverly Hills. Fred Astaire was waiting for his car to be delivered when he saw an old friend. He was Pandro Berman, producer of the Astaire-Rogers musicals at RKO, now retired after a distinguished career. The two old comrades greeted each other warmly.

"Pan, I want to ask you something," Fred said abruptly.

"Sure, Fred, what is it?"

"Well, I'm thinking of getting married again, to a girl who's much younger than I am. Some of my family and friends are against the idea. What do you think?"

"Do you love her?"

"Yes, I do."

"Then what the hell do you care what other people say? They don't have to live with her. They don't have to live *without* her. You do. You have to make the decision. If you love her and you want to marry her, tell them all to go to hell."

"It was difficult for Fred to get a lot of things organized," says Robyn, "in order to make everyone happy. Nothing for me; I had no one. But I didn't push it, because I wanted to ride some more, too. Once I knew that we would eventually get married, I was very, very happy and didn't care when. Everything we did was natural; it was like we had been around each other all our lives.

"Fred is in his eighties and I'm in my late thirties, and there's a big span of years there. It's a very unusual relationship, and if anyone would have said ten years ago that I was going to marry a man forty-some years older than me, I would have said, 'Don't be ridiculous!'"

> FRED: It seems that it was simply, absolutely unavoidable. And when it finally happened, we didn't have much thought about, "Well, how did we do this?" It just happened.

"I didn't think I was capable of love, not like this," says Robyn. "But then, I've always liked older men. When I was ten, I liked men who were thirty. I looked for the father image, no question about it. There's nothing wrong with that; it's a normal thing if you haven't had a father. I always was aware that I had that, but I didn't fight it, I went along with it. Fred's part-father to me, let's face it. But he's part-everything to me."

> FRED: It never occurred to me at all about the difference of age. I was reminded of it quite often, and then I began to realize it. I was seventy-seven, seventy eight when we got serious. All of a sudden came this *eighty* thing. "*Octo*genarian, you son of a —." and I thought, "So what?" because I still had my health.

Robyn Smith and Fred Astaire were married June 24, 1980, in a quiet ceremony at Fred's home in Beverly Hills.

Another movie for Fred. For years, Ava had been encouraging her father to do *Ghost Story,* a book about four oldsters who had been involved in a tragedy in their youths. When Fred's agent, Michael Black, learned that Universal Pictures was planning a film based on *Ghost Story,* he telephoned the studio. "Fred is first on our list," Black was assured. The cast was impressive: Fred Astaire, Melvyn Douglas, Douglas Fairbanks, Jr., John Houseman, Patricia Neal. Also a promising young actor, Craig Wasson. The director was John Irvin, an Englishman who had made *Tinker, Tailor, Soldier, Spy* for BBC.

Fred looked forward to working again, though he was apprehensive about filming in Saratoga Springs in the dead of winter. His biggest concern was Adele. Her vast energy had finally eroded, and in her eighties she railed profanely against the ailments that beset her. Adele's animosity over Fred's marriage to Robyn was submerged when Robyn insisted Fred spend Christmas with Adele in Arizona in 1981. Adele died of a stroke a month later.

The Chowder Society: Douglas Fairbanks, Jr., Astaire, John Houseman, Melvyn Douglas, Ghost Story *(Universal)*

FRED: It happened while I was shooting *Ghost Story.*
There was no way I could have gotten back there.

   She was in a coma for two weeks. It's very
difficult to be trapped in a situation like that. I had
just spent the weekend before with her [in Tucson].
She had had a stroke and had come out of it. She
still was left with some ailments and was in a precarious condition. She had the other stroke just as I was
starting that picture. It was inevitable.

   She was a great girl, a million laughs. I miss her
terribly.

Isolated on the film location in New York State, Fred felt frustrated and miserable. As with Phyllis, he couldn't comprehend the loss of someone who had been such an intimate part of his life. "I can't believe it," he said to young Craig Wasson. "It seems like yesterday that Delly and I were playing vaudeville together." But, of course, that had been seventy years before.

Ghost Story was a misery for several reasons. Saratoga Springs, the racing resort Fred had visited many times, experienced its coldest January in fifty years. The temperature hit twenty degrees below zero, with none of the snow that the film company needed. By mid-February, it had risen to seventy degrees.

The weather affected Fred's ordinarily unchanging good health. Like others in the film company, he had an attack of flu. It was severe enough to make Fred fear he had a worse disease. He didn't.

Adding to his disquietude was the separation from Robyn. He had wanted her to quit her career as a jockey, fearful that she might get hurt.

> FRED: I didn't want Robyn to ride anymore. It's too dangerous. She doesn't think so, but I do. She says, "Oh, I've been thrown, I know what it's like." I say, "Yes, I *know* you've been thrown." I *saw* her thrown one day at Santa Anita. She was going to the gate and the horse got rid of her. I saw her take the fall. She was furious, but she handled the horse beautifully.
>
> Getting into a fall *during* a race—that is something else. It's just awful. They can throw you over the fence, they can pin your leg and break it. What usually happens is the jock goes down and that horse and other horses unwittingly step on him.

Although she knew her racing career was grinding down, Robyn was not quite ready to quit. She wanted one last fling at the circuit. With Fred making a film in Saratoga Springs and his wife riding horses, the scandal tabloids had a field day. One reported that Fred had offered Robyn a mil-

New Partner: Fred dances with Robyn at the 1982 opening of the New Universal Amphitheater (Wide World Photos)

lion dollars for a divorce and was dallying with another young woman on the movie location. Fred, whose entire career had been scandal-free, was appalled to find himself the subject of lurid headlines to attract supermarket shoppers. "How can they print such things!" he exclaimed. He

telephoned Robyn, who was amused. She said she was relieved that Fred was the one reportedly playing around, not
she.

Robyn admits, "I didn't have much of a choice" about
continuing her racing career. She recalls: "Fred said, 'When
we get married, I just want one thing from you. I want you to
stop riding, because I think it's a proper time to wrap up
your career.' He was adamant about my stopping. I had
made up my mind when I started my career that once I
couldn't ride anymore, I would not be one to hang around
the racetrack, and grow old around the racetrack. I made up
my mind to do it first-class and do it right—and get out of it.

"A year before we got married, we made a deal. I almost
stuck to it. I wanted to have one more August at Saratoga,
which was my favorite track and one where I had had success. We were married in June; Saratoga is in August. I said,
'Let me do it one more time to get it out of my system.
Otherwise I will always wish that I had done it. Just one more
time; I promise you I'll stop after that.' He said okay because
he's so good.

"It was really a mistake to go back there. I couldn't get
enough good mounts. I got a few, but they were outclassed.
And you can't look good on a horse that can't run. My very
last mount finished second, so that's not too bad. But I would
have liked to go out with a winner."

Robyn couldn't resist an offer to ride in Argentina.
Then she raced no more.

"I do miss it a hell of a lot," she admits, "but I don't pine
about it. I had nothing left to prove. It was still difficult [to
get good horses] my whole career; it never got easy. I miss it
because it was so much fun. I would have done it for nothing
because I loved it so much. Sometimes I did; to get the
mount I'd give the trainer back his fee."

FRED: You can't just say, "Oh, I think I'll start riding
again tomorrow." It isn't like getting ready to do a
show and you say, "Well, I haven't danced for five
years, but I can get out there and dance again."

Robyn could do it, but there aren't many trainers who would take her on. They'd say, "Well, what

has she been doing?" They know how well she could ride, but they also know she has been gone.

Says Robyn: "I loved riding, but I love Fred more. And I can't have both."

Fred's spirits on the *Ghost Story* location were boosted by the camaraderie with Doug Fairbanks, John Houseman and Melvyn Douglas and by his belief that the role was the best yet to prove himself as an actor. When the end of filming approached and he knew he would be returning to California and Robyn, he became absolutely buoyant.

The final scene took place on the grounds of the Gideon Putnam Hotel, where the company had been quartered. A sudden chill had brought a fresh layer of snow that had hardened into a slippery surface. Astaire and Houseman were assisted to the filming area by escorts, something neither of the actors enjoyed.

"It's a wrap for Mr. Astaire," director Irvin announced at the conclusion of the scene.

"You mean I'm finished?" Fred asked with a wide grin.

"Yes, sir."

To the other members of the company, Fred had seemed frail and fragile during the filming. But as they watched him leave, something miraculous happened. The slow, calculating walk became a rhythmic Astaire lilt. With his own inimitable style, he danced over the glistening snow, all the way back to his dressing room.

Ghost Story fell victim to studio group-think. Concerned about the appeal to the youth market of a film starring actors in their seventies and eighties, Universal made severe cuts and emphasized the youthful love story. Fred Astaire and John Houseman were invited to see the rough cut at the studio.

"Fred and I led the charge against the producer," Houseman recalls. "We were furious when we saw the rough cut, and rightly so. The whole point of the story had been pooped away. The intimate relationship between Fred and me was utterly essential. He seemed to be the weaker, passive brother, and I was the overbearing one. But when the chips were down, the roles were reversed. That was all lost in the editing."

> FRED: I agreed with John when he jumped on the producer. "My dear fellow," he said, "you've ruined your story. You've done it! You *ruined* it."
>
> Somehow or other, they get away with it. They release a picture, get most of their money back and forget it. Write it off.
>
> But they tried. They put a lot of money in the picture, and they're always nice to work with, these people at Universal.
>
> Anyway, we all got out of it without being hurt.

After two and a half years of gentle persuasion over gin rummy, Bill Self finally convinced Fred to accept the Life Achievement Award of the American Film Institute. Self, a trustee of AFI, had pointed out to Fred the good works that the organization did for motion pictures. "It deserves your support, Fred," the producer had said.

The dinner was held April 10, 1981, with a telecast of the event on the CBS network a week later. When Fred walked into the International Ballroom of the Beverly Hilton Hotel, the audience of two thousand rose and cheered. He strode through the tables with his half-dancing gait, then joined Robyn at the place of honor in the center of the ballroom. Also at the table, in a show of familial amity, were Ava and her husband, Richard McKenzie, and Fred, Jr., with his wife Carol. (Ava lives in Ireland with her artist husband; Fred is a flier and rancher. Stepson Peter has retired after a career as a law officer.)

Fred's old chum David Niven came from Europe to be the master of ceremonies. Niven recalled their first meeting, when he arrived in Hollywood in 1934 with a letter of introduction from a mutual friend, a London bookmaker.

"One evening after a hot game of tennis, I decided to present it," said Niven. "So I crossed the street to the Astaire house. Unfortunately, I forgot to put my shirt on. Fred's wife

The AFI Life Achievement Award (AFI, Diana Walker)

opened the door, sniffed like a bird dog, and shut it very quickly indeed. Then I heard her say, 'Fred, come quickly. There's a perfectly dreadful, half-naked man in the garden.'"

Ginger Rogers was notable by her absence. She could not be persuaded to cancel an appearance in New Orleans, but she sent a message: "It certainly was fun, Fred. When they put us together, it was a blessed event. . . ."

Another message came from President Ronald Reagan, recovering from an assassin's wound: "There is nobody like you, and while they say that every generation has its own style, your style reaches and delights us all."

More old friends—

Hermes Pan: "Needless to say, the highlight of my career was having had the wonderful opportunity of working with Fred Astaire on so many wonderful films. . . ."

James Cagney: "There's no doubt in my mind he's the greatest dancer, the greatest dancer I've ever seen in my life. No question about it."

Gene Kelly: "What a lovely evening! For everyone, but especially for all the dancers in the world, because we feel a very strong, a very unique kind of relationship with Fred Astaire. . . ."

And the dance partners—

Eleanor Powell: "Do you know, on 'Begin the Beguine' we rehearsed for two solid weeks on just arm movements so they'd be right together. . . . Of course the reason you work so hard is to make it look easy. And both of us would always say, 'Could we do it just one more time?'"

Audrey Hepburn (on the first day of rehearsing for *Funny Face*): "One look at this most debonair and elegant and distinguished of legends, and I could feel myself turn into solid lead while my heart sank into my two left feet. Then suddenly I felt a hand around my waist and with his inimitable grace and lightness, Fred literally swept me off my feet."

Barrie Chase: "Dancing with Fred Astaire was tough. There were times, Fred, when you were a monster, and I wish I could start it all over again."

Other dancers—

Bob Fosse: "Fred Astaire has been my idol my whole life. . . . I don't think Fred realizes it, but he is responsible for what I do now. When it slowly dawned on me that I could never be the incredible dancer he is—I think the studios realized it before I did—I said I'd better get into another area of this business. So I became a choreographer."

Mikhail Baryshnikov: "Dancers hate Fred Astaire. He gives us complexes because he is too perfect. . . . When I first saw Mr. Astaire's movies, it was very discouraging. I thought everybody in America was that good. I felt, 'You're never gonna dance, kid.'"

The film clips rolled by, from the razzmatazz number with Joan Crawford in *Dancing Lady* to "St. James Infirmary"

Robyn and Fred (© 1984 Ellen Graham)

on television with Barrie. The duets with Ginger, Eleanor, Rita and Cyd, and the fabulous solos—the firecrackers, the magic shoes, the revolving room.

Then it was time for Fred to come onstage. Joseph McBride, who wrote the script with George Stevens, Jr., had prepared a speech for Fred. But, as with his autobiography, Fred had to do it his way. The remarks were entirely his own.

"Oh, my, my, my, my! Now comes the hard part," he

began. "I really have had such a marvelous time. I don't know how to start or how to finish. And I haven't had one drink!"

Adele, he said, "was mostly responsible for my being in show business. She was the whole show, she really was, of all the vaudeville acts and the musical comedies we did together. Delly was the one that was the shining light, and I was just there pushing away.

"Then all of a sudden she got married. I went on by myself and I did all that—I didn't realize I did all that stuff! Yeew, Christmas! I saw things up there [on the ballroom screens] that I don't remember doing. And I'm glad to say I like what I saw."

He told of receiving a letter from Ginger: "Her handwriting is very fancy, but I'm going home and study it. Bless her heart, she's a terrific gal, and she works like crazy all the time, she does. And I love all the beautiful girls I've danced with."

Finally he said: 'Now I'm going to say good night, and if I've forgotten something, it's because I really did forget or have forgotten. There's a lot more to say and I think it's getting late. Oh, my goodness! Thank you so much. I'm thrilled to death. I can't explain it any more than that. I really can't. Thank you."

All his professional life he has maintained this kind of integrity: He takes a job, he works and works on it until he is ready, and then he delivers. And then he goes home. That is the magic formula, and anybody can do the same, provided he is endowed with the physical equipment of a decathlon champion, the imagination of an artist, the perseverance of an expert in dressage, the determination of a gyrene drill sergeant, the self-confidence of a lion tamer, the self-criticism of a neophyte in holy orders, the pride of a man who has created his own tradition—and the ability to go home when he has done his job. On top of which, and throughout which, and at the bottom of which, Astaire is in full possession of a quality amounting almost to an instinct for style, class, taste.

—John O'Hara, 1962

THEATER APPEARANCES

TITLE	PREMIERE	THEATER	PERFORMANCES	SONGWRITERS	ASTAIRE SONGS	OTHERS IN CAST
Over the Top	11/28/17	Forty-fourth Street Roof, New York	78	Charles J. Manning, Matthew Woodward, Sigmund Romberg, Herman Timberg	"Frocks and Frills," "Where is the Language to Tell?" "The Justine Johnson Rag"	Justine Johnson, Mary Eaton, T. Roy Barnes (later, Ed Wynn)
The Passing Show of 1918	7/25/18	Winter Garden, New York	125	Harold Atteridge, Sigmund Romberg, Jean Schwartz	"I Can't Make My Feet Behave," "Squab Farm," "Bring on the Girls," "Quick Service"	Frank Fay, Willie & Eugene Howard, Charles Ruggles, Lou Clayton, Nita Naldi
Apple Blossoms	10/7/19	Globe, New York	256	William LeBaron, Fritz Kreisler, Victor Jacobi	"On the Banks of the Bronx," "A Girl, a Man, a Night, a Dance"	John Charles Thomas, Wilda Bennett, Roy Atwell
The Love Letter	10/4/21	Globe, New York	31	William LeBaron, Victor Jacobi	"I'll Say I Love You," "Upside Down," "Dreaming"	John Charles Thomas, Carolyn Thomson, Marjorie Gateson, Alice Brady
For Goodness Sake	2/20/22	Lyric, New York	103	Arthur Jackson, William Daly, Paul Lannin	"All to Myself," "When You're in Rome," "Oh Gee, Oh Gosh," "French Pastry Walk," "The Whichness of the Whatness"	John E. Hazzard, Marjorie Gateson, Charles Judels, Vinton Freedley, Helen Ford
The Bunch and Judy	11/28/22	Globe, New York	65	Anne Caldwell, Jerome Kern	"Pale Venetian Moon," "Peach Girl," "Morning Glory," "Every Day in Every Way," "Times Square," "How Do You Do, Katinka?"	Johnny Dooley, Ray Dooley, Grace Hayes, Roberta Beatty, Philip Tonge
Stop Flirting	5/30/23	Shaftesbury, London	418	Arthur Jackson, William Daly, Paul Lannin	"All to Myself," "Oh Gee, Oh Gosh," "It's Great to Be in Love," "The Whichness of the Whatness," "I'll Build a Stairway to Paradise" (George Gershwin)	Jack Melford, Mimi Crawford, Marjorie Gordon, Henry Kendall

Show	Date	Theatre	No.	Composer/Lyricist	Songs	Cast
Lady, Be Good!	12/1/24	Liberty, New York	330	Ira and George Gershwin	"Hang on to Me," "So Am I," "Fascinating Rhythm," "The Half of It, Dearie, Blues," "Juanita," "Swiss Miss"	Walter Catlett, Alan Edwards, Cliff Edwards, Gerald Oliver Smith, Kathleen Martin
Lady, Be Good!	4/14/26	Empire, London	326	Ira and George Gershwin	Same as above	William Kent, Buddy Lee, George Volaire, Ewart Scott, Sylvia Leslie
Funny Face	11/22/27	Alvin, New York	250	Ira and George Gershwin	"Funny Face," "High Hat," "He Loves and She Loves," "Let's Kiss and Make Up," "'S Wonderful," "My One and Only," "The Babbitt and the Bromide"	Walter Kent, Victor Moore, Allen Kearns, Betty Compton
Funny Face	11/8/28	Prince's, London	263	Ira and George Gershwin	Same as above	Leslie Henson, Bernard Clifton, Rita Page, Sydney Howard, Eileen Hatton
Smiles	11/18/30	Ziegfeld, New York	63	Clifford Grey, Harold Adamson, Ring Lardner, Vincent Youmans	"Say, Young Man of Manhattan," "Hotcha Ma Chotch," "Be Good to Me," "Anyway, We Had Fun," "If I Were You, Love," "I'm Glad I Waited"	Marilyn Miller, Tom Howard, Eddie Foy, Jr., Paul Gregory, Larry Adler, Claire Dodd
The Band Wagon	6/3/31	New Amsterdam, New York	260	Howard Dietz, Arthur Schwartz	"Sweet Music," "Hoops," "New Sun in the Sky," "Miserable with You," "I Love Louisa," "The Beggar Waltz," "White Heat"	Frank Morgan, Helen Broderick, Tilly Losch, Philip Loeb, John Barker
Gay Divorcée	11/29/32	Ethel Barrymore, New York	248	Cole Porter	"After You, Who?" "Night and Day," "I've Got You on My Mind," "You're in Love"	Claire Luce, Luella Gear, G. P. Huntley, Jr., Betty Starbuck, Eric Blore, Erik Rhodes
Gay Divorcée	11/2/33	Palace, London	108	Cole Porter	Same as above	Claire Luce, Olive Blakeney, Claud Allister, Eric Blore, Erik Rhodes

MUSICAL FILMS

TITLE	DISTRIBUTOR	RELEASE DATE	DIRECTOR	SONGWRITERS	ASTAIRE SONGS	OTHERS IN CAST
Dancing Lady	MGM	12/2/33	Robert Z. Leonard	Harold Adamson, Dorothy Fields, Lorenz Hart, Arthur Freed, Burton Lane, Jimmy McHugh, Richard Rodgers, Nacio Herb Brown	"Heigh-Ho, The Gang's All Here," "Let's Go Bavarian"	Joan Crawford, Clark Gable, Franchot Tone, Robert Benchley, Ted Healy, Three Stooges, Nelson Eddy
Flying Down to Rio	RKO	12/20/33	Thornton Freeland	Edward Eliscu, Gus Kahn, Vincent Youmans	"The Carioca," "Orchids in the Moonlight," "Flying Down to Rio," "Music Makes Me"	Dolores Del Rio, Gene Raymond, Raul Roulien, Ginger Rogers, Eric Blore
The Gay Divorcée	RKO	10/3/34	Mark Sandrich	Cole Porter, Herb Magidson, Mack Gordon, Con Conrad, Harry Revel	"Night and Day," "Don't Let It Bother You," "A Needle in a Haystack," "The Continental"	Ginger Rogers, Alice Brady, Edward Everett Horton, Eric Blore, Erik Rhodes
Roberta	RKO	2/13/35	William A. Seiter	Otto Harbach, Dorothy Fields, Ballard MacDonald, Bernard Dougall, Oscar Hammerstein II, Jerome Kern	"Let's Begin," "I'll Be Hard to Handle," "I Won't Dance," "Smoke Gets in Your Eyes," "Don't Ask Me Not to Sing," "Lovely to Look at"	Irene Dunne, Randolph Scott, Ginger Rogers, Helen Wesley
Top Hat	RKO	9/6/35	Mark Sandrich	Irving Berlin	"No Strings," "Isn't This a Lovely Day?" "Top Hat, White Tie and Tails," "Cheek to Cheek," "The Piccolino"	Ginger Rogers, Edward Everett Horton, Helen Broderick, Eric Blore, Erik Rhodes
Follow the Fleet	RKO	2/19/36	Mark Sandrich	Irving Berlin	"We Saw the Sea," "Let Yourself Go," "I'd Rather Lead a Band," "I'm Putting All My Eggs in One Basket," "Let's Face the Music and Dance"	Ginger Rogers, Randolph Scott, Harriet Hilliard, Lucille Ball, Betty Grable
Swing Time	RKO	8/26/36	George Stevens	Dorothy Fields, Jerome Kern	"It's Not in the Cards, "Pick Yourself Up," "The Way You Look Tonight," "A Fine Romance," "Bojangles of Harlem," "Never Gonna Dance"	Ginger Rogers, Victor Moore, Helen Broderick, Eric Blore, Betty Furness, George Metexa

Film	Studio	Date	Director	Composer(s)/Lyricist	Songs	Cast
Shall We Dance?	RKO	4/30/37	Mark Sandrich	Ira and George Gershwin	"Beginner's Luck," "Slap That Bass," "They All Laughed," "Let's Call the Whole Thing Off," "They Can't Take That Away from Me," "Shall We Dance"	Ginger Rogers, Edward Everett Horton, Eric Blore, Harriet Hoctor
A Damsel in Distress	RKO	11/20/37	George Stevens	Ira and George Gershwin	"I Can't Be Bothered Now," "The Jolly Tar and the Milkmaid," "Put Me to the Test," "Stiff Upper Lip," "A Foggy Day," "Nice Work If You Can Get It"	George Burns, Gracie Allen, Joan Fontaine, Reginald Gardiner, Constance Collier
Carefree	RKO	8/30/38	Mark Sandrich	Irving Berlin	"Since They Turned Loch Lomond into Swing," "I Used to Be Color Blind," "The Yam," "Change Partners"	Ginger Rogers, Ralph Bellamy, Luella Gear, Jack Carson, Clarence Kolb
The Story of Vernon and Irene Castle	RKO	3/31/39	H. C. Potter	Various	Vintage songs	Ginger Rogers, Edna May Oliver, Walter Brennan, Lew Fields
Broadway Melody of 1940	MGM	2/14/40	Norman Taurog	Cole Porter	"Please Don't Monkey with Broadway," "I've Got My Eyes on You," "Jukebox Dance," "Begin the Beguine," "I Concentrate on You"	Eleanor Powell, George Murphy, Frank Morgan, Ian Hunter
Second Chorus	Paramount	12/3/40	H. C. Potter	Johnny Mercer, E. Y. Harburg, Will Harris, Artie Shaw, Bernard Hanighen, Hal Borne, Victor Young	"I Ain't Hep to that Step but I Dig It," "Love of My Life," "Poor Mr. Chisholm"	Paulette Goddard, Artie Shaw, Burgess Meredith, Charles Butterworth
You'll Never Get Rich	Columbia	9/25/41	Sidney Lanfield	Cole Porter	"The Boogie Barcarolle," "Shootin' the Works for Uncle Sam," "Since I Kissed My Baby Goodbye," "A-stairable Rag," "So Near and Yet So Far"	Rita Hayworth, Robert Benchley, John Hubbard, Osa Massen

MUSICAL FILMS

TITLE	DISTRIBUTOR	RELEASE DATE	DIRECTOR	SONGWRITERS	ASTAIRE SONGS	OTHERS IN CAST
Holiday Inn	Paramount	6/15/42	Mark Sandrich	Irving Berlin	"I'll Capture Your Heart Singing," "You're Easy to Dance With," "Be Careful, It's My Heart," "I Can't Tell a Lie," "Let's Say It with Firecrackers"	Bing Crosby, Marjorie Reynolds, Virginia Dale, Walter Abel
You Were Never Lovelier	Columbia	10/5/42	William A. Seiter	Jerome Kern	"Dearly Beloved," "Audition Dance," "I'm Old-Fashioned," "Shorty George," "You Were Never Lovelier"	Rita Hayworth, Adolphe Menjou, Isobel Elsom, Xavier Cugat
The Sky's the Limit	RKO	7/13/43	Edward H. Griffith	Johnny Mercer, Harold Arlen	"My Shining Hour," "A Lot in Common with You," "One for My Baby"	Joan Leslie, Robert Benchley, Robert Ryan, Eric Blore
Yolanda and the Thief	MGM	10/19/45	Vincente Minnelli	Harry Warren, Arthur Freed	"Dream Ballet," "Yolanda," "Coffee Time"	Lucille Bremer, Ralph Morgan, Mildred Natwick
Ziegfeld Follies	MGM	1/11/48	Vincente Minnelli	Various	"Here's to the Girls," "This Heart of Mine," "Limehouse Blues," "The Babbit and the Bromide"	All-star cast
Blue Skies	Paramount	9/26/46	Stuart Heisler	Irving Berlin	"A Pretty Girl Is Like a Melody," "Putting on the Ritz," "A Couple of Song and Dance Men," "Heat Wave"	Bing Crosby, Joan Caulfield, Billy DeWolfe, Olga San Juan
Easter Parade	MGM	6/1/48	Charles Walters	Irving Berlin	"Happy Easter," "Drum Crazy," "It Only Happens When I Dance with You," "Beautiful Faces Need Beautiful Clothes," "I Love a Piano," "Snooky Ookums," "Ragtime Violin," "When the Midnight Choo-Choo Leaves for Alabam," "Steppin' Out with	Judy Garland, Peter Lawford, Ann Miller

Title	Studio	Date	Director	Songwriters	Songs	Cast
					"My Baby," "A Couple of Swells," "Easter Parade"	
The Barkleys of Broadway	MGM	4/11/49	Charles Walters	Ira Gershwin, Arthur Freed, Harry Warren	"Swing Trot," "You'd Be Hard to Replace," "Bouncin' the Blues," "My One and Only Highland Fling," "Shoes with Wings On," "You Can't Take That Away from Me" (George Gershwin, music), "Manhattan Downbeat"	Ginger Rogers, Oscar Levant, Billie Burke, Gale Robbins
Three Little Words	MGM	7/12/50	Richard Thorpe	Bert Kalmar, Edgar Leslie, Arthur Freed, Harry Ruby, Herman Ruby, Ted Snyder, Harry Puck, Herbert Stothart, Nacio Herb Brown	"Where Did You Get That Girl," "Mr. and Mrs. Hoofer at Home," "My Sunny Tennessee," "So-long, Oo-long," "Nevertheless," "I Wanna Be Loved by You," "Thinking of You," "Hooray for Captain Spaulding," "Three Little Words"	Red Skelton, Vera-Ellen, Arlene Dahl, Keenan Wynn, Phil Regan, Debbie Reynolds
Let's Dance	Paramount	8/11/50	Norman Z. McLeod	Frank Loesser	"Can't Stop Talking," "Jack and the Beanstalk," "Oh, Them Dudes," "Why Fight the Feeling?," "The Hyacinth," "Tunnel of Love"	Betty Hutton, Roland Young, Ruth Warrick, Lucile Watson
Royal Wedding	MGM	2/14/51	Stanley Donen	Alan Jay Lerner, Burton Lane	"Ev'ry Night at Seven," "Sunday Jumps," "Open Your Eyes," "How Could You Believe Me When I Said I Love You When You Know I've Been a Liar All My Life?," "You're All the World to Me," "I Left My Hat in Haiti"	Jane Powell, Peter Lawford, Sarah Churchill, Keenan Wynn
The Belle of New York	MGM	2/28/52	Charles Walters	Johnny Mercer, Harry Warren	"When I'm Out with the Belle of New York," "Bachelor Dinner Song," "Seeing's Believing," "Baby Doll," "Oops," "The Bride's Wedding Day Song," "I Wanna Be a Dancin' Man"	Vera-Ellen, Marjorie Main, Keenan Wynn, Alice Peerce

MUSICAL FILMS

TITLE	DISTRIBUTOR	RELEASE DATE	DIRECTOR	SONGWRITERS	ASTAIRE SONGS	OTHERS IN CAST
The Band Wagon	MGM	7/7/53	Vincente Minnelli	Howard Dietz, Arthur Schwartz	"By Myself," "A Shine on My Shoes," "That's Entertainment," "Dancing in the Dark," "You and the Night and the Music," "I Love Louisa," "I Guess I'll Have to Change My Plan," "Triplets," "The Girl Hunt Ballet"	Cyd Charisse, Oscar Levant, Nanette Fabray, Jack Buchanan
Daddy Long Legs	Twentieth Century–Fox	5/4/55	Jean Negulesco	Johnny Mercer	"History of the Beat," "Daydream Sequence," "Sluefoot," "Something's Gotta Give," "Dancing Through Life Ballet"	Leslie Caron, Terry Moore, Fred Clark, Thelma Ritter
Funny Face	Paramount	2/13/57	Stanley Donen	Ira Gershwin, Leonard Gershe, George Gershwin, Roger Edens	"Funny Face," "Bonjour Paris," "Let's Kiss and Make Up," "He Loves and She Loves," "Clap Yo' Hands," "'S Wonderful"	Audrey Hepburn, Kay Thompson, Michel Auclair
Silk Stockings	MGM	5/20/57	Rouben Mamoulian	Cole Porter	"Too Bad," "Paris Loves Lovers," "Stereophonic Sound," "All of You," "Fate to Be Mated," "The Ritz Roll and Rock"	Cyd Charisse, Janis Paige, Peter Lorre, Jules Munshin, George Tobias, Joseph Buloff
Finian's Rainbow	Warner Bros.	10/9/68	Francis Ford Coppola	E. Y. Harburg, Burton Lane	"Look to the Rainbow," "If This Isn't Love," "When the Idle Poor Become the Idle Rich"	Petula Clark, Tommy Steele, Don Francks, Keenan Wynn
That's Entertainment	MGM	6/15/74	Jack Haley, Jr.	Various	"Begin the Beguine," "They Can't Take That Away from Me," "Rhythm of the Day," "I Guess I'll Have to Change My Plan," "Hat Rack Dance," "Shoes with Wings On," "You're All The World to Me," "Dancing in the Dark"	All-star cast

Title	Distributor	Release Date	Director	Music	Others in Cast
That's Entertainment, Part 2	MGM	5/17/76	Gene Kelly	Various	"That's Entertainment," "I Wanna Be a Dancin' Man," "All of You," "Easter Parade," "Three Little Words," "Triplets," "Stepping Out with My Baby," "A Couple of Swells," "Bouncing the Blues." New numbers: "That's Entertainment, Part 2," "Be a Clown," "Shubert Alley," Cartoon Sequence. All-star cast

DRAMATIC FILMS

TITLE	DISTRIBUTOR	RELEASE DATE	DIRECTOR	OTHERS IN CAST
On the Beach	United Artists	12/2/59	Stanley Kramer	Gregory Peck, Ava Gardner, Tony Perkins, Donna Anderson
The Pleasure of His Company	Paramount	5/8/61	George Seaton	Debbie Reynolds, Lilli Palmer, Tab Hunter, Gary Merrill
The Notorious Landlady	Columbia	6/26/62	Richard Quine	Kim Novak, Jack Lemmon, Lionel Jeffries, Estelle Winwood
The Midas Run	Cinerama	5/15/69	Alf Kjellin	Anne Heywood, Richard Crenna, Roddy McDowall, Ralph Richardson, Cesar Romero
The Towering Inferno	20th Century–Fox/Warner Bros.	12/15/74	John Guillermin	Steve McQueen, Paul Newman, William Holden, Faye Dunaway, Susan Blakely, Richard Chamberlain, Jennifer Jones, O. J. Simpson, Robert Wagner, Robert Vaughn
The Amazing Dobermans	Golden Films	1976	Byron Chudnow	James Franciscus, Barbara Eden, Jack Carter, Charlie Bill
Un Taxi Mauve (The Purple Taxi)	Sofracima-Rizzola	1977	Yves Boisset	Charlotte Rampling, Philippe Noiret, Peter Ustinov, Edward Albert
Ghost Story	Universal	12/15/81	John Irvin	Melvyn Douglas, Douglas Fairbanks, Jr., John Houseman, Craig Wasson

TELEVISION APPEARANCES

Imp on a Cobweb Leash, "General Electric Theatre." CBS, drama (12/2/58).

Man on a Bicycle, "General Electric Theatre." CBS, drama (1/1/59).

An Evening with Fred Astaire. NBC, musical special (11/4/58).

Another Evening with Fred Astaire. NBC, musical special (9/28/59).

Astaire Time. NBC, musical special (9/28/60).

"Fred Astaire's Alcoa Premiere Theatre." ABC, dramatic anthology series (1961–1963). Astaire as host and lead in these dramas:

> *Mr. Easy* (2/13/62); *Moment of Decision* (7/10/62); *Guest in the House* (10/3/62); *Mr. Lucifer* (11/1/62); *Blues for a Hanging* (12/27/62).

Think Pretty, "Bob Hope's Chrysler Theatre." NBC musical drama with Barrie Chase (10/24/64).

"Dr. Kildare." NBC, four-part drama (11/65).

"Hollywood Palace." ABC, host-entertainer (9/2/65, 1/22/66, 3/12/66, 4/30/66).

The Fred Astaire Show. NBC, musical special (2/7/68).

"It Takes a Thief." ABC, several appearances (1969–1970).

The Over the Hill Gang Rides Again. ABC, western drama (11/17/70).

Santa Claus Is Coming to Town. ABC, cartoon voice (12/3/71).

'S Wonderful, 'S Marvelous, 'S Gershwin. NBC, musical special (9/9/72).

A Family Upside Down. NBC, drama (4/9/78).

Battlestar Galactica. ABC, adventure (Fall 1978).

Bibliography

BOOKS

Astaire, Fred, *Steps in Time*. New York, Harper, 1959.

Behlmer, Rudy, ed., *Memo from David O. Selznick*. New York, Viking, 1972.

Bordman, Gerald, *Jerome Kern: His Life and His Music*. New York, Oxford University Press, 1980.

Croce, Arlene, *The Fred Astaire and Ginger Rogers Book*. New York, Galahad Books, 1972.

Dietz, Howard, *Dancing in the Dark*. New York, Quadrangle, 1974.

Eels, George, *Ginger, Loretta and Irene Who?* New York, Putnam's, 1976.

————, *The Life That Late He Led*. New York, Putnam's, 1967.

Ewen, David, *George Gershwin: His Journey to Greatness*, Englewood Cliffs, New Jersey, Prentice Hall, 1970.

————, *Jerome Kern*. New York, Henry Holt, 1960.

Finch, Christopher, *Rainbow: The Stormy Life of Judy Garland*. New York, Random House, 1975.

Fontaine, Joan, *No Bed of Roses*. New York, Morrow, 1975.

Fordin, Hugh, *The World of Entertainment*. New York, Doubleday, 1975.

Freedland, Michael, *Irving Berlin*. New York, Stein and Day, 1974.

Gershwin, Ira, *Lyrics on Special Occasions*. New York, Knopf, 1959.

Goldberg, Isaac, *George Gershwin: A Study in American Music*. New York, Ungar, 1958.

Green, Benny, *Fred Astaire*. New York, Exeter Books, 1979.

Jablonsky, Edward, and Stewart, Lawrence D., *The Gershwin Years*. New York, Doubleday, 1958.

Lerner, Alan Jay, *The Street Where I Live*. New York, W. W. Norton, 1978.

Lesley, Cole, *Remembered Laughter: The Life of Noel Coward.* New York, Knopf, 1976.

Levant, Oscar, *Memoirs of an Amnesiac.* New York, Putnam's, 1965.

Minnelli, Vincente, with Hector Arce, *I Remember It Well.* New York, Doubleday, 1974.

Morley, Sheridan, *A Talent to Amuse: A Biography of Noel Coward.* New York, Doubleday, 1969.

Palmer, Lilli, *Change Lobsters and Dance.* New York, Macmillan, 1975.

Richards, Dick, *Ginger, Salute to a Star.* London, Clifton, 1968.

PERIODICALS

Astaire, Adele, "I'm Getting What I Want Out of Life." *Hearst's International Cosmopolitan* (November 1935).

———, "Fred." *London News Chronicle* (April 26, 1936).

Astaire, Fred, "Follow the Feet." *American* (June 1936).

Barnett, Lincoln, "Adele Astaire Comes Home." *Life* (November 19, 1945).

———, "Fred Astaire." *Life* (August 25, 1941).

Baskette, Kirtley, "My Companion Said, 'I'd Just *Love* to Dance with Fred Astaire!'" *Photoplay* (April 1935).

Collins, Frederick, "The Real Romance in the Life of Fred Astaire." *Liberty* (Jan. 25, 1936).

Davidson, Bill, "Fred Astaire." *Look* (November 10–24, 1959).

Deford, Frank, "Beauty and the Beast." *Sports Illustrated* (July 31, 1972).

Eustis, Morton, "Fred Astaire: The Actor-Dancer Attacks His Part." *Theater Arts Monthly* (May 1937).

Green, Adolph, "The Magic of Fred Astaire." *American Film* (April 1981).

Gritten, David, "Couples: Fred and Robyn Astaire," *People* (April 27, 1981).

Howe, Herb, "Tap Happy." *Photoplay* (October 1948).

Jacobs, Mary, "Why Fame Can't Spoil Fred Astaire." *Photoplay* (June 1936).

Janney, John, "A Brother and Sister Who Never Quarrel." *American* (December 1931).

Leamy, Hugh, "The Ascending Astaires." *Collier's* (March 31, 1928).

Lederer, Joseph, "Fred Astaire Remembers Gershwin, Porter, Berlin, Kern and Youmans." *After Dark* (October 1973).

Lewis, Frederick, "The Private Life of Fred Astaire." *Photoplay* (December 1935, January 1936).

McGilligan, Patrick, and McBride, Joseph, "George Stevens: A Piece of the Rock." *Bright Lights* (1979).

Murphy, George, "My Friend Fred." *Photoplay* (March 1940).

O'Hara, John, "There's No One Quite Like Fred Astaire." *Show* (October 1962).

Shipp, Cameron, "How to Dance Like Four Antelopes." *Colliers* (January 8, 1949).

Zeitlin, Ida, "Stepping the Astaire Way to Film Fame." *Screenland* (September 1935).

Index